Gamification Marketing

by Zarrar Chishti

for **dummies**®

A Wiley Brand

Gamification Marketing For Dummies®

Published by: **John Wiley & Sons, Inc.,** 111 River Street, Hoboken, NJ 07030-5774, www.wiley.com

Copyright © 2020 by John Wiley & Sons, Inc., Hoboken, New Jersey

Published simultaneously in Canada

For general information on our other products and services, please contact our Customer Care Department within the U.S. at 877-762-2974, outside the U.S. at 317-572-3993, or fax 317-572-4002. For technical support, please visit https://hub.wiley.com/community/support/dummies.

Wiley publishes in a variety of print and electronic formats and by print-on-demand. Some material included with standard print versions of this book may not be included in e-books or in print-on-demand. If this book refers to media such as a CD or DVD that is not included in the version you purchased, you may download this material at http://booksupport.wiley.com. For more information about Wiley products, visit www.wiley.com.

Library of Congress Control Number: 2020938558

ISBN 978-1-119-66397-3 (pbk); ISBN 978-1-119-66398-0 (ebk); ISBN 978-1-119-66399-7 (ebk)

Manufactured in the United States of America

SKY10020895_090220

Contents at a Glance

Table of Contents

Introduction

What is gamification marketing? After we had run a successful campaign, one of my clients put it simply: "I cannot believe we just gave our customers the *experience* of a game in a campaign that had nothing to do with games."

Gamification is when you apply techniques and concepts from games to any marketing campaign. Today, gamification is everywhere — for instance, companies rewarding their employees, teachers encouraging their pupils to compete for higher marks, and even parents rewarding their kids for washing the dishes.

It's no wonder gamification has worked well for marketing campaigns, too. When any company, large or small, implements gamification properly, the campaign will meet the company's marketing objectives. Why? Because humans have an innate desire to play and compete.

Gamification marketing can have the following end goals:

>> To build brand awareness

>> To increase engagement

>> To drive conversions

>> To boost customer loyalty

>> To encourage brand advocacy

About This Book

This book is for marketers, not developers.

Most books, blogs, and articles on gamification are written for developers. So, I wanted to write this book for people like my clients — people like you! Reading this book should feel like I'm sitting with you in our conference room discussing how you can implement gamification marketing in your next campaign.

This book covers all aspects of developing, launching, and analyzing a gamification marketing campaign. You don't have to read the book from beginning to end. You can use the table of contents and index to find the subject you want more information on. You don't have to remember what you're reading — there won't be a test on Friday, and you can always return to the book to find what you need.

If you're short on time, you can skip anything marked with the Technical Stuff icon, as well as text in gray boxes (called *sidebars*). This information is interesting (some might say fascinating!), but it's not essential to your understanding of the subject at hand.

Within this book, you may note that some web addresses break across two lines of text. If you're reading this book in print and want to visit one of these web pages, simply key in the web address exactly as it's noted in the text, pretending as though the line break doesn't exist. If you're reading this as an e-book, you've got it easy — just click the web address to be taken directly to the web page.

Finally, within this book, you'll find many examples of gamification marketing campaigns from companies around the world. Some of these campaigns will have ended by the time you read this book; others will still be running. For the ones that are still running, I encourage you to sign up and start engaging with them. Experience what they have to offer and try to relate how each gamification element will work with your own campaign.

Foolish Assumptions

This book is for people who work in marketing or are responsible for their company's marketing. Therefore, I do *not* assume that you are knowledgeable in game design or game development. However, I do assume the following:

» You'll be running a campaign for your company.

» You know the basics of marketing.

» You're aware of and have experience in playing online games.

» You have access to your company's analytics program.

» You have an in-house team or can hire a team of developers and designers.

Icons Used in This Book

Like other books in the *For Dummies* series, this book uses icons, or little pictures in the margin, to draw your attention to certain kinds of material. Here are the icons that I use:

Whenever you see the Tip icon, you can be sure to find something that'll save you time or money or just make your life easier (at least when it comes to your campaign).

You don't have to memorize this book, but when I tell you something so important that you really *should* remember it, I mark it with the Remember icon.

I've run loads of gamification marketing campaigns, and I've learned a thing or two along the way. If I can save you from the pitfalls I know are out there, I will! Whenever I warn you about something that could cause a real headache for you and your team, I use the Warning icon.

Occasionally, I dig into some information that's a wee bit technical. If that sounds like your cup of tea, look for the Technical Stuff icon. If you'd rather stick to only the things you *need* to know, you can safely skip these tidbits.

Beyond the Book

In addition to the material in the print or e-book you're reading right now, this product also comes some free access-anywhere goodies on the web. Check out the free Cheat Sheet for information on how games can change your marketing forever, tips on how gamification campaigns differ, and advice on data security for your gamification campaign. To access the Cheat Sheet, go to www.dummies.com and type **Gamification Marketing For Dummies Cheat Sheet** in the Search box.

Where to Go from Here

If you aren't familiar with gamification at all, start with Chapter 1 — a very good place to start. If you already have a good understanding of gamification and you're familiar with the basics, you can probably skip ahead to Chapter 3 and start learning how to kickstart your first gamification marketing campaign. If you're all about the data, head to Part 4. And if you just want some inspiration, check out Chapter 15.

Wherever you start, you'll find information you can use on your next gamification marketing campaign!

1

Introducing Gamification Marketing

Chapter 1

Gamifying Your Marketing Strategy

Thanks to the rise of gamification, marketing campaigns around the world have become increasingly more engaging. Gamification marketing campaigns offer your audience an *experience*, not just content.

Building gamification elements into your marketing will give your next campaign a serious advantage. Gamification enhances user experience and increases your audience's engagement. Another advantage of gamification is that your audience will be more inclined to interact with and share your campaign.

The application of gamification elements in business is catching on fast. Gartner research projects that more than 70 percent of Forbes Global organizations will have at least one game-based application, and that half of all companies that manage innovation processes will have "gamified" them. This opens a wonderful opportunity for you and your team to drive specific behaviors and motivate audiences to perform tasks that would require a lot of effort and time in a non-gamified campaign.

In this chapter, I look at how gamification can help with your marketing and then explore how it gives your campaign an advantage over traditional forms of marketing.

Seeing What Gamification Can Do in Marketing

Using gaming elements in your marketing campaign may sound strange at first. But in my 15 years of gamification and marketing experience, I've found that gamification is a highly effective marketing strategy, no matter which industry a brand is in.

When you gamify your campaign, your audience will have fun interacting with your brand, which means your company will increase its overall engagement. It's a win-win situation!

TIP

The ultimate goal for gamification is to drive your marketing objective to collect big data. I explore this subject in great depth in Chapter 11. But for now, just now that you can analyze big data to glean insights that can lead to better decisions and strategic business moves for your company. So, it's not just about giving your audience a fun experience — it's about gathering data about your audience while they're having fun.

In the following sections, I explain what exactly gamification is, tell you how you can gamify your marketing, and share some examples of successful gamification marketing campaigns.

Understanding gamification

Gamification is simply the process of applying techniques and concepts usually found in games to something outside of games — in this case, your marketing campaign. Chances are, even if you've never heard of gamification marketing before, you've experienced a gamification marketing campaign, whether you realized it or not.

REMEMBER

Gamification can be as simple as incorporating badges or achievement elements (you can find this in the Starbucks Rewards campaign; see Chapter 15). On the other end of the spectrum, you can develop a fully integrated gamification campaign, as when McDonald's and Hasbro teamed up to create the McDonald's Monopoly game.

Adding gamification elements even to a negative situation can make things a little better. For instance, when Google's Chrome web browser can't load a page for some reason, it presents the user with a simple yet highly engaging minigame, as shown in Figure 1-1.

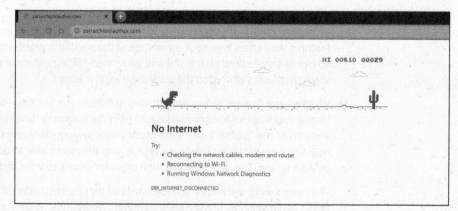

FIGURE 1-1:
Google added
a *T. rex* side-
scrolling
minigame to its
Chrome web
browser.

Gamifying your marketing

Gamification elements can be based off a number of game types that have their own gamification elements, such as trophies, badges, or rewards (see Chapter 2).

In my experience, when marketing content incorporates gamification elements, audience engagement increases. This increase in engagement means that your audience will not only remember your campaign, but also share it with their friends and family on social media. This means you have a bigger potential to increase your brand's awareness to a far larger audience.

When you expose a gamification marketing campaign to your audience, they'll start to think more about your brand, which can lead to a huge increase in news-letter subscriptions and can even lead to purchases of one or more products or services related to the campaign.

The most effective result of gamification marketing is that your conversion rates will spike as audiences become motivated to complete tasks for rewards.

Looking at some examples of gamification

Chapter 15 is all about real-life case studies of gamification marketing campaigns. Let me whet your appetite with just a couple additional examples from brands you've probably heard of:

>> **Verizon Wireless:** Verizon enjoyed a 30 percent increase in login rates due to its gamification campaign. The company did this by adding leaderboards, badges, and social media integration, among other gamification elements, to its website. With this campaign, Verizon managed to engage with its custom-ers on a much closer level.

More than 50 percent of the site's users participated in the new gamification features. And users who took advantage of the social integration spent 30 percent more time on the site and generated 15 percent more page views than users who used the traditional login method.

» **Volkswagen Group:** Volkswagen invited its consumers in China, one of its largest and most important markets, to help the company develop new versions of the "people's car." Participants were given gamification tools to help them easily design their new vehicle, and they were able to post their designs online. The designs were then open for others to view and rate.

The results were tracked on leaderboards so that contestants and the general public could see how the competing designs were faring. Within ten weeks, the online crowd-sourcing campaign had received more than 50,000 ideas! By the end of the campaign's first year, at least 33 million people had visited the site, and the general public had chosen three winning concepts.

This campaign owes its success to the fact that Volkswagen recognized that participation in a popular business initiative needs to be not only enticing and rewarding but also engaging and fun. Because Volkswagen's marketing team using gamification, the campaign went viral in China.

Understanding How Gamification Differs from Other Online Marketing Tactics

When I first started consulting on gamification marketing, traditional marketers viewed gamification as just a temporary fad that wouldn't last. Today, gamification is one of the most profitable forms of marketing worldwide, with engagement from millions of audience members.

Gamification marketing can be very profitable and lucrative for your company. Over the years, I've helped and witnessed companies from all industries successfully implement gamification elements into their campaigns.

In the following sections, I walk you through the advantages of gamification and show you how you can take your user experience to the next level.

Looking at the advantages of gamification

Gamification provides the answer to problems inherent in traditional marketing. Gamification taps into the basic instinct humans have of wanting to play and compete. It also provides a way for all marketing campaigns to provide real value to their audience and a positive digital experience.

When you use gamification techniques, you'll build brand awareness, drive engagement to your brand, and develop a long-lasting loyalty program.

Here are some of the advantages gamification has over traditional marketing:

>> **It enables you to put some fun into your brand or message.** Gamification incorporates elements of fun and competition in any marketing strategy. This is good news for your brand, because your gamification marketing campaign will actively draw people who want to participate, follow, and share your brand's message.

>> **It enables you to get better and more meaningful feedback.** Sadly, we're all inundated with requests for feedback from websites these days. Because of this, generating meaningful customer feedback for a traditional marketing campaign is rare. If you rely on traditional marketing techniques, you'll likely have no clear picture of how your audience feels about your company, brand, and campaign.

Gamification helps make the process simple by offering a more engaging and fun campaign that increases response rates. It generates an emotional and immediate response from your audience because they respond without thinking about their answer. So, as your audience is being bombarded with requests for feedback, gamification helps your campaign stand out by making the process simple, seamless, and fun.

>> **It generates loyalty.** Your audience is inundated with all forms of noise — special deals, offers, and advertising messages everywhere they look. In order for your marketing campaign to be successful, it needs to engage customers, retain their interest, and develop loyalty. With so many options aggressively competing for your audience's attention, this task is becoming more and more difficult.

Gamification can power effective customer loyalty programs, creating a more valuable and sustaining customer relationship. When done well, gamification loyalty programs have an impressive impact.

>> **It personalizes your audience's experience of your brand.** Gamification marketing can create a more personal experience for your audiences during the campaign. Segmentation and personalization are critical to driving conversion, developing trust, and building customer loyalty (see Chapter 9). The more you tailor your marketing to your target group, the more effective your campaigns will be.

You can create custom game experiences targeted to specific audience segments and then develop these game experiences to your brand values. By doing this, your marketing campaign will connect with your audience on a deeper level.

» **It gives you big data.** *Big data* offers insights from all kinds of structured and unstructured data sources to help improve how companies operate and interact with consumers. Gamification, which allows you to connect with your audience in a more interactive and intimate way, gathers valuable data that can be turned into new insights to create detailed market segments for future campaigns.

Gamification creates a lot of data that your company can analyze, especially when users are asked to sign in via social networks where a lot of your audience's public data can be captured. More interestingly, this data can be integrated to provide context with all the other gamification data you're storing.

I look into big data techniques in greater detail in Chapter 11.

» **It enables you to influence customer behavior.** Gamification has a major advantage over traditional marketing campaigns when it comes to influencing customer behavior. A gamification marketing campaign engages universal experiences, such as stimulation and motivation.

Influencing audiences to make the decisions you want them to make is the holy grail of marketing. In Chapter 15, I explain how Nissan's use of gamification influenced drivers to use better driving habits, which is exactly the message Nissan wanted to align itself with.

» **It drives engagement.** If your marketing campaign is engaging, it'll be worth sharing. Gamification can help drive engagement by getting your audience to share your campaign with their family and friends.

Gamification plays on the psychology that drives human engagement — the human desire to compete and improve, as well as wanting to get instantly rewarded. The technology is merely the means to put that psychology to work in the business sphere.

» **It appeals to a younger audience.** By promising a fun and engaging experience, your campaign will grab a younger audience's attention instantly. Younger audiences have been quick to adopt the newer digital and social technology revolutions. This makes gamification an even more important method of marketing if your campaign wants to appeal to young people. Gamification forces your marketing to practice creativity, which is bound to draw younger audiences.

» **It increases reach.** No matter what kind of campaign you run, one of the main objectives will always be to gain new customers. It doesn't matter what market segments you're targeting or which sector your company works in, increasing your consumer reach will always be a fundamental part of your marketing.

The brilliance of gamification marketing campaigns, in which everyday situations are turned into games, is that they're layered and multifunctional, naturally improving both audience engagement and brand reach.

>> **It builds better brand awareness.** By using gamification, you can attract new customers when they notice your branding as part of an innovative and fun campaign. Your audience, old and new, will experience your marketing campaign in a fun and interactive way — an experience that will leave your audience more aware of your company and branding.

By exploiting rewards, points, ranks, leaderboards, and competition, all of which I cover in depth in Chapter 4, you can encourage your audience to follow, share, and like your brand on social media. This way, you can increase your reach and, ultimately, your brand awareness.

Taking your current user experience to the next level

A gamification marketing campaign will trigger emotions that are linked to positive user experience. These emotions can play a very important role in the way you engage with your audience overall.

Here are some ways using gamification elements can affect your audience:

>> **Giving the user control:** Leading your audience toward your desired marketing goals becomes part of the user journey. Nobody likes to be forced to a destination. Most people like to feel in control. This is the core of what gamification is all about. Your campaign will become more like a "choose your own adventure" campaign, which is what'll make people engage with it (see Chapter 2).

>> **Going on a journey:** Gamification elements can help your audience navigate where they're going in your campaign. People like to know where your campaign is heading and where they are in the process. Consider a simple gamification element like badges: You can see how badges can act as progress maps for your audience. They know where they are in the process and what the next steps are. In a way, these elements help break up the journey your audience is taking, which makes it more manageable and engaging — and more likely that they'll keep going.

>> **Giving a real sense of achievement:** Achievement is one of the most powerful driving factors for your audience to remain in your campaign. Whatever they do in your campaign, they'll want to feel like they've achieved something. If you can make them feel a sense of achievement, they'll keep coming back to your campaign. By using gamification elements such as points or rewards, you can create this sense of achievement at regular intervals.

>> **Setting competitive goals:** Your audience will be competitive by nature. Most of them will want to push themselves further and harder. By applying elements such as leaderboards, you can convince your audience to come back and try again. Competition is the driving factor behind the popularity of the Nike+ app (see Chapter 15).

>> **Exploring:** When you give your audience the freedom to explore, it creates intrigue and excitement, which are two very powerful and positive emotions. Of course, the gamification element should be carefully structured so your audience is neither overwhelmed nor bored. With a combination of levels, strategy, and storyline elements (see Chapter 2), you can transform any campaign into one that allows your audience to feel like they have room to explore inside your campaign.

>> **Giving rewards:** People love rewards. Earlier, I explain the importance of creating a sense of achievement. But this sense of achievement should be supplemented with a tangible reward. Consider the Starbucks Rewards program, in which Starbucks offer rewards after a certain number of purchases (see Chapter 15). Create your rewards in a way that your audience will go out of their way to get their hands on them.

>> **Offering exclusivity:** Your audience will do just about anything for exclusive gamification elements, such as status levels. Exclusivity creates intrigue and curiosity. Your audience will work hard to achieve that status. This is akin to unlocking the secret level on a video game.

>> **Creating collaboration:** Another key driver is community and collaboration. Community elements allow audiences to collaborate in order to achieve bigger and better things than they could on their own. If you can make your audience feel like part of a team within the campaign, you'll create loyalty and a positive user experience.

Stepping Up Your Current Marketing

Using gamification elements in your campaign can be a great way to increase the amount of engagement with your brand. And brand engagement will go a long way toward influencing an audience's purchasing decisions.

Here are some ways you can step up your current marketing strategy by incorporating gamification:

>> **Figure out what type of gamification elements might appeal to your target audience (see Chapter 3).** If you don't look at this aspect first, you may not engage them to get the return you're seeking.

REMEMBER

Not every gamification model and element will be suitable to your target audience. In fact, you may find that only one or two really resonate with them. Before deciding which ones to use, you need to understand how gamification models perform with various audiences.

If your audience spans a larger demographic, you could combine several popular gamification elements to appeal to a more general audience.

>> **Do your research.** Check out the examples in Chapter 15 to get a sense of how gamification works, what type of rewards companies give, and how the campaigns incorporate companies' marketing objectives.

TIP

Nothing helps shape your own gamification strategy like trying out what others have done before you. See if you can identify best practices that would fit *your* marketing objectives.

The gamification elements that often do the best are social sharing, scoring, and rewards. I've investigated numerous quiz, trivia, puzzle, and skills gamification models before knowing what would work for my client's brand and audience. This more hands-on strategy also provided me with a way to better understand what was engaging based on my *own* reactions.

>> **Think about establishing incentives.** Consider what you want to give away as an incentive. It could be a new product, digital content, or promotional coupons, for example. Whatever it is, you need to offer a clear incentive in order to make the gamification work with your audience. Your audience needs a *reason* to aim toward earning the coveted gold badge.

Research what works with others in your industry or ask your audience what they would like to receive from your next campaign.

>> **Keep it as simple as possible.** A complex gamification marketing campaign may get lost on your audience. Look at the campaign from your audience's point of view. If they can't figure out your gamification elements quickly, they'll move on. These days, people have relatively short attention spans and many distractions, so consider making each achievement or gamification milestone relatively short.

>> **Start thinking about who you'll want to work with for your creative and technical tasks.** Define your ideal time frame for developing and launching your gamification marketing campaign, and set your budget. Gamification

may be new to your marketing strategy, so look to outsource talent that specializes in gamification (see Chapter 5).

>> **Plan your launch.** Your audience cannot play your awesome gamification campaign if they don't know it exists. By using a combination of a planned successful launch, a targeted email campaign, social media promotions, and a researched media outreach, you can ensure your game reaches everyone who would love to play it (see Chapter 9).

>> **Don't be afraid to experiment with your gamification elements.** There is no bible or "best way" to creating gamification marketing campaigns. Gamification elements are designed to personalize the experience and continually increase the challenge involved for your audience. The only way you'll know which element is right for *your* audience is to take the plunge and make educated choices.

TIP

Stay up to date on new gamification elements to keep your marketing strategy fresh for your audience. Subscribe to gamification blogs written by industry experts. Here are a few I recommend:

>> **Gamelearn** (www.game-learn.com/serious-games-gamification-blog): Gamelearn's blog explains how games can apply to business environments.

>> **Gamification Nation** (www.gamificationnation.com): This blog offers fresh gamification content presented in a fun way.

>> **Gamified UK** (www.gamified.uk): Gamified UK is a great place to start learning about gamification and game theory more broadly.

>> **Yu-kai Chou** (https://yukaichou.com): Yu-kai Chou is an author and international keynote speaker on gamification and behavioral design, and his blog is a great resource.

Chapter **2**

Getting to Know Gamification Models

You and your team have lots of gamification options and elements. The key is understanding all these options and how they can benefit your campaign.

Be sure to keep your intended audience in mind when you're building your campaign. Understanding your audience will help you make the right choices and, ultimately, the most engaging campaign.

In this chapter, I walk you through the various settings you can make for your gamification campaign and fill you in on some of the mistakes I've come across in gamification marketing.

Exploring Your Options

When you're just starting to think about developing a gamification marketing campaign, you'll be glad to know that you have lots of options! But the options may be overwhelming. There is no definitive list of all the options at your disposal, but over many years working with many clients, I've come up with ways to make sense of all this information. And that's what this section is about.

Here, I introduce you to the six game types you have to decide on:

>> Classic

>> Enterprising

>> Disrupting

>> User experience

>> Contributing

>> Community

In the following sections, I walk you through each of these game types in greater detail.

Discovering game types

In this section, I walk you through the six game types that have individual elements that you can choose from. As you read the sections that follow, think about your target audience. First, rank the game types that your campaign associates with best. Then choose the elements that will work best for your audience from each of the game types. For instance, if your target audience is made up of other businesses, you'll probably want to base 70 percent of your campaign on the enterprising game type and the rest on user experience and classic. Alternatively, if your clients are in the 18- to 25-year-old market, you'll want to focus more on the community and user experience game types, because that's what 18- to 25-year-olds are into.

Classic

The classic game type includes gamification elements that are intuitive. You can add these gamification elements to your campaign and know that your audience will be able to easily engage with it.

TIP

If this campaign is your first gamification marketing endeavor, I recommend using the classic game type.

Here are some elements commonly found in the classic game type (not every classic game will have every one of these elements, so you can pick and choose what works for you):

>> **Strategy:** Strategy involves skillful thinking and planning, in which your audience must plan a series of actions against one or more opponents.

Players win through superior planning, but the element of chance is involved, too (in a much smaller role). If you'd like strategy to be a part of your game, be sure to incorporate a challenge for your audience so they can explore or manage their environment.

» **Investment:** The goal here is to get your audience to invest their time and emotions into your game. If you achieve this goal, they'll value your campaign. This game type typically involves more development at the design stage to ensure there is enough to engage your audience for the long term. Ultimately, you want your game to get them racing back to your campaign to ensure their progress is maintained.

» **Consequences:** If you include this element in your classic game type, there will be a consequence for every one of your audience's actions. Each significant action (or nonaction) should result in a visual consequence, such as rewards, badges, or points.

» **Progress and feedback:** I cover this element in the coming chapters, where I discuss the importance of giving your audience some sort of measure of progress and feedback as they progress in your game.

» **Tutorials:** The last thing you want is for your gamification campaign to leave your audience feeling helpless. To alleviate this problem, you can include a visual tutorial, as well as help sections at each major part of your campaign. This way, your audience will know how everything works right at the start and throughout the campaign.

» **Achievements:** As opposed to progress and feedback, where the audience can see a positive progression, here the fear of losing points and achievements can be a powerful motivator. With gamification marketing, getting your audience to your campaign is the easy part. Getting them to return and value their status in your campaign can only be done through regular, meaningful achievements.

» **Storyline:** In a classic game type, you may want to consider adding a storyline in the form of a narrative or a theme. This strategy can help your audience be more engaged.

The storyline may be linked with some existing narrative associated with your company or industry. It could be anything from your company values to topical industry themes. Whatever you decide on, make sure your audience will be able to understand and make sense of it. Otherwise, they'll feel an immediate disconnect with your campaign.

» **Time:** Including time pressure in your classic game type can help create a sense of urgency with your campaign. Reducing the amount of time your audience has to complete tasks can focus them on your campaign. You can increase engagement through increased time pressure, too.

For instance, by default, you can give them 15 minutes to solve a particular task, which is plenty of time. However, whenever the audience makes a mistake, not only are they penalized with lack of achievements, but their time remaining is also reduced. This increase in time pressure adds an interesting tension to the classic game type. The idea is that your audience will remain engaged because they'll want to solve the task faster.

>> **Rarity:** There should always be levels of rarity to the achievements you offer in a classic game type. Making something rare can make it all the more desirable. For instance, if you're offering colored badges, there should be a badge that is very much coveted but extremely rare to achieve.

Enterprising

You should incorporate at least one enterprising game type element in your campaign. The enterprising game type is all about points and status. It creates the type of engagement where your audience will want to show their friends how they're progressing (for example, through badges).

An example of an enterprising game type is British Airways Avios air-mile program, where every additional mile collected is an achievement in its own right. Flyers can gain points by purchasing tickets, shopping at one of British Airways' partner sites, and using an American Express credit card. However, British Airways also awards badges for purchasing a certain number of flights every year. These badges give flyers privileged access to lounges across the world, among other benefits. Flyers then have to ensure they complete the journeys every year to maintain their badge status.

There is a good chance that your audience will respond favorably to the enterprising game type: someone who boasts they have a higher status or achievement than their friend did.

Here are some elements of the enterprising game type (not every enterprising game will have every one of these elements, so you can pick and choose what works for you):

>> **Levels or progression:** In an enterprising type game, giving your audience a chance to work their way up levels (such as status levels) and goals can help them to visually map their progression through your campaign. Employing levels will ensure that your audience remains loyal to your campaign and company.

>> **Learning new skills:** The idea here is to give your audience an opportunity to learn something new about your company, products, services, or industry.

Gamification can be a very effective way to achieve this goal in a marketing campaign. For instance, if you want to highlight the fact that your company uses a unique method or ingredient, make sure this lesson is learned during people's engagement with your campaign.

» **Symbolic rewards:** Symbolic rewards are different from general rewards like badges. Symbolic rewards are a physical symbol of achievement, such as a free coffee or a free companion ticket on someone's next purchase. Make sure they carry meaning and status and are useful to the campaign.

» **Challenges:** In an enterprising game type, you want to challenge the audience. Don't be afraid to create challenges. In fact, look to incorporate them in increasing levels. Challenges help keep your audience interested and engaged, especially after the initial phase. Look to test your audience's knowledge and give them an opportunity to apply it. Overcoming challenges will make your audience feel like they've earned their achievements.

Disrupting

Elements of the disrupting game type help create a gamification marketing campaign that displaces the existing marketing trends and eventually replaces them. Disruptive campaigns are generally more entrepreneurial in design and outside the norm in functionality.

TIP

Try to identify gaps in your industry's current campaigns that fail to see how the marketing trends are evolving. With a game-changing element, you can create a disruptive campaign that will allow your company to stay ahead of the rest. Plus, your audience will welcome a disruption to the current marketing campaigns being thrown at them.

Here are some elements of the disrupting game type (not every disrupting game will have every one of these elements, so you can pick and choose what works for you):

» **Creativity tools:** Give back control to your audience. For instance, allow them to create their own content and express themselves. There could be a number of reasons to do this, outside of your campaign, including for personal gain, for pleasure, or to help other people.

An example of this element of a disrupting type of game is the popular ElfYourself gamification campaign from Office Depot/OfficeMax. ElfYourself is a native app (available for download from the mobile app stores) that allows users to upload photos of their friends and family from Facebook or their mobile phones. Then users select a dance, and the app creates a custom video that users can share to social media.

- » **Innovation:** Giving your audience a way to think outside the box and outside the boundaries of your campaign is a great element of a disrupting type of game. This approach allows them to channel innovation and helps you understand what your audience wants and expects from your company and industry. For instance, you could allow your audience to develop a system that creates the results *they* would like to see. You can then use this data to see if your company is currently producing these results for your customers.

- » **Chaos:** I get funny looks from clients when I suggest chaos as a gamification element. But in games, chaos is symbolic. It's a core element that keeps the player immersed and engaged. For your disrupting type of game, it's not about burning your company's image to the ground. Instead, think of this chaos element as throwing out the rulebook for your campaign. For instance, in your gamification model, consider running "no rules" events.

- » **Random rewards:** The key here is to surprise your audience — pleasantly, of course. You can do this with unexpected rewards. If done correctly, you'll see an increase in engagement in the long run. Everyone likes to be given a nice surprise, especially if it's unexpected and random. This element of a disrupting campaign will keep your audience engaged in a more positive way.

- » **Voice:** I find giving your audience a voice an extremely effective element of a disrupting type of game, especially in industries where the customers are seldom heard from. However, it isn't enough to simply give your audience a voice. They need to feel that their voice is being heard. You can do this by incorporating feedback tools into your game, which allow you to gather data as you hear back from your audience. This data can be extremely powerful for your company and industry as a whole because it gives you a greater insight into your audience's voice and generates opportunities to create better relationships with them.

- » **Invisibility:** If used properly, the invisibility element of a disrupting type of game can work in your gamification campaign. Essentially, it's about encouraging total freedom and lack of inhibitions. Why? It allows your audience to be far more open and honest in their opinions. Be careful, though — invisibility can bring out the worst in your audience.

User experience

The user experience game type involves designing your campaign around the psychology of your intended audience. You can go further and consider their behaviors, thought processes, and capabilities as well.

I like to think of *user experience* as creative design elements that create a unique and long-lasting impression on your player. The ultimate goal here is data collection (see Chapter 10). You gather data is by tapping into the behaviors and thought processes your intended audience will respond positively to.

TIP

Before I look into the various specifics of user experience elements, let me offer some tips on user experience in general:

>> **Learn as much as you can about your intended audience (see Chapter 9).** This is the best advice I can offer to my clients. For instance, if you're thinking your audience is men from 18 to 30 years old, go back to your research because that's too vague. There are so many types of players with different tastes and expectations when it comes to the complexity of the game. You can't appeal to them all. So, it's best to be more specific and design the campaign for those who will most likely engage positively.

>> **Less is more.** When you're looking to add elements to your game, you may be tempted to add as many elements as you can. This impulse is natural. As a marketer, you want to add extra mechanics to ensure maximum engagement. But using fewer elements is the core of the user experience discipline.

>> **Your campaign's gamification user experience should feel seamless.** This is harder to achieve than it may sound. When designing your game, make sure to prevent any discontinuity in the user experience. You want the gameplay to be compelling and the feedback to be instantaneous in order to keep the campaign flowing. An example of this is to employ the same level of responsiveness in every element you design. Anything that the player interacts with should respond with visual and audio cues.

>> **As with any marketing campaign, try to keep your user experience consistent.** Create a user experience bible that contains the core principles of your user experience. Then make sure all designers and developers adhere to this bible. Consistency helps your audience find their way around the gamification campaign more easily because they'll have fewer rules to figure out and remember.

TIP

To gather as much behavioral and personal information as possible on your campaign's audience, along with the relative objective data, you have to use an analytics program (see Chapter 11). The data you collect will allow you to spot issues with your campaign's user experience design very clearly.

Here are some elements of the user experience game type (not every user experience game will have every one of these elements, so you can pick and choose what works for you):

>> **Badges and achievements:** Gamification badges and achievements are a recognition of the commitment that your audience makes to your campaign.

Using them appropriately will motivate players to work through all your challenges and actively promote your campaign to others. The prospect of earning more badges is one of the best audience engagement tools. Use badges wisely and in a meaningful way to make them more appreciated by your audience. For instance, make your audience earn each badge instead of just giving it to them for simply registering their details. But don't make it *too* hard and rare for the audience to earn a badge either.

>> **Leaderboards:** Leaderboards are a useful element to increase engagement in your campaign. They're commonly used to show your audience how they compare to others and so others can see how they're faring. In its simplest form, a leaderboard is a high-score listing. It's the visual representation of a real-time competition within your campaign. Leaderboards encourage your audiences to compete and set goals for themselves. Finally, leaderboards allow players to keep track of their progress in relation to the other players.

>> **Experience points:** Just like badges, experience points are feedback elements. You can use them to allow your audience to track progress and as a way to unlock new elements within the campaign. Experience points should be based on the audience's achievement within the campaign. In your campaign, players should earn experience points by doing tasks and completing objectives.

>> **Skill or chance:** This element promotes the idea that your audience has a good chance to win something within your campaign. Skill and chance are deeply rooted in game design. They're a way for players to win rewards with very little effort.

>> **Easter eggs:** An *Easter egg* is a hidden feature, level, or bonus that your audience wouldn't normally encounter while playing. They can only be found by searching levels and exploring your campaign. Easter eggs are a fun way to reward and surprise your audience just for engaging with your campaign. They encourage audiences to spend more time interacting with your campaign. The harder Easter eggs are to find, the more exciting and viral your campaign will become.

Contributing

Not all game types have to be visual or gamified to be effective in your campaign. A contribution game helps your audience provide for others. This may seem strange, but it's best to view this game type giving your audience a way to give back.

Here are some elements of the contributing game type (not every contributing game will have every one of these elements, so you can pick and choose what works for you):

>> **Being responsible:** Giving your audiences the chance to be responsible for looking after other people can be very fulfilling. This can be done by creating roles within your campaign. For instance, you can award administrator or moderator rights to certain audience members. You can develop a multi-layered hierarchy that allows for certain positions of power within certain geographical locations.

>> **Access:** Award access to special features and abilities within your campaign. In this way, your audience will have more ways to help others and to contribute. It also helps them feel valued by your company, which will in itself foster a more meaningful and earned role in the campaign.

>> **Collect and trade:** This element taps into people's love of collecting things. If you can, try to give your audience a way to collect and trade items in your campaign. For instance, they could use their points to get discounts on products and services. If you do, you'll build relationships and engagements of purpose and value.

>> **Gifting:** Gifting offers your audience the ability to gift items to other players, helping them achieve their goals within your campaign. For instance, some campaigns allow users at a certain achievement level to gift membership benefits to family and friends. This element can be difficult to incorporate, but the potential for reciprocity can be a strong motivator.

>> **Sharing knowledge:** This element has become important in gamification lately. You incorporate in your game a way for your audience to answer questions and teach other audience members. When they share their knowledge, your campaign offers them an in-game reward.

Community

The vast majority of your intended audience like to be part of a community. The community game type can create a fun environment through interaction with other members.

Community elements allow audiences to collaborate in order to achieve bigger and better things than they could on their own. Community elements make sense in gamification marketing campaigns because community elements are widely used in popular gamification models. For instance, if you have a FarmVille-type game (www.zynga.com/games/farmville/), audiences will be happy to water someone else's farm in exchange for new crops for their own farm.

Here are some elements of the community game type (not every community game will have every one of these elements, so you can pick and choose what works for you):

>> **Guilds or teams:** Guilds allow your audience to share common scenarios and skills, and to be recognized as a trusted, trained resource. Entry into the guild

should be through invitation or proof of time spent in the campaign overall. When adding this element, give your audience the ability to build close-knit guilds or teams themselves. Small groups can be an effective way to increase engagement. Finally, you can consider ways to allow team-based competitions.

>> **Social networking:** Allow your campaign to connect with social networking platforms, not only to allow your audience to connect with their current friends but also to become visible to other audience members. This can help create opportunities for new relationships within your campaign. In this way, your campaign can create new mini-communities within each social network platform.

>> **Social discovery:** This element is extremely similar to the social networking element, but it goes one step further. It's a way for your audience to be found and build new relationships. You do this by using your data to help match your audience members based on their choices and status within your campaign.

>> **Customization:** It is almost the norm now to give audiences the tools to help customize their experience within your campaign. This allows your campaign to be more personal and increases overall engagement. You can offer avatars, allow players to upload profile pictures, and even allow them to upload their own background images. The idea is to allow your audience to customize their environment, letting them express themselves and choose how they'll present themselves to others within your campaign.

>> **Time-dependent rewards:** Time-dependent rewards may include things like birthday gifts. You can go one step further and design time-dependent rewards that are only available for set period of time (for instance, if audiences come back next Wednesday, they'll get a reward).

Creating the Perfect Gamification Campaign Settings

In addition to working out what your gamification campaign will include, you need to decide how your campaign will run. This includes thinking about the demographics, duration, and frequency of your campaigns. This information will help you shape the final shape of your campaign and create a consistent message both for your team and your audience.

Choosing the right game for your audience

Deciding which gaming elements will work with your audience is essential. One method for finding the right elements is to look at the Bartle player types (see Figure 2-1), a classification of game players based on a 1996 paper by Richard Bartle. According to the Bartle player types, there are four different kinds of players, each motivated by a different incentive for playing:

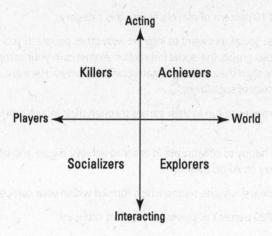

FIGURE 2-1:
The Bartle
player types.

>> **Achievers:** Achievers are all about points and status. Here are some characteristics of achievers:

- They want to be able to show their friends how they are progressing.

- They like to collect badges, trophies, and in-game status.

- They respond well to incentive schemes, such as air miles.

- They want to gain points or get to the next level.

- They like proof of success, such as points, possessions, or prizes.

- They seek rewards and prestige with advancement in the campaign.

- Around 10 percent of players fit into this category.

>> **Explorers:** Explorers want to see new things and discover new secrets. They aren't as concerned with points and badges. Here are some characteristics of explorers:

- They value discovery more value than in-game status, such as badges.

- They're okay with repetitive tasks as long as they eventually "unlock" a new area of the campaign.

- They enjoy the surprise element that is possible in a gamification campaign.

- They want to discover new things; they love to find hidden treasure.

- They like to dig down and find something new or unknown. Secret pathways and rare finds excite them much more than prizes do.

- They care more about the gameplay than the end result.

- Around 10 percent of players fit into this category.

>> **Socializers:** Socializers want to interact with other people. If you want to appeal to this group, the social interaction elements in your campaign will count more than the campaign's gamification strategy. Here are some characteristics of socializers:

- They experience fun in their games through their interaction with other players.

- They're happy to collaborate in order to achieve bigger and better things than they could on their own.

- Their reward is in the relationships formed within your campaign.

- Around 80 percent of players fit into this category.

>> **Killers:** Killers have strong competitive instincts. Here are some characteristics of killers:

- They like scoring points, competing against people, taking part in challenges, winning, and showing off their knowledge.

- They're similar to achievers in the way that they get a thrill from gaining points and winning status. What sets them apart from achievers is that killers want to see other people lose.

- They're highly competitive; winning is what motivates them.

- They want to be the best players in your campaign.

- Less than 1 percent of players fit into this category.

To attract killers, include elements such as leaderboards and ranks. Consider having audiences compete against each other if possible.

TIP

If you know the Bartle player types of your target audience, you'll be able to meet their needs when designing your campaign. To increase the success of your campaign, look at ways you can attract *more than one type* into your campaign.

There are other demographic factors to consider when developing your next gamification marketing campaign, including the following:

>> **Gender:** My research consistently shows that gender differences exist when considering the motivations for game playing in marketing campaigns. For instance, female audiences have been found to be less attracted to competitive elements. Male audiences are more likely to enjoy action games. Interestingly, women are more attracted to games that involve long-term relationship building, whereas men tend to respond more to task- and achievement-oriented elements.

TIP

Avoid gender stereotypes. You could end up alienating your audience with the wrong research data.

>> **Age:** Your main concern should be if your audience will instinctively know what to do when they get to your campaign. What does your current customer data tell you? A younger, more tech-savvy audience will hit the ground running. If you're seeking an older audience, you'll need to make sure to include multiple explanation elements along with a simpler graphics and mechanics.

Determining duration and frequency

Consider the longevity of your gamification marketing campaign. How long will your campaign last? This is especially important for gamification campaigns, where you've invested huge resources creating a unique marketing vehicle. Ideally, you want your campaign to last long enough for your target audience to engage fully.

WARNING

If your campaign is shorter than one month, you'll be seriously reducing the likelihood of your audience seeing, understanding, and engaging with the gamification elements you're marketing. Similarly, you don't want your campaign to go on more than six months because you run the risk of your gamification elements becoming stale. If a gamification campaign becomes too familiar to your audience, it eventually loses its appeal. Even legacy brands like Coca-Cola and Nike change up their gamification campaigns frequently in order to keep their audiences interested in their marketing messages.

TIP

When considering the duration of your campaign, keep in mind the following:

>> **What's popular today may not be popular tomorrow.** Gamification works best when it's based on trends, but you need to identify a sensible longevity for those trends.

>> **Try to provide a means for getting customer feedback (see Chapter 10).**
This can be through forms, chat bots, and social media platforms. Then keep track of public interest in your campaign and make adjustments accordingly. Being able to show your audience you're listening will produce a positive reaction on social media.

>> **Be flexible.** Don't be afraid to end the campaign sooner than you thought, if you identify interest going stale or, worse, you're getting negative feedback. Figure out what's working in your current marketing efforts. You may not need to change everything — just adjust anything that's causing negative reactions.

>> **Be innovative.** Innovation is what gamification is all about. Be creative with your gamification elements. Pay attention to what's current. Don't be afraid to be a trendsetter!

After you've worked out the ideal duration for your campaign, consider the frequency of it. How often will you bring out a new campaign? Gamification elements are expensive to design and develop, and gamification campaigns can take a lot of effort.

REMEMBER

All the elements you create — from the animation to the designs to the coding — can be reused over and over again. These elements are assets for your company. The first development will involve the biggest cost. After your first campaign, it will cost considerably less to revamp and recode new campaigns. Think about how you'll be reusing the gamification elements when developing your first gamification campaign.

TIP

There are three frequencies I recommend considering:

>> **One-off:** When the campaign ends, so does the narrative for the gamification elements. When reusing the gamification elements for the next campaign, you'll produce a brand-new narrative. This approach works well when your audience is exposed to your campaign over longer periods. In this case, a new narrative will reignite their interest in your marketing efforts each time you launch.

>> **Series:** Just like a TV series, your campaign's narrative continues from where it left off with the last campaign. This approach can be extremely profitable in marketing terms. Your message is repeatedly pushed to your audience with minimum effort (after the first launch). This approach works for campaigns that are short, leaving your audience wanting more.

>> **Seasonal:** Here, you deck your campaign with the seasonal themes. The most popular version is Christmas, which has historically been the most engaging time for gamification campaigns. This approach can work for medium to short-term campaigns. It can even work for long-term ones as long as the seasonal theme is incorporated within the campaign rather than treated as a relaunch.

In Table 2-1, I compare the various frequencies against the gamification models I look at earlier in the chapter.

TABLE 2-1 **Determining the Best Frequency for Your Gamification Model**

Game Model	Cost	Development Time	Best Frequency
Action	Low	1 to 2 weeks	Series, seasonal
Simulation	High	3 months	One-off
Interactive storytelling	Very high	4 to 6 months	One-off
Adventure	Medium	2 to 3 months	One-off, seasonal (incorporated)
Puzzles	Low	2 to 3 weeks	Series, seasonal
Word-based	Low	2 to 3 weeks	Series, seasonal
Skill-based	Medium	1 month	Series, seasonal
Multi-player	High	2 to 3 months	One-off
Educational	High	2 to 3 months	One-off, seasonal (incorporated)
Role playing	High	2 to 3 months	One-off

Avoiding the Big Mistakes

In this section, I share some of the mistakes I've made so you can avoid making them yourself. Believe it or not, the list was originally much longer — I've shortened it to the most important mistakes I believe can be easily avoided with a little care from the start.

Depending on desktop

Mobile phones and tablets are everywhere, so as a marketer you need to make sure your gamification elements are developed using mobile-friendly interfaces.

As I explain in Chapter 6, having a responsive game design means that it can be played on different types of devices. You can achieve this goal using HTML5, which is a web-based framework that, in my opinion, is the best way to ensure games will run correctly within any device.

Going rogue

This is when you try to add more elements after the final functional spec has been agreed upon. You see something new and creative and you just *have* to incorporate it into the development. Most of the time, this only delays your final product and inevitably creates a muddled and confused gaming experience.

TIP

Stick to your functional spec and create a "wish list" when you come across a new idea. The wish list will come in handy for the next phase or launch.

Complicating the gameplay

Making the gameplay more unique or more complicated doesn't mean your campaign will be better. The ultimate goal for your team is to get your audience to engage with your campaign. Overly complicated gameplay causes confusion, and confusion means minimal overall engagement. Another downfall to adding too many elements is the adverse effect on loading times. If your campaign doesn't load quickly, your audience will quickly lose patience and give up.

REMEMBER

Keeping the gameplay simple will create a fun, interactive, and easy-to-play campaign. It's always better for games to be simple and quick, so your audience will pick up the campaign and play right away without paying too much attention to the rules.

Creating too many rewards

Throughout this book, I go on a lot about rewards. After all, rewards are the ultimate goal for gamification marketing campaigns. But you can have too much of a good thing. If your audience is being rewarded for every little action, the rewards won't mean anything. Your entire reward system, along with your entire gamification campaign, will be rendered null and void.

Try to limit the ways your audience is awarded points, badges, and rewards. By doing this, your audience will take them more seriously, and the rewards themselves will feel special.

Also, keep both the objectives and the rewards simple. Choose two or three actions that you want your users to carry out. By rewarding users for carrying out these specific behaviors, you can motivate them to do exactly what you want.

Misusing game mechanics

Game mechanics are the vehicles that drive your marketing goals and objectives. Use too many, and your message becomes over-saturated and your audience will start to become confused over the goals being communicated to them. Use too few, and the message won't be clearly communicated.

As an example, you can use badges to communicate achievements to your audience. Badges keep them motivated to reach the next level or earn another badge. Badges, which mark special achievements, give your audience a way to feel connected to your campaign.

However, a common mistake I see is when my clients force their audience to earn their next badge by making them do something they don't want to do. For instance, maybe the only way to progress is by sharing their progress on their social media platforms. Not everyone will want to do this, and some people will bail.

In this example, the game mechanics of badges should be looked at as a way to recognize an achievement, not the reason for your audience to do something.

Banking on virality

Gamification marketing may be more likely to go viral than ordinary marketing campaigns. However, you can't *bank* on this happening. It will either happen or it won't. I never create a gamification campaign for virality.

The sheer volume of campaigns that contain online videos, photos, cartoons, memes, infographics, posts, and other easily sharable content is so enormous that it unlikely for *any* campaign to go viral.

Most companies I work with have to acknowledge that the primary goal of their gamification marketing campaigns is to create a buzz within their industry.

You can't control the outcome, but you can control the development, design, and launch. Work on this, and the buzz within your industry will be guaranteed.

Creating a campaign that can't be played at work

WARNING

No one will want to play your campaign if game elements (for instance, sudden loud sound effects, annoying track music, or full-screen animation) can cause sudden embarrassment at work. These elements may be the norm in online games, but use them with caution in your campaign.

When designing a gamification campaign, I like to imagine that the audience is sitting one desk away from their manager. If you think of it this way, the elements you develop will be subtle and stress-free so that everyone can enjoy and engage with your campaign, wherever they are.

Assuming your audience will understand games

Unless your company is in the gaming and entertainment industry, your audience may not be familiar with gamification campaigns. I see this as a major plus.

All marketing campaigns are looking for some way to create a disruption within their industries. Gamification helps to get your audience's attention and promote your message. If you suddenly launch a game to an audience who isn't usually presented with this type of marketing, you'll pique their interest.

The mistake I see is assuming your audience will understand the point of the gamification elements. They won't. To overcome this hurdle, introduce as many help elements as you can. These may include videos, FAQs, in-game instructional messages, and a chat window.

If you accomplish this goal, once-unknowledgeable audiences will see your company as the pioneer and voice of authority in gamification marketing. For me, this is the best possible result for your team's hard work.

Beginning Your Gamification Marketing Quest

Define your audience and deliver a uniquely engaging campaign to them.

Explore the various types of gamification engagement tools available for your campaign.

Assemble a dream team to help you design, build, and maintain your gamification model.

Understand the technology that will power your gamification marketing campaign.

Chapter 3

Identifying Your Target Audience

I deally, your gamification marketing campaign will deliver a personalized experience to as wide an audience possible. To accomplish this goal, you can't afford to take a global and generalized approach to your marketing efforts.

You need to gather key data on precisely who your target audience will be. After you find this data, you can target your campaign directly to them. However, to obtain the best results, you'll need to exhaust all data channels you have on your existing customers and social media followers. These are people who already know about you and have engaged with your company.

After you've mined this data, your campaign will be sending messages that are customer-centric and content that targets your audience. Identifying your target audience will make your gamification marketing campaign far more efficient and successful.

TIP

In almost all ad campaign managers, you can drill down on exactly whom you want to see your ads. So, identifying and perfecting your target audience to advertise and promote your campaign, will greatly reduce wasted expenditure on ads.

Defining Your Audience

The key to defining your target audience is to be as specific and as visual as possible so that your marketing message feels very personal to them, almost as if you had written to them personally.

Start by defining one specific group of people you want to reach with your marketing message. This group should be interested in your solutions and very likely willing to purchase your products or services. The more specific you can be, the better.

By defining your audience, you'll have a group of people who are most likely to lead to conversions after encountering your campaign. Keep narrowing down this audience in as much detail as possible.

In the following sections, I walk you through how to define your audience.

Throwing out everything you think you know about your audience

Companies often are blind when trying to create target audiences. They feel like they already know who their target audience is, instead of conducting independent audience research.

WARNING

Assuming who your audience is and what they like can cause your gamification marketing campaign's content and strategy to seriously miss the mark. You could experience the following:

>> Poorly judged creative decisions

>> An unengaging campaign style and personality

>> Misjudged promotional strategies

>> A campaign that doesn't resonate with your audience

REMEMBER

Although you may already have a detailed image of your target audience in mind, actively challenge your thought processes. This means gathering hard evidence to substantiate your thoughts. When you do this, you're in the best possible position to offer value to your audience.

Conducting research to find your audience

In a perfect world, every single person on the planet would love your gamification marketing campaign. But this isn't possible because your campaign needs to deliver a personalized experience, and not every consumer is the same.

TIP

There are a few methods you can use to better identify and analyze your target market:

» **Conduct your own primary research.** You can do this by conducting surveys and assembling focus groups to analyze your campaign's objectives. Surveys are efficient because you can receive a large volume of customer feedback without investing a lot of money. Although focus groups are expensive, time consuming, and resource dependent, they encourage productive, interpersonal discussion, which leads to far more productive feedback. I look into this form of research in more detail in Chapter 10.

» **Look into your competitors.** What are their customers saying about their campaigns on social media? You can identify a whole host of things *not* to do by looking at what has annoyed and put their audience off.

» **Exhaust your existing resources.** Do you have mini client databases in other departments of your company? Collect them all and analyze them for key data points.

» **Conduct A/B testing.** Create two versions of your core message and measure the difference in performance. After you've created your two versions, give one version to one group and the other version to another group. You can then monitor and review the responses and level of engagement each version received.

» **Be as specific as possible.** Drill down on who your audience truly is, and study their online attitudes and pain points. By identifying a specific target audience, you can make decisions that are dictated by your customers, which sets your campaign up for long-term success.

» **Segment your audience (see Chapter 9).** Locate all the data you can about how the target customer behaves and any basic information about them. This will help you identify your audience. This data can include the following:

- Age
- Location
- Gender
- Income level
- Education level

- Marital or family status
- Occupation
- Ethnic background
- Interests
- Hobbies
- Values
- Attitudes
- Behaviors
- Lifestyle preferences

Taking a Closer Look at Your Current Customer Base

By knowing your target audience, you can maximize the results of every campaign launch. This means that as you launch more gamification marketing campaigns, you'll find that it'll take less effort, giving you the opportunity to grow and evolve your audience comfortably.

How do you even know what your target audience might look like? Instead of going through experimentation and trial and error, you should look to your existing, loyal customer base. Also, a large portion of the audience who will visit your campaign will be people like your existing customers. Defining these customers can help you refine your campaign's messages to deliver a more personal experience.

You'll gain the following benefits by successfully targeting your gamification marketing campaign to existing customers:

>> You can tailor your campaign's content to ensure that it will appeal to the right people.

>> You can gain a better understanding of the needs of your audience.

>> Your campaign will provide a more beneficial and engaging experience.

>> There will be a higher rate of conversions and call-to-action (CTA) engagements within your campaign.

Establishing existing data points

Initially you need to look at your existing database, whether that's in the form of your company's customer relationship management (CRM) system, SQL/MySQL database, or even Microsoft Excel spreadsheets. Make sure you have each customer's contact information, as well as their purchase and engagement history with your company. Using this information, you need to identify customers by:

>> **Purchase history:** How much they've spent over their lifetime and the most they've spent on one order

>> **Referrals:** The customers who provide the most identifiable referrals

>> **Feedback:** The customers who have provided feedback or reviews regarding your company, products, or services

After you've identified this information, you can perform an analysis to discover and understand your customers' defining characteristics. From there, you can create your audience profiles and then target people who fit the same mold.

REMEMBER

Starting to work through the vast amounts of profiles can be overwhelming. Depending on how your customers have connected with your business, you may not have a lot of information about them. Don't worry about what you don't have — just gather all the information you *do* have about your existing customers into a small database or spreadsheet so that you can start tracking trends.

Here are some of the data points you'll want to include in your analysis:

>> **Personal information:** This kind of information includes your audience's age (a rough age bracket), gender, income, and occupation.

>> **Geographic information:** This is where your existing customers live, as well as their time zone.

>> **Language:** Don't assume your customers speak the same language as the one that's dominant in the place they live. Identify their native language.

>> **Interests:** Interests are a hugely varied piece of the target audience. What do your customers like to do, besides using your products or services?

>> **Purchasing potential:** This not only includes the amount your current customers spend but also their income. It's better to have a set bracket of income (for example, $50,000 to $65,999).

>> **Stage of life:** Are your customers likely to be college students? New parents? Retirees?

By the time you've analyzed your data points, you'll have defined an understanding of each of the following:

>> Who is going to engage with your campaign

>> Which gamification platform will appeal best to your customers

>> Why your audience should choose to click on your campaign

Tailoring for B2B

If your campaign is targeting a business-to-business (B2B) audience, you'll want to change the data points:

>> **Contact's details:** Define the ideal position you're looking to engage with (for example, marketing managers or sales managers).

>> **Communication:** Don't assume that email is the best way to communicate. With certain professions, it may be more appropriate and engaging to inform them of your campaign via LinkedIn.

>> **Company:** This information includes the industries your audience are typically working in, as well as the size, location, and department.

>> **Decision making:** Look at what decision criteria your customers have when it comes to finally making a purchase. It would be ideal if you could understand what was most attractive and unique about your product.

These points can help you tailor your campaign to better appeal to and engage with your B2B customer base. To do this, your campaign will need to contain the same unique features and benefits you'll find in these data points.

TIP

If you can't gain meaningful data points from your existing database or there isn't enough sales from your product or service, find the information from a third party. For example, consider tasking a survey or polling company to find out the information for you. Alternatively, you can do it yourself using an online survey creator platform, such as SurveyMonkey (www.surveymonkey.com), shown in Figure 3-1.

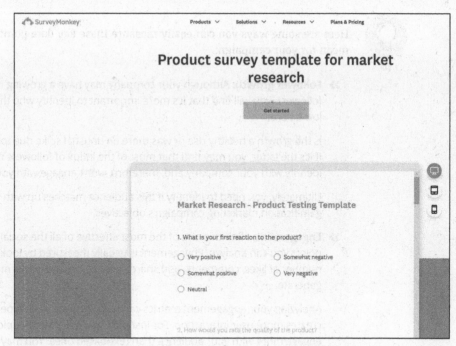

FIGURE 3-1:
DIY online
sites such as
SurveyMonkey
allow you to
obtain important
data points via
polls and surveys.

Mining Your Social Media Accounts

Your existing social media data can provide in-depth insights on strategy and growth for your gamification marketing campaign. Social media data is the collected information from all your social network channels that show how your users share, view, and engage with your company.

In this section, I look at how to target the key data points in your social media data, and then look at a few individual social media platforms. Then I look into the difference between meaningful social media data versus useless vanity metrics.

Identifying key data points

The data from your social media channels will contain key data points for you to analyze. These key data points show the overall progress your company is making on social media. By analyzing these data points, you and your team will be able to make far more informed decisions on your future campaign's content.

TIP

Here are some ways you can easily measure these key data points and what they mean for your campaign:

>> **Follower growth:** Although your company may have a growing number of followers, you will find that it's more important to identify who these followers are.

Is the growth a healthy rise or was there an unusual spike due to a viral post? If it's the latter, you may find that most of the influx of followers may not identify with your company and, therefore, won't engage with your campaign.

Ultimately, you need to identify if this audience matches up with your gamification marketing campaign's objectives.

>> **Engagement:** I find this one of the most effective of all the social media data points you can analyze. Engagement is usually measured by looking at the number of likes, comments, and shares your company's social media posts generate.

Analyzing your engagement metrics can help illustrate what type of posts creates more user interaction. For instance, you may find that picture posts engage more with your audience than text-based ones. You may also find that articles or blog posts that focus on your industry create more shares than ones that talk about your company. I've even noticed that an interesting article can generate more engagement than special-offer blog posts.

Generally, a high engagement rate indicates your company is connecting well with your audience.

>> **Social reach:** Your social reach metric will show you how many people have seen your messages and how far your messages have traveled. Social reach is a good indicator of how well your social media accounts and content attract new audience members.

By analyzing your social reach, you can work out if your company is, in fact, connecting and interacting with the right people.

Your social reach metrics are usually easily accessible on the insights page on each of your social media channels.

>> **Impressions:** This can be an extremely complex metric to obtain. Impressions show how many times your company's posts showed up on an audience's news feed or timeline. In some instances, audiences may see your posts several times on their newsfeed due to some of their friends sharing it. So, one user can have multiple impressions.

>> **Follower count:** In my experience, this is the one metric that, when analyzed on its own, is the most useless. You'll probably be looking at this metric to see how big your company's social media audience is reaching. However, if all those followers are not constantly engaging, then this metric holds little to no value.

>> **Likes and shares:** Likes given to your social posts indicate a very key engagement metric. The more likes your social updates receive, the more engagement they'll cultivate. This key data will show which of all your social content deserves more attention and has authority over the others.

Shares demonstrate a more powerful metric than likes because they're an indicator of loyalty. Audiences can like a post without even reading it. But a share means that the audience has genuinely engaged with your social content. This key data will measure the amount your customers want to recommend your company to their peers.

>> **Mentions:** I always liken mentions to what people say about you behind your back. I find that most times a company is given a "mention" on social platforms, the original commenter doesn't even follow the company. You need to capture and acknowledge what people say about your company via mentions on all channels. Analyzing this key data can help to measure your social media growth.

TIP

Although comments are not a direct key data metric, they're an excellent opportunity to engage with your audience and learn key data from them. Valuable and relevant posts will always generate comments. Even if the comments are negative, you can still learn something about the commenters' experience with your company.

Tracking unique metrics from each platform

To get a true measure of all metrics, you need a solid understanding of how well your company is performing on all the social media platforms. The good news is that most social networks offer their own native analytics, which makes mining metrics much easier. In this section, I look at some of the ways the popular social media channels offer this data.

Facebook Insights

If your company has created a Facebook Business page (and if you haven't, get on that!), you can analyze some key data metrics within the social network's channel, as shown in Figure 3-2:

>> **Engagement:** The number of likes, clicks, and shares your posts have generated. One useful feature allows you to compare metrics from one week with metrics from another week.

>> **Post Reach:** The number of people who have seen any of your content.

>> **Impressions:** The number of times your company's page is displayed.

>> **Organic Page Likes:** The number of people who like your page without coming from an ad campaign. This metric highlights the total amount of likes, as well as the number of new page likes on a week-by-week basis. It also helps you understand if your Facebook presence is growing at a healthy rate.

>> **Paid Likes:** The number of people who have liked your page who came from your ad campaign.

>> **Reactions:** The number of people who have engaged with your posts by using the various Facebook reaction emojis.

>> **Unlikes:** The number of people who unliked your Facebook page this week. If this metric ever spikes, it's worth investigating the reason, such as a controversial post.

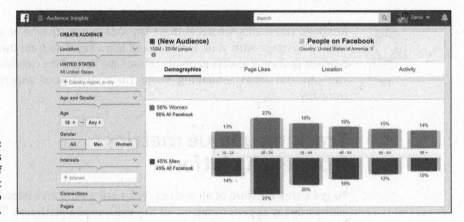

FIGURE 3-2:
Facebook Insights offers a wealth of audience metric data for you to analyze.

Instagram Insights

Instagram Insights provides in-depth key data metrics broken down into two sections — one focused on your individual posts and the other on your profile as a whole. Here are some of the key data metrics to capture:

>> **Account Impressions:** The number of times your posts and stories were viewed

>> **Total Reach:** How many unique accounts have viewed your posts and stories

>> **Website Clicks:** The number of people who have clicked the website URL in your profile

>> **Profile Visits:** The number of people who have clicked to view your account page

>> **Post Likes:** The number of likes your posts have received

>> **Post Comments:** The number of comments accumulated on any given post

>> **Posts Saved:** The number of times your posts have been saved

>> **Follows:** The number of people who have started following you over a period of time

Twitter Analytics

Twitter for Business allows you to have in-depth data access to your analytics, as shown in Figure 3-3. The dashboard gives you a summary of your content and other key data. Here are some of the key metrics to analyze:

>> **Engagement Rate:** A whole array of data, including link clicks, retweets, favorites. and replies to your tweets

>> **Followers:** The total number of Twitter followers your company has gained, with the ability to compare the rates over a period of time

>> **Link Clicks:** The total number of people who have clicked the website URL in your profile

>> **Mentions:** The number of times your username was mentioned by others

>> **Profile Visits:** The number of people who have visited your Twitter profile

>> **Replies:** The number of times your tweets received replies

>> **Retweets:** The number of retweets received by others with a date comparison features

>> **Tweet Impressions:** The number of times your tweets have been viewed, whether they were engaged with or not

LinkedIn Analytics

You can access LinkedIn Analytics through your company page, which shows you all the social media data going into your LinkedIn page. Here are the top metrics to look out for:

>> **Interactions:** The number of comments, likes, and shares your posts and overall company profile have received over a period of time

>> **Clicks:** The number of clicks on your posts and on your company page

>> **Engagement:** The number of interactions compared to the number of impressions

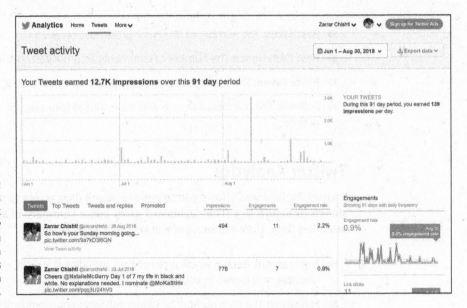

FIGURE 3-3:
Twitter Analytics helps you break down your key data to help you understand which types of posts resonate with your audience.

» **Followers:** The number of new followers, which includes any that came through a sponsored post

» **Impressions:** The number of times your posts were visible to other LinkedIn users

Choosing meaningful social media data versus vanity metrics

It's easy to get carried away with metrics without really understanding what they mean in context. In other words, it's just as important to analyze your data as it is to collect it.

I, too, am guilty of becoming obsessed with *vanity metrics* (any social media metrics that make your company's presence look good but do very little in terms of engagement), such as follower counts and likes. The fact is, the data from vanity metrics can't help you measure your company's past and current performance in a way that allows you to create a strategy for your gamification marketing campaign. These data points can look impressive when you're looking at them on a report. But, unfortunately, they may mean very little without some context.

REMEMBER

Your company having thousands of followers will mean very little if those same followers aren't translating into sales. Similarly, it's pointless posting interesting news and content if the majority of your followers fail to engage with it.

Not all is lost, though. There must be a reason for your company to have gained all these followers. The cause may have been a popular hashtag you used or created in the past or it may have been a popular post or article. By identifying the reasons for the followers you have, you can use the same tactics in your marketing campaign's launch strategy.

REMEMBER

Vanity metrics are ultimately useless because they're too easy to measure and contain no context. This can mean they're often misleading and, more important, don't really help your gamification marketing campaign in any meaningful way. They *look* impressive, but sadly, they're devoid of substance.

Sure, go ahead and take pride in your earned metrics. There's absolutely nothing wrong with sharing this data to demonstrate how well your company is doing online. But just know that the data can't be used as evidence for your campaign. Best to leave it for website headlines and press releases.

Arguably any of your social media data can be a vanity metric. The good news is: You can identify which metrics are meaningless. The central question to ask yourself when considering a metric is whether it will help your business achieve its goals. Here are three questions you can ask yourself to identify vanity metrics:

>> **Can you make meaningful decisions for your gamification marketing campaign using this metric?** Dismiss the metric if your answer is "no."

Actionable metrics can help you make decisions for your campaign. This is because the data provides meaningful feedback and context for what your campaign should be doing and whether it has a chance of working.

Smart data can also help you adjust your campaign strategies so that the campaign attracts a bigger audience. Any social media data you collect should help make your campaign's launch better.

>> **Can you reproduce the results?** Any social media data that was produced as a random occurrence will not be helpful to your campaign. When it comes to viral posts in social media, lightning rarely strikes twice unless you can identify a cause and effect within the data.

Make sure the metrics have been reproduced more than once. If you can't reproduce a statistically similar metric, then you can't use it to improve your campaign. This means that although the metric looks great, the data and knowledge behind it won't do anything to help your campaign.

>> **What caused the metrics to look so good?** Did someone with a large following notice one of your company's posts and repost it to his followers? If so, try reaching out to him over a private message and ask how he noticed your campaign — and be sure to express your gratitude, too.

Was a third-party algorithm (that your company has no control over) responsible for the spike? Engage with the owners/developers of this algorithm to see if you can utilize it for future campaigns.

Was seasonality a factor (where a particular month was responsible for the majority of the metric)? This will be an invaluable source of information when you come to analyze your campaign further using big data (see Chapter 11).

Did someone in your company pay to increase the numbers of likes or even followers? If so, determine whether this spending was a good return on investment (ROI) for your campaign.

DON'T IGNORE THE SILVER SURFERS

If executed properly, your gamification marketing campaign can appeal to all ages. Recent reports have shown that the number of *silver surfers* (generally, people over 50, although that age can vary by country) on social media is on the rise. This is excellent news for your campaign because you have a new channel to target, an all-too-often ignored audience.

Instead of trying to target this demographic directly, use Facebook. Facebook is the silver surfer's preferred mode of social networking (35 percent of people over 65 are on Facebook, compared to the 2 percent of them on Twitter and 1 percent on Pinterest). So, quite clearly, the bulk of your marketing will rely on Facebook.

Also, bear in mind that older people will take their time to research campaigns. For this reason, it's important to invest in your campaign's content. Although silver surfers search for campaigns the same way anyone else does, they also tend to use Bing over Google. Bing users tend to be 55 to 64, so include Bing in your marketing strategy.

In terms of your actual gamification content, because this demographic is more likely than the average Internet user to read articles and web pages in full, you should employ more CTAs, such as "learn more." Your user experience (UX) is a very important element in ensuring that your campaign is effective. If a silver surfer comes to your campaign only to be faced with a complex and confusing landing page, he most likely won't engage with it. Plan your landing pages to make them easy for anyone to access — use large fonts, clear buttons, and clear navigation.

Chapter **4**

Increasing Engagement in Your Campaign

Thinking of ways to maximize engagement for your gamification marketing campaign is not only beneficial but critical — and this is true before the launch and long after the launch. In this way, your company will build a far more meaningful and engaging experience for your customers.

REMEMBER

The audience's experience must be much more than just a sales campaign. Your audience should not only feel like the campaign was designed for them but also feel actively rewarded for their loyalty and participation. If you accomplish these two goals, they'll feel a connection to the campaign.

Campaigns that focus on audience engagement are focused on creating value, which give their audiences a meaningful experience. In this chapter, I offer specific strategies you can use to increase your campaign's engagement.

Establishing User Rewards and Achievements

One of the main advantages of using gamification marketing is the real-time audience engagement. Your audience gets real-time feedback and statistics that are influenced by their engagement on your campaign. Rewards and achievements will motivate your audience to keep coming back to your campaign so that they can complete or proceed with a challenge or task.

Gamification marketing allows your audience to see immediate progress. This is the edge that gamification marketing has over traditional marketing. With traditional marketing, your audience doesn't instantly and visually receive any form of feedback and reward for their efforts. With gamification marketing, you can reward every action or task that your audience completes.

Rewarding your players

Your audience should receive points or earn experience as rewards for their actions within your campaign. Essentially, your campaign should be designed to encourage your audience with strategically clever rewards throughout the campaign. These rewards will entice them to return over and over again. In the following sections, I introduce you to a variety of rewards you can offer your players, from points to progress bars to badges and more.

Points

Points are relatively straightforward to design into your campaign. The concept is simple: Complete a task, and earn points. Some websites use points as a way to encourage users to post in web forums, which helps the forum owners get more content on their site.

Points are the simplest way to reward a player. Every mission or action that you want to include in your gamified campaign can be rewarded by a specific number of points. You need to choose carefully the number of points depending on the difficulty of a mission or action.

In most campaigns, points act as a measure of how well the user has mastered the game. So, the points signify the level of skill a person has managed to accumulate. You might award points for the following:

>> **Clicking on call-to-action (CTA) buttons:** For instance, downloading the app, signing up for an account or even just clicking the Start button on your game could be CTAs that garner points for a user.

>> **Completing a level:** You can even award points in areas *within* a level.

>> **Spending time playing the game:** If the user logs a certain number of hours playing the game, he can be awarded points.

>> **Sharing the game with friends:** If the user clicks your specially designed Share buttons, she can earn points for herself and/or for the person she has shared the campaign with.

>> **Offering feedback:** Give the audience a reason to give you valuable feedback on your campaign. Did something go wrong technically? Was it too hard or too easy? Would they like to see more levels?

You can use points to create a leaderboard (see "Leaderboards," later in this chapter), which is a running list of users who have the most points.

Levels and progress bars

Progress bars are graphic visualizations that show your audience their progress within areas of your campaign. For instance, they may show the progress the user has made to get to the next level. Progress bars can also be used to denote the number of points the user has to obtain in order to earn a badge.

No matter their context, progress bars help keep your audience motivated.

Levels can help keep users motivated, too, but they also give the audience a sense of direction for their motivation. Users are more focused and determined if they can see where they'll end up if they keep playing. Levels and progress bars can do the following:

>> Give the user a sense of progress.

>> Give the campaign a more structured design.

>> Help keep the user motivated.

>> Help you design specific challenges within the campaign.

Badges

Badges are extremely important in gamification marketing campaigns because they make your audience feel important and skilled. In my experience, badges strengthen the audience's connection with the campaign.

TIP

When designing your gamification campaign, tie the points you're allowing the audience to earn to the badges you'll be awarding. Badges boost the audience's engagement because they're a visual representation of the points they've earned. Plus, badges are just more entertaining and fun than points (which are just numbers).

Many gamified apps and sites have used badges for high user engagement. For instance, Waze, a very popular driving app, uses ranks, which come with visual badges, as shown in Figure 4-1.

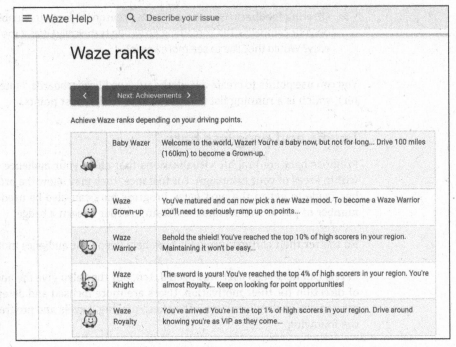

FIGURE 4-1: Waze, a popular driving app, has created innovative badges to keep its audience engaged.

TIP

When designing your badges keep in mind the following tips:

>> Badges should be designed to acknowledge specific audience behaviors.

>> Use a limited number of badges so your audience will feel appreciated and valued. If you shower your audience with badges, the badges won't mean as much.

>> Brand your badge names and icons to your campaign's theme and content.

>> Create multiple levels within badges, which can be accompanied by points.

Leaderboards

The points your audience collects can be used to create a leaderboard in your campaign. A *leaderboard* is a running list of users who have the most points. This kind of friendly competition can act as a motivating factor for audiences to keep returning to your campaign.

TIP

If executed correctly, leaderboards can be powerful motivators. Here are some tips when designing your own:

» When you have a large number of players, show just the top players, but give people the option of seeing where they rank in comparison.

» Give points and possibly a special badge for the top three players. You could give a separate badge to players who retain their high ranking for a certain period of time.

» Offer the option for players to receive an alert if they get knocked out of the top positions.

» If a user is positioned lower than the top ranks, visually show her how far she is to the next position up.

Creating loyalty

Creating loyalty in your audience will not only keep them coming back to your campaign, but also increase the likelihood that they'll actively promote it to everyone they know. In fact, loyal audiences go on to subscribe to future campaign, actively follow your company's social media channels, and are more likely to buy from your business.

In order to create loyalty, you need to have a relationship with your audience. Relationships convert audiences into customers and spokespeople for your campaign. In the following sections, I offer tips on how to build the kind of relationship that will engender loyalty.

Making customer service a priority

To create a loyal audience, you need to provide consistently amazing customer service. Your audience will evaluate every interaction they have with your campaign based on the service you provide them.

Here are some examples of where this interaction could originate:

» The contact form on your landing page

» An email or phone call

>> A tweet directed to your Twitter profile

>> A question posted on your campaign's Facebook page

>> A direct message received through Instagram or other social media channels

Make sure your replies are friendly and that you convey to the user that you hear them and are working to resolve their issue. Your support, regardless of how the audience reaches you, should have the same energetic and positive tone. The replies should aim to solve their problems in a timely fashion.

TIP

Your campaign's responses should be engineered to answer questions or address problems quickly, on all platforms. Most people on social media expect a response within an hour. I advise, particularly on Twitter, to aim to respond within half an hour.

Polling and questioning

Requesting and responding to your audience's feedback is the best way to build loyalty. The sad fact is that most of your audience won't give feedback unless they've run into a problem with your campaign.

For this reason, you want to get ahead of any potential issues and design different ways to actively obtain feedback from your users. This will demonstrate to your audience that you *want* to hear from them, regardless of whether they had a good experience or a bad one. Also, the responses you get will go a long way toward perfecting your *next* gamification marketing campaign.

Another positive outcome of actively soliciting feedback is being able to identify the reasons audiences are *not* returning. What's making them leave? Why are they not wanting to return? On the flipside, you may learn what you're doing *well*. What does your audience love about your campaign? Why do they keep coming back?

TIP

There are few different strategies for getting your customers to give you this feedback:

>> **Feedback polls on social media channels:** Most social media channels offer forms, polls, and questionnaires that you can send to your followers.

>> **Customer satisfaction surveys:** Customer satisfaction surveys are a straightforward way to collect feedback from your audiences. Send them out a few days after the campaign's launch so you can identify any technical or functional issues right away.

>> **Requests for reviews:** These work really well if your campaign has a mobile app. Typically, it's better to ask for a customer review after your audience has

engaged with your game a few times. You want to give your audience enough time to have familiarized themselves with the campaign.

» **An emoji-themed survey:** These surveys are becoming very popular because they allow your audience to give their feedback simply by clicking the emoji that represents their mood. Typically, response rates are far higher than with text-based surveys. Some great online tools, such as Customer Thermometer (www.customerthermometer.com), shown in Figure 4-2, can help you quickly implement this type of survey in your campaign.

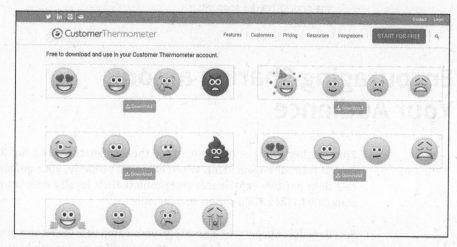

FIGURE 4-2: Customer Thermometer helps you implement emoji-themed surveys in your campaign.

Celebrating on social media

Make sure that you take the time to celebrate your most loyal audience members on your social media channels. After you've given them a voice to express their feedback and experiences, you may want to make them feel special for supporting you.

Showcase their thoughts and ideas on your social media platforms like Instagram and Twitter. This will not only promote loyalty with your current audiences, but also let other people know that you value your audience.

Referring the love

One of my favorite methods to encourage loyalty is to offer your audience referral programs. Referral programs reward your audience every time one of their friends joins the campaign.

People who love your campaign will naturally want to share it with their friends through word of mouth. A referral program goes one step further and *encourages* that behavior with incentives for both the referrer and the referred friend.

TIP

Design your incentive program to:

>> Offer points to both parties (referrer and referred) if they share a special code.

>> Award badges to referrers who hit a milestone of referrals.

>> Create attractive and eye-catching images that your audience can share on their social media accounts.

Encouraging Sharing among Your Audience

Encouraging your customers to share their experiences is a highly effective and crucial form of engagement. When executed properly, your audience will broadcast their positive experiences and promote their loyalty with your campaign and company to their follower on social media.

Social media engagement also allows your campaign to connect and form valuable relationships with your audience. If you utilize as many channels as possible, you'll increase your overall engagement, which results in long-term benefits for your gamification marketing campaign.

Using a unique hashtag

Hashtags are a way for people to discuss specific events, products, services, and issues on social media. They're used by millions of social media users on a daily basis, and they're fast becoming an integral component of any marketing campaign.

A *hashtag* is a word, or group of words with no spaces in between, with a pound sign (#) at the start. Using hashtags, online users can easily search for any topic and participate in the conversation.

With user content being posted on all social media networks faster than ever, using a hashtag to raise awareness is not as easy as adding # to your company name. Your gamification marketing campaign will need to create its own unique hashtag and get people to use it. By successfully creating a unique hashtag, your team will be able to track and control the flow of the discussion generated on social media channels.

Seeing how hashtags work on the various social media platforms

Hashtags got started on Twitter, where they were used for "tweet chats." As "tweet chats" became more prominent, marketers began to see the importance and relevance of using hashtags in their campaigns.

Today, most major social media platforms support hashtags. Knowing how to create and use them on each platform can help put your campaign directly in front of your target audience. In the following sections, I take a look at how hashtags are best utilized on the major social networks.

TWITTER

By using relevant hashtags in your tweets, you can increase your campaign's engagement. Twitter hashtags can be used to denote specific topics. If these hashtag-driven topics become immediately popular at a particular time, they're referred to as a *trend*. Trending topics appear on the sidebar of your audience's Twitter feed. A trending topic is a very powerful marketing tool because it can bring a mass volume of traffic to your campaign.

In the past, hashtags have been the subject of mass abuse by marketing campaigns. As a result, Twitter immediately filters out posts that are blatantly spamming a hashtag. Any tweets that use a trending hashtag but do not add value to the conversation are also filtered out. Tweeting about a trend and then linking it to something totally unrelated is a violation of the rules. An example of spamming would be deliberately adding a trending hashtag like #SuperBowl to your tweet just to receive traffic to your message when your content has nothing to do with football or the Super Bowl.

TIP

I recommend using a maximum of three hashtags per tweet.

INSTAGRAM

As opposed to Twitter, where hashtags should be used sparingly, on Instagram, using more hashtags often leads to *more* engagement. Instagram does place a limit on the number of hashtags you can use in each post (the limit is 30 hashtags). You may not need to use 30 hashtags in a post, but you can do so without being penalized.

TIP

Try using the maximum number of hashtags so you can experiment with which hashtags work for your campaign. Instagram is the best platform for using multiple hashtags, so try a wide variety of them, and use them on posts, photos, and comments.

Hashtags can be used to encourage users to submit their images and experiences with your gamification marketing campaign. For instance, some hashtags were created specifically for Instagram photo campaigns like #ThrowbackThursday (more recently #TBT), which encourages audiences to post past photos of themselves.

FACEBOOK

Facebook was a late adopter of hashtag support and, because of this, the practice has not been picked up by its users as much as it has been with the other platforms. Nevertheless, Facebook will group your campaign's posts containing the same hashtag. Even better, the results from hashtag searches are not limited to people you know.

WARNING

On Facebook, try not to use too many hashtags. I recommend using a maximum of two hashtags per post on Facebook. If you use more than that, your campaign is in danger of appearing unprofessional and will most likely annoy your Facebook audience.

TIP

If you're using a Facebook hashtag strategy, make sure all your campaign's posts are public. This will enable your audience to find and share your posts and hashtags.

PINTEREST

Using unique and relevant hashtags on Pinterest can help expose your campaign to a brand-new audience. On this platform, nonspecific keywords aren't likely to do any good. So be sure to create unique hashtags that are specific to your campaign.

Pinterest hashtags are placed in the pin description. When users click them, they're taken to pins that contain the exact hashtag, plus pins with the same word or phrase in the description.

LinkedIn

Up to a couple of years ago, LinkedIn didn't emphasize the use of hashtags. But recently, LinkedIn has made some important updates to its algorithm, which has resulted in a 50 percent increase in viral activity. Today, more than two million posts, videos, and articles are filtered, ranked, and displayed in the feeds of LinkedIn's members.

When you publish content on LinkedIn, use a maximum of three hashtags in the body of your post.

The use of unique hashtags on LinkedIn will get your campaign in front of people outside your network, making it a great way to increase awareness.

Creating unique hashtags for your gamification marketing campaign

If your hashtag is unique, it will stand out, and your campaign will gain a lot more engagement on social media channels. The goal is to come up with something unique that is shareable and memorable, and that instantly connects with your audience. In the following sections, I provide essential tips to keep in mind when creating a keyword.

MAKING IT BRIEF BUT UNIQUE

In general, when it comes to unique hashtags, the shorter the better. One good reason for this, apart from the fact that shorter phrases are more readable and notable, is that a longer hashtag may be unpopular with Twitter users because tweets are limited in terms of the number of characters. Plus, longer hashtags are just harder to spell and more likely to result in typos. If in doubt, just remember that less is more. Try to stick to no more than three words. And try to avoid two of the same letters in a row (for example, #marketinggamification), because it's just harder to read.

Starbucks used a unique two-word hashtag, #StarbucksRewards (see Figure 4-3) to promote its gamification marketing campaign on all its social media platforms (see Chapter 15).

EVOKING AN EMOTION

If you craft your hashtag to evoke an emotion with your audience, you'll instantly connect and leave a lasting impression. Not only will your hashtag catch their attention, but it will motivate them to share your posts.

Here are some ways to evoke emotions with hashtags:

>> **Create a sense of belonging.** In order to do this, you need to have a deep understanding of your audience. Try to include interests into your hashtag that are specific and unique to your company or industry. For instance, if your campaign is targeting one city or state, include that as a hashtag.

FIGURE 4-3:
The #Starbucks
Rewards
hashtag in use.

>> **Create a sense of thrill.** Motivate your audience to take action on exciting events or issues.

>> **Celebrate local pride.** Do your homework and see if you can connect with specific locations. Playing to an audience's local team or event will evoke strong passions.

>> **Challenge your audience.** If you can empower your audience to take up challenges, you'll evoke a sense of independence and freedom.

GOING TOPICAL

Carefully structuring your hashtag to incorporate a viral topic can boost your campaign instantly. A trending topic will already be generating a lot of buzz, and you may be able to redirect all that traffic to your campaign. For example, many campaigns piggyback on the Academy Awards season. Charmin capitalized on the public tweeting and messaging over which Oscar nominees wore the best dress by tweeting a picture of a red dress with toilet paper trailing behind with the caption "Good luck to the nominees tonight. Don't forget to look down before your speech."

WARNING

Tread with care. Most trends can turn negative just as quickly as they went viral. Plus, trends don't last forever, so you can't bank on them to last for the duration of your campaign.

BEING CLEVER

If you can craft your hashtags to be catchy, funny, and clever, your campaign is more likely to catch on quickly and spread like wildfire. A clever hashtag will be easier for your audience to remember.

An excellent example is Charmin's #TweetFromTheSeat, shown in Figure 4-4, which was both fun and actionable (because Charmin tied it in with a contest).

FIGURE 4-4: Charmin's #TweetFromTheSeat hashtag was funny and encouraged its audience to get involved with a contest.

BEING CONSISTENT WITH YOUR BRAND

While you're generating your catchy and clever hashtag, make sure that it still fits with your company's overall brand. Take into consideration what your audience expects from your company. Think of the tone your business adopts across all its social media accounts, and make sure your hashtag is consistent with that tone.

You can come up with a catchy and clever hashtag that fits your brand, no matter what area of business your company operates in. For instance, the frozen pizza company, DiGiorno, was able to showcase its personality in a fun and clever way with the hashtag #DiGiorNOYOUDIDNT.

PROOFREADING HIDDEN MEANINGS

TIP

If you're using more than one word in your hashtag, make sure to not fall victim to a serious hashtag fail. Check to make sure it doesn't spell something other than what you intended. Back in 2012, a unique hashtag (#susanalbumparty) was created to promote singer Susan Boyle's album launch (see Figure 4-5). Unfortunately, this ended up creating a huge stir internationally, and not the kind Ms. Boyle was after. (Read it a few times and see if you can find the double meaning.)

FIGURE 4-5:
To promote Susan Boyle's album, the promoters failed to double-check this very unfortunate hashtag.

Susan Boyle
@SusanBoyleHQ

Susan will be answering your questions at her exclusive album listening party on Saturday. Send in your questions Susan HQ

When a hashtag has an unintended double meaning, it can wreak havoc on your campaign and cause embarrassing damage to your brand. Proofread and triple-check your hashtag to ensure that there is absolutely no potential for any double meanings. Get as many people in your company as you can to try to find hidden meanings.

You can't assume users will use capital letters in your hashtag, so look at it with all lowercase letters, as well as with the first letter of each word capitalized, to see if anything stands out.

TIP

RECYCLING HASHTAGS

You may find an existing hashtag works perfectly for your campaign. As you would if you were using an existing company name, do your homework and make sure there are no preexisting negative associations attached to the hashtag.

WARNING

Use an online tool, such as Hashtagify (http://hashtagify.me) to actively check out existing associations with any hashtag.

TIP

Providing more than just a link to share

Successful campaigns usually become popular thanks to the active contributions of their audiences. When your audience connects to and engages with your marketing content, they'll actively look to promote and champion the campaign's messages.

Fortunately, there are a number of ways to ensure that your campaign's messages create the right level of interest and engagement. In the following sections, I look at some methods of achieving this goal.

Creating great content

Content creation is a vital element for any gamification marketing campaign's strategy. However, it's imperative that you and your team produce interesting content that your audience will want to share and like. Without this level of engagement, your content will have failed to support your campaign.

A number of psychological triggers can inspire your audience to engage with your content:

>> **Focus on quality.** Invest time into research and content creation. If you do this, you can expect your audience to be interested and engaged. Content development can take time and effort and is worth outsourcing to professional copywriters if you have the budget.

>> **Break up your text.** You audience will be impatient and will tend to read very quickly. This means that they'll be turned off by a block of text. Try to format your content intelligently by using numbered lists, bulleted lists, and headers to easily highlight key information points.

>> **Generate infographics.** Infographics are informative and easy to understand. Plus, they're convenient for people to share on social media. If you don't have the time or resources to create the graphics yourself, you can use online tools like Piktochart (https://piktochart.com) to quickly create high-quality infographics, as shown in Figure 4-6.

>> **Offer incentives.** Your audience will love free and special offers. You can experiment on what level of engagement you want from your audience to win (for example, asking them to share, like, or follow your campaign page). Or you can go one step further and request audience submissions in the form of text, images, or videos. If executed properly, your campaign will create a viral ripple effect that will have your audience doing all the hard work for you.

Scheduling your social media posts

Once you have great content (see the preceding section), you're ready to share it! But spontaneously sharing amazing content is tough to do. The good news is, you can schedule your social media content so that it's posted when your audience is most likely to engage with it.

Every social media channel is different when it comes to the best times of day to post (see Table 4-1). This is due to a number of factors, such as when users are most active. Try to schedule your social media messages to be posted at the best times. If you're covering an area that spans more than one time zone, you can repeat your messages so that they fall in the local times for the majority of your audience. That way, you're much more likely to engage with your followers.

TABLE 4-1 **The Best Times to Post on Social Media**

Social Media Channel	For Business-to-Consumer Campaigns		For Business-to-Business Campaigns	
	Days	Local Times	Days	Local Times
Facebook	Monday, Tuesday, and Wednesday	11:30 a.m. to 12:30 p.m.	Monday and Thursday	9 a.m. to 2 p.m.
Twitter	Monday, Tuesday, and Wednesday	Midnight to 1 p.m.	Tuesday, Wednesday, and Thursday	9 a.m. to 4 p.m.
Instagram	Monday, Tuesday, and Friday	9 a.m. to 1 p.m.	Monday and Friday	Noon to 3 p.m.
LinkedIn	Monday and Wednesday	11 a.m. to 1 p.m.	Tuesday and Wednesday	7 a.m. to 9 a.m. and noon to 5 p.m.

TIP

How *often* you should post to social media depends on the platform. Here are my recommendations:

>> **Facebook:** One or two times per day

>> **Instagram:** One or two times per day

>> **LinkedIn:** Once per business day

>> **Pinterest:** Five to 30 times per day (This number is higher than the other platforms because, on Pinterest, you're pinning original image content for other members to pin rather than a wall of text or original witty tweets.)

>> **Twitter:** Five to ten times per day

REPOSTING YOUR OWN CONTENT

On average, you can get 30 times more click-throughs when you share your content on social media more than once. For this reason, you should schedule reposts of your content on social media channels more than once during your campaign.

If you're worried that your audience will get bored if they see the same content more than once, keep in mind that only a very small portion of your audience will see your content. The majority probably never saw your content the first time you posted it.

I recommend reposting your content on social media at least once every two weeks after the first publication, for the duration of the campaign. A good way to do this is to mix up the appearance of the content:

- You can change the image associated with the text.

- You can change the heading.

- You can tailor the content to the platform. Some platforms allow you to add a CTA. For instance, on Twitter, you can add a poll within the content.

Try to identify posts that your audience loves — these are the reposts that consistently get likes and comments. Your audience is more likely to share this content, so when it comes to reposting these messages, make sure you engage with them, encouraging them to share it with their friends.

Using photographs and videos to your advantage

Social media messages with visuals get more engagement. In fact, posts with images get approximately 20 percent more click-throughs than those with just text. Depending on your campaign, you could use screenshots of your campaign, stock images, funny memes, and animated GIFs to increase overall engagement.

Posts with GIFs get over 150 percent more click-throughs than posts with static images. Memes bring humor to busy news feeds and result in a far higher percentage of shares than any other type of image posts.

You can create themed videos to give your audience a chance to learn more about the campaign. Here are some ideas for video content:

>> How-to play videos that guide your audience on how to participate in the campaign

>> Viral entertainment videos — anything from a fun and engaging advertisement to user submissions of people winning the game

>> Behind-the-scenes videos, showing off the technology and team behind the campaign

>> Customer testimonials showing the fans talking about how much they enjoyed the campaign

Use your social media channels to get your audience excited to watch and share the videos.

The best video length for social media channels is around one and half minutes long.

Building a community with a Facebook group

A Facebook group is an ideal way to build an online community. You can engage with your community by asking questions, getting valuable feedback, and asking them to share your campaign's content.

After you've created a large community, you may want to make your group public, closed, or secret depending on the kind of community engagement you're hoping to achieve.

Write a campaign intro to help your following understand the purpose of the group. You can also select additional admins to help you manage your group.

Chapter **5**

Budgeting Your Development

F or traditional marketing campaigns, the majority of the budget is assigned to costs incurred from the point the campaign is launched — things like ad spend, public relations, and online promotions. This isn't the case for gamification marketing campaigns, though. A gamification marketing budget needs to include the upfront planning, development expenditures, and ongoing IT support for your campaign. If you factor these expenses in, you'll create an engaging campaign that remains in budget every step of the way.

In this chapter, I look at the major areas of cost during development — namely, your developers and testers. But I start things off by helping you set your budget.

Setting Your Budget

Your marketing budget is the amount of money you have to spend to make your gamification marketing campaign a reality. You need this piece of your marketing plan right at the start.

Estimating the costs

When planning your budget at the start of your campaign, try to estimate various costs, including the following:

>> **Market research:** Market research includes efforts such as developing a customer profile and examining your current audience preferences. Include administering surveys and buying research studies to best determine the perfect gamification model for your campaign.

>> **Development:** This will be the bulk of your pre-launch costs. This includes the designers, developers, database developers, and testers.

>> **Launch day:** You need to estimate the costs to launch your campaign successfully (see Chapter 9). This includes testing different marketing strategies you may not have tried before, such as Facebook ads.

>> **Monitoring:** Try to estimate the costs of tracking and monitoring your communications efforts. This includes hiring (possibly someone in-house) to track the vast amounts of analytical data you will be gathering.

>> **On-going support:** You need to factor in the server and website support your team will need for the duration of the campaign.

Aligning your budget with your goals

At some point you and your team will have set goals for your gamification marketing campaign. Now is the time to plan your budget to make those goals a reality. I find this is the best method for setting a realistic budget that will, in turn, help you run a successful campaign.

The way to do this is by determining each of your marketing goal's acquisition costs. This means working out how much money you'll need to spend to get one goal conversion.

I look into specific goals in Chapter 7, where I explore how to embed your goals into your gamification marketing campaign.

Anticipating risks

When your campaign's budget is defined and the plan is in place, it's helpful to try to identify any risks that could potentially harm your campaign's budget.

Here are some examples of risks I tend to see with gamification marketing campaigns:

- **Key staff:** One example I find all too common is when the campaign relies too much on one person. If that person gets sick or quits or is otherwise unavailable, you're out of luck. The solution is to budget for more staff. Key team members should train at least one or two other staff members on how they perform their duties *before* they win the lottery and head off to Fiji.

- **Viral success:** Another example I see too often, especially with gamification models, is the unexpected viral success of a campaign. If your service agreements don't account for a burst of traffic in the millions, that's another risk. To combat this risk, invest in a content delivery network (CDN), which will ensure your traffic is spread across nodes around the world. Also look at the various options your current web host offers. Look to upgrade vital elements of your server, like bandwidth allowance and memory.

- **Untested technology:** Your developers may have used new and untested frameworks or application programming interfaces (APIs). This represents risk because your campaign may not work when certain browsers get an upgrade. The solution is to budget for continual testing. Unfortunately, there are no specific times in the year browsers will upload upgrades so you just have to stay on top of this issue.

  TECHNICAL STUFF

  An API is a software intermediary that allows two applications to talk to each other. Typically, an API includes a list of operations that developers can use, along with a description of what they do. The developer doesn't necessarily need to know how the API works; she just needs to know that it's available for use in her gamification app.

- **Junk folder:** Communicating to your audience during your campaign is key. However, what if your legitimate email campaign is being filtered as spam? This can suddenly happen after a few people, by mistake, send your emails to spam. Unfortunately, fixing your email reputation will take time — possibly beyond the duration of your campaign. Look to invest in something like Amazon Simple Email Service (Amazon SES), a cost-effective email service built on the reliable and scalable infrastructure that Amazon developed. With an email service like Amazon SES, you can send marketing messages with confidence.

- **Content creation:** If you're planning to create quality content such as videos, photos, or even blog posts in-house, at some point you and your team will become too busy to continue. Budget how much money will go into creating the same level of content with an external agency. This will ensure the quality content will keep coming.

>> **So-called "acts of God":** Pandemics, weather, natural disasters, and other catastrophic events represent unforeseen risks and complications. Although I admit this is a low-level risk, it still happens from time to time. So, look into options where your key staff can work from home if coming to the office isn't possible. This includes issuing laptops and ensuring they have good Internet connections. Also, look to hold regular meetings during the day via video conferencing services such as Skype.

After you've identified potential risk factors, you can easily prioritize their threat levels and place an appropriate contingency budget for them. By anticipating and planning for anything major, you'll increase the likelihood of success for your campaign to meet its objectives on budget.

Gathering Your Team

Depending on your company's infrastructure, you may or may not have some talent in-house that you can turn to. For the purposes of this chapter, I assume you do *not* have these resources and will need to budget for it all. Also, I'm assuming that you're planning to run a temporary campaign to test out the gamification marketing strategy, so you'll want to contract agencies and freelancers rather than bring in a permanent staff.

TIP

If you're thinking of hiring permanent skilled employees, you'll want to budget for high-performance computers and licenses for their software technology.

Accounting for your gamification model

Depending on the gamification model you select, you can estimate the number of key staff you need to hire for the development (see Chapter 8). In Tables 5-1 through 5-4, I cover the four main gamification models and summarize the development skills you need to account for.

Outsourcing talent

The key to making your campaign's gamification development successful is deciding which tasks to do in-house and which to outsource. In my experience, the right call can be different for every industry, so there is no one-size-fits-all rule.

TABLE 5-1   **Typical Personnel Required for Action Games**

Role	Typical Time Required on a Project	Specific Role Requirements	Typical Cost of a Freelancer or Agency per Project
Project manager	1 month	An action game will typically take a month for development.	$2,000–$4,000
Artist	1 week	Artists work before development starts and work closely with the game designers. For action games, there won't be a huge resource requirement because most assets can be outsourced and also will be reused between levels.	$750–$2,000
Game designer	3–4 weeks	Game designers will be brought in right at the start to create the concept, but when development begins they won't be required on a full-time basis.	$1,500–$3,000
Level designer	1 week	Typically, the level designer is required up until the designs begin.	$750–$1,500
Game developer	3 weeks	For action games, the development team can use widely available reusable code.	$2,000–$3,500
Sound engineer	1–2 days	Sound engineers work after the development has finished.	$350–$750
Game tester	3–4 days	Because there aren't too many complex permutations in action games for testers to test, they can typically complete their task quickly.	$450–$950
UX designer and web developer	1 week	Action games typically don't have complex page structures.	$1,500–$2,500

TABLE 5-2   **Typical Personnel Required for Simulation Games**

Role	Typical Time Required on a Project	Specific Role Requirements	Typical Cost of a Freelancer or Agency per Project
Project manager	3 months	A simulation game typically takes 3 months for development, but it can take longer depending on your objectives.	$4,000–$8,000
Artist	3–4 weeks	Artists work before development starts, but they continue to work after development begins in order to create custom graphics for later levels and stages. For simulation games, there is a very large resource requirement because most assets are custom developed.	$2,500–$4,500

(continued)

TABLE 5-2 *(continued)*

Role	Typical Time Required on a Project	Specific Role Requirements	Typical Cost of a Freelancer or Agency per Project
Game designer	2 months	Game designers are brought in right at the start to create the concept and are required on a full-time basis until the development ends.	$4,500–$5,500
Level designer	3–4 weeks	Typically, the level designer works even after development starts.	$1,550–$3,000
Game developer	2–3 months	For simulation games, a lot of custom code needs to be developed.	$4,000–$6,500
Sound engineer	5–7 days	Sound engineers can be brought in as each level is completed.	$750–$1,250
Game tester	2 weeks	Simulation games involve an extensive amount of complex permutations, all of which need to be tested and retested on multiple devices.	$2,500–$3,500
UX Designer and web developer	2 weeks	Simulation games typically have complex page structures, which need to be integrated with the website.	$3,000–$4,500

TABLE 5-3   **Typical Personnel Required for Interactive Storytelling Games**

Role	Typical Time Required on a Project	Specific Role Requirements	Typical Cost of a Freelancer or Agency per Project
Project manager	3 months	Interactive storytelling games typically take 3 months for development, but they can take longer depending on your objectives.	$4,000–$8,000
Artist	2–3 months	Artists work for the duration of the project because each level will require fresh graphics.	$4,500–$6,500
Game designer	1 month	Interactive storytelling games feature more graphical content, which means the game designers will be supporting the work provided by the game artists.	$2,500–$3,000
Level designer	Not required	Interactive Storytelling games don't have levels because the user follows the story sequentially.	$0
Game developer	1–2 weeks	Interactive storytelling games feature more graphical content and fewer gaming elements. For this reason, most of the work is done by game artists and game designers. Some gaming elements will need to be custom coded.	$1,000–$2,500

Role	Typical Time Required on a Project	Specific Role Requirements	Typical Cost of a Freelancer or Agency per Project
Sound engineer	2–4 days	Sound engineers can be used for the overall music score and the individual sound effects.	$350–$750
Game tester	3–5 days	Interactive storytelling games don't involve any complex permutations because the flow is very sequential.	$750–$1,500
UX designer and web developer	3–4 weeks	Interactive storytelling games require the flow of the game to be embedded into the website.	$3,000–$4,500

TABLE 5-4   **Typical Personnel Required for Adventure Games**

Role	Typical Time Required on a Project	Specific Role Requirements	Typical Cost of a Freelancer or Agency per Project
Project manager	2 months	Adventure games typically take 2 months for development, but they can take longer depending on your objectives.	$4,000–$6,000
Artist	2–3 weeks	Artists work on the initial stages of the project, ensuring each level has custom graphics.	$1,500–$3,500
Game designer	2 months	Adventure games feature a lot of graphical content, which means the game designers will be supporting the work provided by the game artists.	$4,500–$5,500
Level designer	3–4 weeks	The level designer will be working to ensure the objectives are met for each level.	$1,550–$3,000
Game developer	1–2 months	For adventure games, although there is a lot of custom code required, typically a lot of the code can be reused as the levels progress.	$2,000–$3,500
Sound engineer	1 week	Sound engineers can be used for the overall music score and the individual sound effects for each level.	$950–$1,500
Game tester	2 weeks	Adventure games involve an extensive amount of levels, all of which need to be tested and retested on multiple devices.	$2,500–$3,500
UX designer and web developer	3–4 weeks	Adventure games require the flow of the game to be embedded into the website.	$3,000–$4,500

If your company is smaller, with a limited budget, you'll need to do as much of the work in-house as possible. However, if the budget allows, it's usually far more cost-efficient to outsource some work to agencies and freelancers.

Which agency or contractor you choose will come down to your budget (are you sensing a theme here?). The cost difference between selecting an agency from the Unites States and choosing one from Southeast Asia is huge. Locating an offshore agency or freelancer is easier than ever nowadays thanks to portals such as Guru (www.guru.com).

But is outsourcing your gamification development a good strategy? The answer depends on your unique business situation. For instance, is your business regulated and required to keep all suppliers continually vetted? Or is it important to keep the development of this campaign under wraps?

Recognizing the benefits of outsourcing

Here are some of the most important benefits of outsourcing:

>> **Saving money:** The primary reason to outsource is the cost-efficiency, even if you're only outsourcing a portion of the campaign's development. Hiring an offshore company to develop part or all of your gamification model can be significantly less expensive than hiring full-time in-house developers.

   To put this in perspective, on one of the projects I worked on recently, my client saved 40 percent by outsourcing compared to the cost of getting the same work completed in the United Kingdom, where they were located. They found the overall process minimized their costs, which allowed them to concentrate on launching their campaign.

>> **Overworking in-house staff:** If you have a team of in-house developers or designers, chances are they'll be working on other company projects. Getting your campaign developed probably isn't a priority for them. They have their own day-to-day deadlines to meet, and your project will be almost like a distraction. Unfortunately, this can lead to your campaign being inefficient and riddled with errors.

   Outsourcing your development means your project will be delivered without distraction because the people you've hired will only take your work when they have the time for it.

>> **Accessing advanced technology:** Software design and development, especially for gamification, can require high-end software. Purchasing all the necessary licenses for an in-house team can be prohibitively expensive. On top of that, you may find that your team won't even be using the full extent of the software you're purchasing.

REMEMBER

Online gaming technology constantly evolves, and keeping up can be challenging. By outsourcing your development, you can get access to people who stay ahead of the technology curve. You can get the benefits of cutting-edge gaming technology without sacrificing a large percentage of your marketing budget.

>> **Diversifying your thinking:** Keeping all your development work in-house may feel safe, but it can lead to circular thinking and lack of creative vision.

Outsourcing, especially to an offshore provider, can give you access to fresh perspectives on your campaign's options. You'll likely see innovation from your outsourcing team; differing opinions can encourage your in-house team to be more adventurous as well.

>> **Maintaining quality:** One of the ways to ensure your campaign succeeds is to ensure that you produce a high-quality gamification option. However, between staff benefits, minimum wage requirements, and the current software development job market, it can be difficult to find expert developers who are available to work within your budget and limited time requirements.

Of course, you could consider training your employees, but I find this will just delay your campaign's launch considerably. Outsourcing gives you immediate access to top-level developers who won't need additional training.

Identifying the downsides of outsourcing

Nothing is perfect. Outsourcing comes with some potential pitfalls you'll want to avoid. Here are some common hurdles you may have to overcome if you decide to outsource:

>> **Difficulty with communication:** One benefit of outsourcing development is being able to gain access to a global pool of talent for a lot less money. However, this can result in issues with communication.

I'm not talking here about their grasp of the English language — you'll likely find that their spoken English is top-notch. The issue to overcome is the vast difference in time zones and cultures.

Establishing regular channels of communication with your outsourced team is essential. At the start, it will be essential for them to understand your campaign's objectives and requirements. But as the campaign evolves, you need to ensure you can clearly communicate any changes in real time.

TIP

One way to ensure effective communication is to use collaboration tools like Asana (www.asana.com). Regular engagement with the remote team via video or audio communication and stand-up meetings at regular intervals are best practices for establishing communication channels with the outsourced development team.

>> **Misunderstandings:** I find that before outsourcing development, it's important to clearly document your campaign's requirements and deliverables. Essentially this document should include:

- Exactly what your team will expect

- The expected timeline (which includes the deliverable milestones)

- An explanation of the overall scope of the campaign

Failure to communicate these details could result in your development being completely misaligned with your campaign's objectives. When this happens, you'll find an impossible gap between your expectations and the actual deliverables.

TIP

To eliminate this issue, you should look to establish a *software requirements specification* (SRS), which describes exactly what should be developed and implemented. An SRS contains a full and detailed description of intended purposes, system behavior, and user and system requirements. Also, an SRS defines the expected system performance and capabilities. A typical SRS includes the following:

- The purpose of the campaign

- An overall description of the development required

- Specific requirements

This document can be an excellent starting point that gives the team clear insights into your campaign's requirements. However, drafting this kind of document can be daunting. I recommend using an SRS template website like SRSCreator (www.srscreator.com), shown in Figure 5-1, which can help with the documentation process.

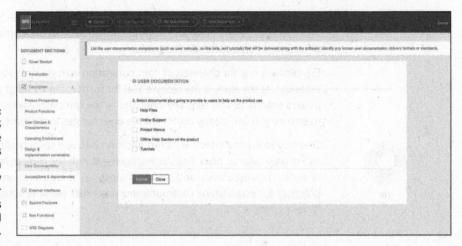

FIGURE 5-1: Using an SRS template website such as SRSCreator can help clearly document your campaign's requirements and deliverables.

>> **Coding quality issues:** Unfortunately, *code quality* is a very ambiguous term because there are arguably no strict definitions for what qualifies as high-quality or low-quality code. Setting standards for the quality of your coding is a challenge, one that's significant when you're trying to ascertain an offshore company's coding expertise.

In my experience, quality code needs to have two key qualities: readability and maintainability. This means the code needs to be well documented and well tested. It also need to be formatted using the best practices and coding conventions of the programming language the application is being written in.

Maintaining code quality when outsourcing development to offshore teams requires communication of expectations, laying down the quality benchmarks in advance, and regular briefings with the team to stay on top of the development efforts.

A coding standard ensures that all the developers working on the project are following certain specified guidelines. The code can be easily understood and proper consistency is maintained. However, the team that you're outsourcing to should have checks in place to ensure consistency in code quality.

The code should be such that anyone should be able to understand it even after returning to it after several months. To do this, the developers should:

- Take measures to continually review their code review.

- Perform functional and unit testing.

- Ensure that there is a consistency in the naming convention of variables and files.

- Name each function according to what it performs.

- Ensure that the code contains descriptive commenting throughout.

If the coding standards are not defined, developers could be using any of their own methods, which might lead to certain negative effects such as:

WARNING

- **Security concerns:** Your campaign could be vulnerable to attacks if it has been coded with bugs and errors in its logic.

- **Performance issues:** Poor coding has an adverse effect on the performance of the site, which includes server response issues and reusability of the code.

When the coding standards are implemented, these problems can be easily overcome, giving you a secure campaign with minimum or no performance issues.

>> **Conflict over who's responsible for the code:** Disputes often occur over who's responsible for fixing faulty code, and this usually boils down to the ultimate ownership of the code. It most often happens when the outsourcing partner you pick goes on to outsource some of the work to other agencies and freelancers. When this happens, it becomes almost impossible to agree on the actual code ownership.

If you don't know who "owns" your code, your campaign's deliverables can be inconsistent with the objectives set out because no project leader or team can be held accountable for the work. When outsourcing development of a software project, make sure you understand who will be working on it and try to ensure that at least a few of the project managers stay consistent throughout the entire process.

Drafting a contract

The phrase "get it in writing" is vital in gamification development. A properly drafted contract acts like a road map for the outsourced agency or freelancer to follow. It also safeguards you from bearing the brunt of losses in case the agency or freelancer you hire fails to deliver.

Always seek legal advice when drafting a new contract.

Here are some best practices when it comes to signing an outsourcing contract:

>> **Try to draft a contract that ensures that you won't miss out on any of the objectives your campaign is promising.** Avoid using a boilerplate template. Instead, actively try to customize your contract to include the features and objectives you want delivered.

>> **Outline the deliverables and the time frames.** The contract needs to clearly state the deliverables expected in the form of a list of objectives. From here, you should establish an estimated timeline to deliver the work. An outsourcing agency that follows Agile development (see Chapter 8) can help give you an accurate picture of the development progress.

>> **Ask for objectives-based deliverables instead of time-based deliverables.** An objectives-based contract will help you judge the quality of the deliverables. It can also help identify any flaws or errors in your planning early on so you can communicate changes to the developers.

>> **Agree to milestone-based payments.** Breaking down the campaign development into distinct milestones and defining the payment schedule in accordance with the achievement of these milestones simplifies the payment structure. Plan regular follow-ups for achieving milestones and schedule stand-up meetings with the team.

>> **Insist on code guarantees.** Don't sign a contract without some form of code guarantee. The contract should specify that the code you receive is free of any errors and device-related responsiveness issues. A period of one to two weeks is a reasonable time frame within which any bugs found in the application need to be fixed at the developer's expense.

>> **Make sure the contract covers support.** A maintenance support contract should clearly state the duration for which they'll provide your team support for the software they built and delivered. Specifying support in the project also results in an enhanced sense of ownership for the developers working on building your application.

>> **Pay attention to intellectual property rights.** Make sure your contract spells out that you have complete intellectual property rights to your project. This will save you from legal issues related to rights in the future. It will also prevent the contractor from reusing the code written for your campaign when working for a possible competitor in the future.

>> **Require them to sign a confidentiality agreement.** You need to ensure that all information and proprietary information of your company remains confidential. Nondisclosure and confidentiality agreements should be signed not just with the outsourcing agency but with any individual developers they go on to employ.

>> **Include a termination clause.** You hope development goes to plan, but be prepared for worst-case scenarios. Make sure you include a termination clause in your contract that clearly states the course of action that you'll take if development fails to reach completion.

Chapter **6**

Getting to Know the Technology

amification marketing campaigns are heavily dependent on knowledge of the latest technology. Although the actual development will be done by skilled developers and designers, knowing what *can* be done is invaluable, regardless of your role.

In this chapter, I fill you in on the common platforms and technologies used in gamification marketing campaigns. I walk you through how to make sure your email communications are being delivered. And I show you how to test your campaign to make sure it's working as it should.

Choosing a Foundation for Your Campaign

Gamification has quickly become the most popular platform not only for creating stunning, high-quality games, but also for generating loyalty and meeting engagement objectives in marketing campaigns. To do this, marketing teams have had to decide how they want their gamification models to be delivered.

The two choices currently are either to develop for the web using HTML5 (so your campaign will live on the web and be accessed using a web browser, like Chrome, Firefox, or Safari), or developing a native app (which is downloaded by the user from a mobile app store like any other app, and used only on their mobile device).

Building in HTML5

HTML5 is made up of the following three components:

>> **Hypertext Markup Language (HTML):** The basic building block of the web

>> **Cascading Style Sheets (CSS):** Adds style (for example, fonts and colors) to multiple web pages all at once, saving you lots of time

>> **JavaScript:** A scripting language that enables you to create dynamic content and animation

HTML5 delivers almost everything you would want to develop on an online platform without requiring any additional software (such as browser plug-ins) or hardware. You can use HTML5 to build incredibly complicated gamification applications that will simply run on your audience's browsers, no matter what browsers they're using.

HTML5 is cross-platform, which means it works whether you're using a smartphone, a laptop, a desktop, or even a smart TV. Plus, you don't have to pay anything to use HTML5 — it's free!

TIP

HTML5 is an evolving standard, so there is an ever-increasing list of features you can use for your gamification campaign. For instance, your campaign can respond differently depending on where your audience is physically located. However, bear in mind that it takes time for these new features to be adopted by all browsers. Websites such as Can I Use (www.caniuse.com) provide up-to-date browser support tables.

You're probably assuming that your audience will need to be online to engage with your gamification marketing campaign. Fortunately, with HTML offline web applications, your audience can continue to engage with your campaign regardless of whether they have an Internet connection.

An *offline application* is a packaged group of your campaign's web pages, style sheets, and scripts files that are available to the audience whether a web connection is present or not. In technical terms, the new HTML5 offline storage saves files in a cache and allows users to access their materials when they're offline. In other words, HTML5 allows your audience to engage with your campaign anytime, without limitations.

Your audience can't *always* be offline. Your campaign will still need to sync with your cloud server. Aim to keep certain information — for instance, the user's music preference — locally on your audience's device. Your developers will let you know various situations where local storage is a better alternative to server-based storage. By offloading data storage to your audience's device, you avoid the hassle of syncing data on your server all the time. Only store noncritical data offline.

Pay attention to security and privacy with *host-proof hosting* (in which applications are designed so that they don't have to trust the web server that stores your data). With host-proof hosting, the servers that hold the encrypted data don't *also* possess the key to decrypt that data. In the unlikely scenario that someone were to obtain access to your database, it would be useless, because the data can't be understood without the key.

Consider whether offline support is justified — there is a high price and level of complexity to online-offline applications. Here are some of the arguments for developing this complex concept into your campaign:

>> **Your campaign will be playable when your audience goes into airplane mode.** If your audience knows they can still keep playing when they're offline, you'll see an increase in play time.

>> **Servers go down and network outages occur.** Unlike websites, your app should be able to continue despite not having a connection to the online server database. In this way, your audience will be able to keep engaging with your campaign even if they experience network issues.

>> **It creates a faster experience for your audience.** Offline technologies support caching, so web apps can boot quickly and show your campaign instantly.

On the other hand, despite network data being much faster these days, there are still noticeable limitations for certain applications, especially in terms of both throughput and latency. For instance, if your campaign involves high-density videos and editors, you'll probably find the video is too big to fit into memory at once. In this case, you're far better off storing the video offline and pushing changes to the server as and when they happen.

>> **If your campaign goes viral, your server will experience a burst of unmanageable traffic.** When this happens, your app will no longer be able to register new users. However, by creating an offline feature, you allow all your registered users to continue uninterrupted.

In the following sections, I cover the technical aspects of developing offline features for your campaign, starting with the options available to you for storing data on your audience's devices.

Application cache and offline storage

As opposed to mobile applications, an offline application is a packaged group of web pages, style sheets, and JavaScript files that are saved on your audience's device. These files are actually stored in the application cache.

When a request for a file (for instance, a CSS file) is initiated by your campaign, instead of requesting the file from your web server, the file is taken from this application cache.

Pages loaded into the application cache are served from the cache regardless of whether a connection to the Internet is available. There are primarily two offline capabilities in HTML5; the difference is what type of data they store:

» **Application caching:** Saves the campaign's core logic and user interface

» **Offline storage or client-side storage:** Captures specific data generated by the user, or resources the user has expressed interest in

In a gamification marketing campaign, application caching would retain the initial HTML document, the JavaScript, the CSS, frequently used icons and images for game characters and scenes, and sound samples. Then the next time the user visited your campaign, the game would load immediately. In addition, there are application programming interfaces (APIs) that control what can be cached from your campaign, which is not the same as regular browser caching.

TECHNICAL STUFF

An API is a software intermediary that allows two applications to talk to each other. Typically, an API includes a list of operations that developers can use, along with a description of what they do. The developer doesn't necessarily need to know how the API works; she just needs to know that it's available for use in her gamification app.

Additionally, if you wanted to let the user to continue playing your game from a previously saved position, your campaign's code would return the previous state of the game instantly. This kind of data is not held in the application cache, because it's user specific, so it's handled by offline storage.

Your developers will ensure that whenever the user presses Save, the data is not only uploaded to the cloud server but also stored on the device at the same time. A good example is when you want to save the player's badge or loyalty status. Your developers will want to keep a loop running to store the game data offline so that the latest changes are still there even if the user suddenly loses battery or connectivity. It also takes less bandwidth than continuously uploading the user's state to the server.

Data storage alternatives

Here are some of the alternative methods of storing data locally:

>> **Cookies:** Most applications only store identifying information in cookies; they store the rest of the user's data on the server. Still, the fact that cookies can store some data does put them in the category of offline storage. Unfortunately, the data capacity of cookies is extremely limited and, on occasion, cookies can slow down network activity because they're transferred to and from the server inside HTTP headers. So, your developers should use them judiciously.

>> **Plug-in storage:** Plug-in storage has been supported by several plug-ins, and offline storage was one of the main selling points right from its inception. There are some downsides of plug-in storage, though:

- *You have to assume the plug-in is present and that the user has the right version of the plug-in.* It isn't uncommon for company firewalls to block plug-ins and for plugin releases to lag behind, or not exist at all on certain operating systems.

- *You have to have rely on the plug-in developer keeping up the plug-in quality.* You have no control over the plug-in.

>> **Web storage:** Web storage is a very convenient form of offline storage, because it's a simple structure of key-value pairs like any other JavaScript object. Web storage works well for gamification situations, such as saving a user's rewards or loyalty points. Although technically speaking, the values can be any type, this isn't the case in practice. Browsers currently support only string values. There is also a variant where the data is removed when the window is closed; this is known as *session data*.

For many offline storage scenarios, web storage may be all you need for your gamification campaign, and it's the most compatible format of storage available. However, the data isn't structured, so if you wanted to locate all games at level 10 or above, for example, you have to iterate through every single game item manually.

My main concern with web storage is the unreliability when it comes to multiple tabs. The issue is with the integrity of your data and the accuracy of any queries. For instance, a user may have your campaign open in two or more tabs. One tab could be writing several things to the storage, and the other tabs could be reading the partially updated data.

>> **Web SQL Database:** A Web SQL Database is an offline SQL database. It's a general purpose open-source SQL engine that comes with all the pros and cons of traditional databases.

It comes with a fully relational structure, allowing you to rapidly query and manipulate data. It also includes database optimization, which gives it a powerful performance advantage. Plus, there is support for transactions, which means that no data integrity issues can arise with web storage.

However, a Web SQL Database comes at the cost of complexity. Does your campaign need a full relational database in your front-end web client? For most campaigns, this option is overkill.

The other issue is compatibility with browsers. Unless your campaign will only need to target a particular browser, I would pass on this option.

>> **IndexedDB:** IndexedDB is a compromise between web storage and Web SQL Database. It's relatively simple and capable of being very fast. IndexedDB can provide more storage capacity and, as with Web SQL Database, there's support for transactions, which means no data integrity issues. Best of all, it's supported on all modern browsers.

>> **FileSystem API:** FileSystem API fills a niche not supported by the other techniques. It gives you a way to store binary content (as well as plain text), create folder hierarchies, and store potentially huge data structures.

With the FileSystem API, a web app can create, read, navigate, and write to a sandboxed section of the user's local file system. A sandbox section is an isolated testing environment that allows you to test the campaign settings. If your campaign needs a directory structure, use this API to store large chunks of data (for example, large text documents or even entire movies).

Unfortunately, as of the time of this writing, the FileSystem API is supported by just the Chrome, Edge, and Opera web browsers.

Offline storage has many potential applications, such as wanting your campaign to run when your audience is using airplane mode. However, the challenge is to decide which option to use when, and to use them in the right way. Your developer should be able to determine the right path for your campaign based on your marketing objectives and goals.

Recognizing the downsides of building an app

Many marketers' first thought is to push their gamification model onto a mobile game app, and it's not hard to see why. Native mobile apps have seemed like the "cool" development platform for the last few years. Gamification apps can utilize the latest device capabilities, load graphics fast, and perform equally well offline, in addition to presenting the game play on a silky-smooth interface.

On the other hand, the global demand for the HTML5 game development platform has expanded so fast that it's currently the far more preferred platform to launch gamification marketing campaigns. With the relentless backing of the giants of the industry, including Apple and Google, HTML5 is rapidly becoming the leading technology for gamification.

There are an equal number, if not more, reasons for marketers to "go native" with apps, and I explore these options in Chapter 9. But the more I work as a consultant in the commercial world, the more I see that HTML5 is the better option. If you're looking to launch an effective and engaging gamification marketing campaign, I would passionately steer you toward HTML5.

Here are some ways HTML5 will be better for your campaign over native app development:

>> **You only have to worry about launching on one platform with HTML5.** If you go with a native app, your campaign will have to be developed for all the different mobile platforms. Not only do you have to get your gamification model developed using different programming languages, but your developers will potentially also need separate computers. In contrast, nearly every mobile device, tablet, and computer system offers full support for the latest games developed in HTML5.

A few years ago, I was approached by a marketing director to consult on a new range of interactive storytelling campaigns that would be developed over the next two years. Throughout the first meeting, he kept insisting that they would need apps for the games to play on their iPad-mounted displays. You can understand his initial disbelief when I explained that if they were to develop in HTML5, the games would not only be instantly available to be deployed on the display units in the museums but also on their websites, the handheld (Android) devices handed out for tours, and in their promotional USB devices — all for a fraction of the cost of native app development.

>> **It's easier to update your campaign with HTML5.** Need to update your gamification campaign urgently? With HTML5, your audience will see the new updates in about the length of time it takes to click Upload on your developer's FTP program. With native apps, you're at the mercy of the app store. Although the app update approval process has sped up considerably in recent years, there is still a waiting period, which can be problematic, particularly if the updates are urgent.

>> **Users can find your campaign more easily with HTML5.** It can be hard to be noticed among the millions of apps in the app stores. In contrast, HTML5 campaigns are essentially websites. And websites can be optimized from day 1 of your campaign's launch. In other words, the page your campaign sits on will be known to search engines when you launch your game.

Plus, as your campaign gains traction, other sites will be able to link to or embed your game into theirs. Even better, you can publish your HTML5 games onto Facebook in a few easy steps (see Chapter 9). This means an ever-increasing number of link-backs, resulting in higher search engine ranking.

Finally, you aren't limited to promoting your campaign on app stores. Instead, you can advertise and promote your campaign everywhere, taking advantage of the web's inherent shareability to reach new customers.

Remember: The ultimate goal of any gamification marketing campaign is to find audiences who will not only play but also recommend, share, and even promote the campaign. HTML5 campaigns can do all that easily.

>> **You don't have to worry about running out of memory with HTML5.** Every time there is another major iOS update, some apps stop working. What are the chances your campaign will face that problem? Add in the towering number of photos saved from apps like Instagram, Snapchat, and the default camera app, and memory becomes precious to the user.

HTML5 campaigns require no memory or device permissions. They run seamlessly on the user's browser and, as a bonus, can even be saved as an icon on the user's desktop or mobile start screen.

Keeping Up the Communications

Email is a fact of life for many gamification marketing campaigns, even in this age of social media. Every campaign should communicate with its audience with official emails. The problem is that email is also a complex endeavor for companies that need to send tens of thousands of messages per week for their campaign.

One of the worst points in any marketing campaign is when you realize your emails are going directly into your audience's spam folder. Time-critical campaign updates are not getting through, and there is nothing you can do about it.

In this section, I tell you how to avoid this scenario in the first place and then look at ways you can resolve it if you do find yourself in this unfortunate position.

Checking your email deliverability

Being blocked by just one major mail client (like Google) can impact your entire email marketing campaign. By tracking delivery to all major Internet service providers (ISPs), you can work out where your marketing email ends up: inbox or spam.

I recommend the following kinds of email deliverability tools:

>> **Email spam checkers:** Spam checkers let you analyze the content of your emails and check them against spam filters. They're looking at various elements inside your email message (like the amount and types of links, images and their size, coding, what's inside the headers, and so on). The results are usually presented on a scale from 1 to 5, where 5 means your chances to hit the junk folder are the highest. Many sites will perform an email spam check, but I recommend Email Copy Checker (https://emailcopychecker.com), Mailgun (www.mailgun.com), and Mail-Tester (www.mail-tester.com).

>> **Seed list testing:** In seed list testing, you send your email individually to a sample list of email addresses yourself, before launching it to your whole database. These sample email addresses are usually set up to include different ISPs (like Outlook or Google), devices, and web browsers. After sending your email campaign to a seed email list, you should know whether your email is delivered to the inbox of all major email clients.

>> **Reputation monitoring tools:** These tools help you monitor your Internet Protocol (IP) address and domain name reputation. Your IP address is the unique address that identifies your mail client's server on the Internet, and your domain name is the name of your website (like dummies.com). You can see whether your IP address or domain name is listed on one of many blacklists that ISPs use when evaluating the incoming emails. An example of such a service is GlockApps (www.glockapps.com), which can help check to see if your IP address or domain name is set up correctly and has a good reputation with the major ISPs.

Table 6-1 outlines some of the advantages and disadvantages of these tools.

TIP

If you can, include all three of these tools in your email campaign workflow. But if you don't have the time or the resources to do that, here are my recommendations:

>> If this is a new email campaign, use a spam checker and a seed list.

>> If you're relaunching one of your older campaigns, use a seed list.

>> If you've been experiencing deliverability problems (such as high bounce rate and complaint rate), use all three tools.

TABLE 6-1 **Advantages and Disadvantages of the Deliverability Tools**

Deliverability Tool	Advantages	Disadvantages
Email spam checker	Very quick, usually taking just a few seconds. Easy to use. Very powerful because it's based on hundreds of various tests.	Extremely limited scope because it only looks at the content of your emails, excluding factors like the recipient's behavior or the ISP's filters.
Seed list testing	Can help you identify email display issues. You can see what your email looks like on different email platforms. Can help identify important issues (for instance, display problems) that would not come up in spam checker tests.	Not based on real people. The results from seed list tests are not perfect, which may give you a false confidence in your deliverability.
Reputation monitoring tool	Gives you an insight into the more technical side of email marketing. Gives you information about potential deliverability issues quickly.	Doesn't give you insight into your email content or how it renders in popular email clients. Can be confusing, which results in falsely alarming you when everything may be fine.

Making sure your emails don't end up in the spam folder

Spam filters have a list of elements that they consider to be key spam criteria. Whenever any of these elements is present in your email, it will earn your email a certain number of points. Earn enough points, and your message will be filtered as spam. The points limit varies across ISPs, so there's no way to know exactly how much you can get away with — for this reason, you want to pay attention to all the following:

>> **Text and images:** Pay attention to your text-to-image ratio. Sending an email that is too image heavy is the most common cause of campaigns going to spam. This can be a particular problem if your campaign is one big image containing hardly any text at all. Aim for a good balance of text and images.

>> **Keywords:** Certain words and phrases often trigger spam filters. There are plenty of obvious ones such as *risk-free* or *100% free,* but terms like *limited* or *click here* can cause problems even when used legitimately. You can see a list of common email spam trigger words and phrases to avoid at www.simplycast.com/blog/100-top-email-spam-trigger-words-and-phrases-to-avoid.

- >> **All caps:** This may seem obvious, but I see it used in major campaigns all the time. Using all caps in an email is game-over with all major ISPs.

- >> **Punctuation:** Like emails with all caps, emails with exclamation points go directly to spam, especially when the exclamation points are in the subject line. Try to moderate your enthusiasm. Too many exclamation points will definitely earn you some spam points.

- >> **Subject line:** Avoid using a long subject line — it can sometimes earn you spam points.

- >> **Different colored fonts and/or styles:** Spam filters look for variations in colors and font styles. Try to keep your email simple and use no more than three font styles/colors in total. Less is more on this front.

- >> **Links:** Having a large number of hyperlinks in your campaign can trigger spam filters. If you have more than three links, decide if they're all strictly necessary and delete the rest.

  REMEMBER

  Any link in your email counts toward your link count, even it's the same link in multiple places in the same email. Keep in mind that if you link your logo to your home page, that counts in your link count.

- >> **HTML quality:** Spam filters are on the lookout for bad coding. This is due to the fact that real spammers are notoriously bad coders. Make sure your HTML code has been formatted and coded well. Try using an email editor to create your emails. Most email service providers have an email editor for creating email campaigns where no coding knowledge is needed.

- >> **Plain text:** Going one step further, ditch the HTML and go for plain-text emails if you can. They'll stand a better chance of getting through.

- >> **Unsubscribe link:** Give your audience a way to opt out. Some of the major ISPs will penalize your email if they don't detect an unsubscribe link.

TIP

Take a look through your own spam folder and look for the violations I list above. You may be surprised to see emails from some major companies in your spam folder just because they fell into one or two of these traps.

Continuing with your campaign

If your IP address or domain name has been blacklisted, you'll need to take some steps to fix that. Being blacklisted is more common than you may think.

In this section, I define what a blacklist is, tell you how to know if you've been blacklisted, and give you steps you can take to improve your deliverability and get off a blacklist.

Checking to see if you've been blacklisted

An email blacklist is a real-time database that uses criteria to determine if an IP address is sending email it considers to be spam. Unfortunately, there are several blacklists and each has its own unique criteria for what it considers to be spam. However, all blacklists can impact deliverability for your gamification marketing campaign's emails. If you're on one of the blacklists, your emails could end up in spam or not delivered by being actively rejected. Essentially, your messages won't show up in your audience's inboxes.

TIP

Here are a few tools you can use to check your email reputation:

>> **Barracuda Central** (www.barracudacentral.org/lookups): Its reputation system is simple, with only a good or poor rating, but results are tabulated in real time, which could help if you've noticed your deliverability failing fairly recently.

>> **Cisco Talos Intelligence Group** (https://talosintelligence.com): This tool has a three-tier ranking system (good, neutral, and poor) instead of a number system.

>> **McAfee Trusted Source** (www.trustedsource.org): McAfee's reputation tool provides a bit more information. It provides information on your domain's email and web reputations, as well as affiliations, domain name system (DNS), and mail server information.

>> **Sender Score** (www.senderscore.com): Sender Score allows you to view your reputation on a 0- to 100-point scale. The higher your score, the better your reputation. It is compiled with a monthly rolling average and is probably the best-known tool in this list.

>> **WatchGuard ReputationAuthority** (www.borderware.com): My preferred tool, ReputationAuthority provides a reputation score based on automated antispam and antivirus analysis of data sent previously from the IP address.

Getting off the blacklist

Each blacklist database has its own criteria for flagging IP addresses. Those criteria could be due to:

>> **Technical listings:** These occur mostly from mail server configuration issues, such as missing or incorrect reverse Domain Name System (DNS) records, missing or incorrect banner greetings, and mail servers operating within a suspicious range of IP addresses.

- **Policy listings:** These are based on an operator who doesn't want to receive email from certain countries or ISPs that have a history of not honoring unsubscribe requests.

- **Evidence-based listings:** These are based on an operator that has received direct evidence that an IP address has been involved in sending unsolicited emails.

If your IP address has been blacklisted and you want to investigate, you'll need to visit the blacklist's website and do a lookup on your IP address. Most blacklist databases provide general listing reasons, but won't list specific email addresses tied to blacklisted IP addresses. For a blacklist checklist, visit `https://whatismyipaddress.com/blacklist-check`.

Ideally, you'll be able to find out why you were blacklisted. You can then try to get your blacklisting status reversed. To start with, take the time to ensure your network and mail server are configured correctly and all the details are in order for resolving the issues, as prescribed by the blacklist. For instance, they may ask you to correct both forward and reverse DNS records, as well as Simple Mail Transfer Protocol (SMTP) banners.

You want to be removed from any blacklists because ISPs often share IP addresses that have been listed. If you think you've fixed the issues on your end, go back to the blacklist's site and follow its instructions for the IP address removal process.

TIP

Here are some common ways to reverse your blacklisted status:

- **Do it yourself.** Some blacklists have a do-it-yourself (DIY) removal feature that lets you take your IP address off the list without much trouble. However, your team will want to make sure you've resolved any issues before doing this. If you don't resolve the issues, and your IP address gets blacklisted again, it won't be easy to get it removed the next time.

- **Give it time.** Most blacklists have a scheduled automated process that removes low-level listings. So, if your IP address is a light offender, you can wait a week or two, by which time you may be dropped off the list. If your IP address is a repeat offender, the time period will be longer.

- **Be nice.** You'll get a lot farther if you follow the rules and cooperate. When you're trying to get off a blacklist, be honest with them. If you're truly innocent of any deliberate wrongdoing or if your team made an honest mistake, just let them know. The more open and direct you are with a blacklisting database, the simpler it may be to have your IP address taken off the blacklist.

REMEMBER

Spam is a serious problem. ISPs just want to reduce the spam on their email platforms for their customers. Their goal isn't to prevent you from sending emails. ISPs won't blacklist your IP address lightly. If they do, it's their way of trying to identify and prevent real problems.

When you do get your IP address removed from a blacklist — either from a blacklist site or an ISP server — make sure to do the following:

>> **If your team made a mistake, don't make the same mistake again.** You probably won't be forgiven a second time.

>> **If you find yourself blacklisted a second time, consider calling the blacklist administrators.** Try to discover the issue and resolve it on a more personal level.

>> **Start to invest a little time and effort into data management at the start of your gamification marketing campaigns.** Improve your lists to ensure you have robust and reliable data.

>> **Develop a plan for data quality.** Ask yourself what kind of information you're trying to collect. Your data management tools will give you a better overview of your *data hygiene* (the process of ensuring all incorrect, duplicate, or unused data is properly classified and removed) so that you can put those plans into practice. Try using your data management tool to pinpoint the areas where data errors are most likely to occur. For instance, maybe you're collecting duplicate lead information from a specific form online.

>> **Standardize your data at the point of entry.** Make sure that you're gathering your information correctly. Ultimately, this means coming up with a standard operating procedure (SOP) with your team about the kind of information you're going to gather and where you're going to collect it from.

>> **Identify and stamp out duplicates.** Duplicates go hand in hand with blacklisting. No one wants to hear from you twice with the same message. The more you collect the same information on a customer, the more you waste your time and send your insights spiraling in the wrong direction.

>> **Check in with the blacklist sites.** Don't just forget about all the sites you visited to check if you've been blacklisted. Bookmark them and revisit them regularly to make sure you aren't on them.

>> **Validate the unsubscribes.** If someone has asked to be unsubscribed, make sure there are mechanisms in place to ensure he never gets an email again. Ideally, you'll delete him from your database, but this may not be feasible (for instance, you may still need to keep their details so they can continue with your campaign).

WHEN YOU NEED TO GET OFF THE BLACKLIST IMMEDIATELY

If your IP address is blacklisted and you need to start sending campaign emails urgently, you may want to look into using a cloud-based email service such as Amazon Simple Email Service (SES; https://aws.amazon.com/ses). Amazon SES is a cost-effective email service built on the reliable and scalable infrastructure that Amazon developed to serve its own customer base.

Amazon SES has the back-end infrastructure to keep your campaign's communications running smoothly. It uses cutting-edge content-filtering techniques, reputation management features to guard against any issues with regulatory compliance, and a vast array of analytics and reporting functions. Amazon SES is a console app that you can manage and configure for your campaign's needs. With Amazon SES, you can both send *and* receive emails. And Amazon takes reputation and whitelisting seriously by supporting all three authentication mechanisms (DKIM, SPF, and DMARC). In addition, you can track your sending activity and manage your reputation.

For me, the most important benefit is that Amazon SES uses a pay-as-you-go model, so the costs are extremely economical for campaigns that process thousands of emails per week. As of this writing, the cost is about 10 cents per 1,000 emails.

Amazon SES isn't perfect, though. It doesn't provide much in the way of documentation at the start, which makes configuration complicated for most marketers. In addition, there is an initial limit on what you can send; you'll need to get your campaign approved and verified before the limits are lifted. Amazon SES is a simple sending service, not a marketing platform, so you'll need to have your emails prepared beforehand. Finally, Amazon SES won't provide you with a place to store your email lists.

There are several alternatives that are similar to Amazon SES in terms of functionality. You may want to check out the following, too:

- **ClickSend** (www.clicksend.com): ClickSend is a dedicated email sending service that you can integrate via API and SMTP, or you can use its dashboard for marketing emails.

- **Elastic Email** (https://elasticemail.com): Elastic Email is an all-in-one email delivery platform. It offers an SMTP relay, a robust HTTP API, and a user interface that has a complete suite of tools and features for managing contacts, templates, campaigns, and reports. It specializes in delivering transactional and marketing emails for campaigns.

(continued)

(continued)

- **Mailgun** (www.mailgun.com): Mailgun is an email service for developers, which allows them to easily integrate their service into your campaign via API or SMTP. In addition to email sending, Mailgun offers email list management and validation. Mailgun is much more expensive than Amazon SES.

- **Mandrill** (https://mandrill.com): Mandrill is an affordable, scalable, and secure email infrastructure service for Mailchimp clients. It is easy to set up and integrate with existing apps. With servers all over the world, it claims to be able to deliver your emails faster than the others. Mandrill provides detailed delivery reports and real-time analytics, which means your team can easily monitor and evaluate your email campaign's performance.

- **Pepipost** (https://pepipost.com): Pepipost provides a cloud-based transactional email delivery infrastructure that's reliable, scalable, secure, and easy to use. This email sending service can be integrated via API or SMTP relay. It offers competitive pricing as well.

- **Salesforce Email Studio** (www.salesforce.com/products/marketing-cloud/email-marketing/): Marketers can use Email Studio, part of Salesforce Marketing Cloud, to quickly build and send personalized emails — everything from basic newsletters to complex campaigns. Salesforce delivers promotional, transactional, and triggered messages with robust real-time reporting to track and optimize performance.

- **Sendinblue** (www.sendinblue.com): Sendinblue is an extremely popular service for business-to-business (B2B) campaigns. Its pricing is based on the number of email messages sent, rather than the number of contacts you keep in your account. Sendinblue offers free accounts that allow you to send up to 300 emails per day (9,000 emails per month) free of charge.

Complying with the General Data Protection Regulation

The General Data Protection Regulation (GDPR) is a European Union (EU) regulation that aims to enhance the protection of personal data for EU residents. This includes increasing the obligations of companies that collect, store, or process personal data; the GDPR has stronger penalties for regulation violations.

Even if you're not actively targeting the EU with your gamification marketing campaign, EU residents may visit your website, subscribe to your campaign, or be on your email marketing list. If any of this is happening, you're processing and storing personal data for EU residents.

According to Article 3 of the GDPR, the territorial scope of the regulation applies to the processing of personal data for EU residents (including U.S. citizens living in the EU) "regardless of whether the processing takes place in the Union or not." In other words, GDPR has implications for your marketing even if you're not based in the EU.

TIP

Check out the GDPR legal documentation at https://gdpr-info.eu. It may seem overwhelming, but it's worth your time and effort to know what's involved. Understanding the GDPR will give you better insight into changes your legal team may recommend. In the following sections, I cover some of the key issues related to the GDPR and marketing.

Obtaining permission

Data permission is about how you manage *email opt-ins* (people who request to be kept informed about your gamification marketing campaign).

People need to express consent to be contacted in a "freely given, specific, informed, and unambiguous" way, which is reinforced by a "clear affirmative action."

What this means is that your campaign's audience needs to physically confirm that they want to be contacted. Don't use a check box that automatically opts your audience into your email list. Instead, make sure people have to deliberately *select* that check box in order to opt in to your email list.

Accessing data

The GDPR gives people the right to be forgotten, which means your audience has the right to have outdated or inaccurate personal data removed.

The GDPR offers your audience a method to gain more control over how their data is collected and used. This includes the ability to access and remove the data.

In your gamification marketing campaign, you need to ensure your audience can easily access their data and remove consent for its use. Practically speaking, this can be as straightforward as including an unsubscribe link within your email marketing template and linking to their customer profile that allows users to manage their email preferences.

Focusing on data

GDPR requires you to legally justify the processing of the personal data you collect. Ask yourself whether you really need to know all the data listed on your registration form before giving access to your campaign.

This means focusing on the data you need and no longer asking for anything superfluous. For instance, if you really *need* to know your audience's favorite color, and you can prove why you need it, then you can continue to ask for it; otherwise, let it go.

Knowing what happens if you fail to comply

Unfortunately, the cost of failing to comply is high — and the Information Commissioner's Office (ICO) has started to clamp down even harder on the misuse of personal data. In fact, the ICO has already reported several incidents that involve well-known brands that tried to use well-known email activation strategies to reach out to their database.

Table 6-2 lists several campaigns that ran afoul of the GDPR. As you can see, the fines are serious.

TABLE 6-2   **GDPR Marketing Fails**

Company	Description	Fine Amount
Flybe	Flybe sent an email to 3.3 million people in its database with the subject line "Are your details correct?" In theory, this sounds like a smart strategy, but unfortunately, these 3.3 million people had previously opted out to marketing emails and gave no consent to be contacted again. Flybe also gave people the chance to enter a prize draw.	$83,000
Honda	Honda sent 289,790 emails to clarify customers' choices for receiving marketing but did not secure their consent. According to the ICO, "The firm believed the emails were not classed as marketing but instead were customer service emails to help the company comply with data protection law." This email was sent to individuals who had specifically opted out.	$15,500
Google	Sweden's Data Protection Authority (DPA) fined Google for "failure to comply" with the GDPR after the Internet giant reportedly failed to adequately remove search result links under right-to-be-forgotten requests. In a notable twist, the DPA also demanded that Google refrain from informing website operators that their URLs would be de-indexed.	$8 million
The Royal Dutch Lawn Tennis Association	The association was fined for selling data to sponsors without consent of data subjects. In 2018, the association sold personal data of a few hundred thousand of its members to two sponsors without legal basis.	$570,000
Morrisons	Morrisons, a leading supermarket in the UK, sent an email to all 230,000 members from its database, asking subscribers to update their account preferences. Unfortunately, this included 131,000 subscribers who had previously opted out and unsubscribed.	$12,500

Considering Testing Issues

Gamification testing is the most important part of your campaign's development process. This is the final component that analyzes whether your gaming application is ready for launch. Unfortunately, testing is not something game developers are known for doing particularly well. If your budget allows for it, I recommend hiring a separate testing company.

Looking at testing methods

You and your team can implement some key tests even before you bring on an outside testing company. These methods ensure that the end result has been thoroughly tested and give a critical eye to focus on constant searches like inconsistencies and errors.

Here are some game testing techniques that you should develop with your development team:

>> **Combinatorial testing:** Combinatorial testing can reduce cost and significantly improve test effectiveness for many gamification campaigns. This method of experimental design is done to generate test cases. Applying combinatorial testing to game testing increases test execution efficiency, provides better quality, reduces cost, and provides better *phase containment* (the number of defects that are detected and prevented in a given phase). Every possible testing scenario combination is covered using this test. It identifies distinct attributes that can be varied either in data or configuration. Parameters are selected from your game functions, elements, events, settings, play options, and marketing objectives.

>> **Clean room testing:** Clean room testing produces games with a certifiable level of reliability. The focus of the clean-room process is on defect prevention, rather than defect removal. This approach combines mathematical reasoning, design refinement, and statistical reasoning during test case generation and testing. The main aim of this method is to produce minimal defect software.

>> **Functionality testing:** This method identifies bugs or errors in a game that may affect the user experience. Types include:

- *Unit testing:* Tests individual components of your game.

- *Integration testing:* Individual units are combined and tested as a group. The purpose of this level of testing is to expose faults in the interaction between integrated units.

- *System testing:* This type of testing validates the complete game package and verifies that it meets the original specified requirements.

- *Sanity testing:* Ensures that the code changes that are made are working as expected.

- *Smoke testing:* This is a non-exhaustive set of tests that aim to ensure that the most important functions work.

- *Interface testing:* This type of testing verifies whether the communication between two different software systems is done correctly.

- *Regression testing:* This type of testing is done when changes have been made to the software to make sure that the change hasn't broken any existing functionality.

- *Beta/acceptance testing:* This type of testing is performed by real users in a real environment. It's usually the final test before launching your campaign.

Functionality testing determines whether the campaign is working according to the original specifications and objectives. It takes more time to execute because testers look for game play issues. It validates whether the campaign will work with all social networking options, payment gateways, and other features.

>> **Compatibility testing:** Compatibility testing is used to find out whether your gamification campaign is functioning properly with respect to all the various hardware devices and browsers that are built within them. It validates whether the user interface of the campaign works with the screen size of each device. It ensures whether the text is readable for all users. Compatibility testing ensures that the product meets all necessary requirements set by the original objectives.

>> **Play testing:** Play testing is a method of game testing in which testers play the game to analyze nonfunctional features like fun factors and difficulty levels. Typically, a selected group of users plays the unfinished versions of the game to check the game flow. Play testing is an integral part of game design; it's used commonly in PC games and character-playing games. It's more about judging the game than the facts.

>> **Ad hoc testing:** Ad hoc testing is an unplanned testing method generally used to break down the system. Testers randomly test the app without test cases or any documents. Ad hoc testing is randomly done on any part of the campaign. Unfortunately, because the defects are not mapped to test cases, it's quite difficult to reproduce the defects.

Checking on browsers

Many web browsers are out there, including Edge, Firefox, Chrome, Safari, and Opera. And dozens of mobile browsers are available, with more in development as each new device arrives on the shelves. Not all browsers, and versions of those browsers, work the same. Your campaign may not look or function identically on each browser, which can lead to lost audience share.

For instance, recently I was made aware of Opera Mini. Opera Mini is a web browser designed primarily for mobile phones, which lets you do everything you want to online without wasting your data allowance. Unfortunately, it does this by compressing content and stripping certain APIs. This means your campaign will need to be refined to operate properly on this browser.

Thankfully, there are many browser compatibility testing tools on the web. These tools can test speed and function across operating systems and geographies, at high and low traffic levels:

>> **Browsershots** (http://browsershots.org): This free cross-browser solution tests approximately 80 versions of widely used browsers. Browsershots is a simple tool that allows you to see screenshots of a given web page in different operating systems, including Linux, Windows, Mac, and open-sourced Berkeley Software Distribution (BSD). All the major browsers are available, with the (major) exception of Internet Explorer (IE). The test can take anywhere from three minutes to two hours, depending on the number of browsers you select. You can bookmark the page and come back at any time to see how the tests are progressing. As each browser test completes, a screenshot appears in your queue on the Browsershots web page.

>> **PowerMapper SortSite** (www.powermapper.com/products/sortsite/): This test checks accessibility, broken links, browser code compatibility, search engine optimization, and other usability issues on ten pages of a given website. When the testing is complete, a report is generated with graphs of the issues discovered during testing. The free trial gives you a good idea of what issues a website may have; more data is available if you purchase the full version.

>> **Perfecto** (www.perfecto.io): Perfecto is a testing service that allows you to test a website for mobile compatibility across hundreds of real mobile devices. You can also test across geographical locations, including the United States, United Kingdom, Canada, France, and Israel. You make a reservation for a testing session on a specific date and time for testing across the selected variety of mobile devices. When your testing session begins, you can control the devices you've selected and test your website's look and function across these multiple device platforms. When mobile browser testing is complete, Perfecto also offers testing of individual apps in the same cloud testing environment across the same geographical locations.

3

Executing Your Gamification Plan

» Figuring out who you want to play your game

» Creating goals for your campaign

» Rewarding your players' loyalty

Chapter **7**

Making Your Game a Reality

You need to create a solid concept for your campaign right at the beginning; otherwise, you may end up creating a game that doesn't deliver your marketing goals. Your campaign's chances of success are greatly determined by the planning you put in at the start. I like to encourage my clients to spend more of their time on this part of the gamification marketing campaign than they put into the development of the game itself.

The options I cover in this chapter may appear overwhelming, so I point out the strengths and weaknesses of each. This information will help you determine which options are right for your campaign. I liken this to cooking, where you may have the options of using a multitude of spices that are in your kitchen cabinet. Some may be too overpowering, while others may not be suitable to the dish you're making. Selecting the right ingredients will help you develop the perfect campaign for your target audience.

Choosing the Perfect Gamification Model for You

The success of your gamification marketing campaign will depend on whether the gamification model you've selected appeals to your core audience. Not every gamification model will be suitable to your audience. In fact, you may find that only one or two really resonate with them. Before deciding which model is right for you, you need understand how gamification models perform with various audiences.

I covered the fundamentals of gamification models in Chapter 2. In this section, I show you how to match the right model with your intended audience. If more than one appeals to you for your campaign, you may want to consider jotting down the alternatives for future campaigns.

Here's a rundown of the various models:

>> **Action:** The key factor with action games is that everything has to be quick. These campaigns can be quick to develop, too, especially if you grab a white-labeled game already developed and tested. This means less development time and less cost overall.

The game itself should allow your audience to easily learn the controls, quickly get into the playing screen, and start collecting rewards. However, if you don't provide these things quickly enough, your audience will be just as quick to leave your game.

To counter this high bounce rate, consider adding a leaderboard so you can create a competitive environment. In addition, when designing the game, make sure that the game's mechanics aren't too complicated and, instead, are intuitive for your audience.

>> **Simulation:** In development terms, simulation is almost the opposite of an action game. It takes much longer to design and develop, and it costs a lot more, too. But before you dismiss this option, think about the many success stories for simulation games! If you can create a niche virtual world for your campaign, a dedicated army of players will find their way to your game, eager to invest their time.

Audiences will invest their time in playing a good simulation game. You just need to make sure the game is designed with plenty of rewards and objectives so your users will keep playing. Simulation games require a lot of time during the storyboarding phase, to make sure you keep your audience interested.

>> **Interactive storytelling:** Interactive storytelling an exceptional option because it gives everyone a unique story experience, centered around your brand. The audience becomes hugely invested as they customize their experience. Typically, an interactive storytelling campaign will leave a more lasting impression than action games do. Of course, this all comes at a huge expense in terms of staff, development time, and ultimately cost.

Interactive storytelling campaigns can be extremely expensive and take many months to develop. The main costs will come from the custom and multilevel designs along with the expert advice required during the story-building development phase. However, your gamification marketing campaign can last for an entire quarter.

>> **Adventure:** I find adventure games to be an excellent hybrid of action, simulation, and interactive storytelling. They require your audience to be willing to invest a lot of their time. But if you execute the game correctly, the experience can be extremely rewarding for both the audience and your campaign.

Apart from the costs, the game usually requires your audience to invest their time to advance in the game and at the same time expose your branding. This can be done with consistent goals and objectives for the audience to continually achieve and aim for.

>> **Puzzles:** These types of games are used in gamification marketing campaigns that want to associate puzzle solving around their campaign. These types of games involve some form of problem-solving skill for your audience where your campaign's message can be embedded into the logic, pattern recognition, or sequence solving. I find that it's usually easier to source a white label solution due to the vast number of puzzle games available to buy from good developers.

TIP

To give the audience a reason to come back, it's better to give a slightly unrealistic amount of time or attempts to solve the puzzle. Your campaign won't be very effective if your audience manages to complete the game in one sitting.

>> **Skill based:** This is my personal favorite type of game option to use in a gamification marketing campaign. With skill-based games, the outcome is determined by the audience's reactions, mental abilities, strategic thinking, or trivia knowledge. This type of game is easy to fit into almost any campaign because there is no rigid formula. This means that you can develop one of these types of games to suit most budgets. Spot the Ball (shown in Figure 7-1), developed by www.spotheball.software, is a good example of a skill-based game; players have to use their skill of looking at where all the players are looking to determine the location of the ball.

FIGURE 7-1:
A skill-based
game called Spot
the Ball.

Image labels: UNDO   SELECT   PROCEED   X: 1202 Y: 894

One favorable aspect of skill-based games is that there doesn't necessarily need to be a right or wrong answer (as opposed to puzzles). Although this type of game mechanics falls into the "game of chance" category, players won't see it as "gambling" as long as your campaign isn't asking them to pay to play. With gambling or lotto-type games, users typically play a game that they have no control over. An example is a card-based game like blackjack. On the other hand, a skill-based game gives the user control by allowing him to use his skill to increase his chances of winning.

» **Multi-player:** As the name suggests, a multi-player game allows more than one person to play in the same game environment at the same time. The game should allow your audience to compete against one or more human contestants as well as the computer.

TIP

I find it important to develop a multi-player game to allow audiences to partner up with other individuals instead of just competing against them. This provides the social communication element that's missing from single-player games.

Interestingly, by using the latest HTML5 technology, this kind of game can be developed to be played locally (over a local network like an office). This allows your audience to create competitive environments without having to constantly open their connections to the Internet (a security concern for professional environments).

>> **Educational:** Usually dismissed as a game for educational establishments, this type of game is an extremely effective tool for any gamification marketing campaign. An educational game provides a useful way for your audience to learn something valuable about your product or business, all in an entertaining platform. The game should be educating your audience while they're playing. At the end of the game, the audience should leave more educated about your business or product.

TIP

This type of game is especially successful if there is some aspect of your product or service that is being used wrongly or is being queried by your customers. Also, educational games can help educate audiences in instances where there is some service or value that your company provides that isn't widely known.

>> **Role playing:** A role-playing game (RPG) is the least common type of game selected for gamification marketing campaigns. The audience controls the actions of a character immersed in a branded world. This world should be full of elements that are centered around your campaign's objectives.

Many RPGs come from tabletop games, such as Dungeons & Dragons. Try to emulate and use much of the same game mechanics to create an engaging game. Depending on your budget, you can develop a game as simple as a text-based console entry game, all the way up to a 3D version that can be played on a virtual reality (VR) device.

Table 7-1 lists the strengths and weaknesses of various game models when used in gamification marketing campaigns.

TIP

Many companies discover that their marketing budget won't cover the type of game they want to use. If that's where you find yourself, don't scale down the game to fit your budget. Instead, go for a cheaper game option and scale that game *up* with the remaining budget you have. If a game is scaled down, audiences will be able to tell right away. On the other hand, a less expensive game that has been upgraded in terms of design and development is more likely to be championed by audiences through social media channels.

TABLE 7-1   Determining the Best Game Model for Your Audience

Game Model	Cost	Development Time	Brand Exposure	Audience Interest Retention
Action	Low	1 to 2 weeks	**	1 week
Simulation	High	3 months	***	1 to 2 months
Interactive storytelling	Very high	4 to 6 months	****	3 months
Adventure	Medium	2 to 3 months	*****	1 month
Puzzles	Low	2 to 3 weeks	***	1 week
Skill based	Medium	1 month	***	2 weeks
Multi-player	High	2 to 3 months	***	2 to 3 weeks
Educational	High	2 to 3 months	***	2 to 3 months
Role playing	High	2 to 3 months	****	2 to 3 months

Determining Your Target Market

Determining your intended target market will help shape the game option for your gamification marketing campaign. The *target market* is the specific group of people you intend to reach with your campaign — the people who you intend to play and share your game. These people have common characteristics, like demographics and behaviors, which will help you to determine which game option to develop.

The more clearly you define your target market, the better equipped you'll be to decide which game option to select. Don't be afraid to get specific at this stage. You need to be specific to target your gamification marketing efforts effectively. Anyone who is not included in your target market can still enjoy the game; they just aren't the focus when it comes to crafting your marketing strategy.

Conducting your own audience research

You can't target the whole world with your campaign. You couldn't even if you wanted to — it would be impossible to find a game that would cater for everyone. By focusing on a specific audience, you can comfortably and confidently choose which game to use for your gamification marketing campaign. As with any traditional marketing campaign, you should be conducting audience research to determine your target market.

To do this you need to look at your current customers — people who have purchased or used your company in the past. With all the data you have on them, you can start figuring out their defining characteristics so that you can create a unique character template to use for your campaign.

Here are some data points you'll want to consider:

- **Age:** You don't need specific date of births. It won't make a difference whether your average customer is 34 or 37, for instance. But by identifying whether they're in their 20s or 30s or 40s, you can determine the type of games they'll be more likely to want to play.

- **Location and language:** Where in the world do your existing customers live? Understanding which geographic areas to target will help eliminate certain game options. For instance, if you're targeting multiple countries and languages, it may not make sense to develop an interactive storytelling game.

- **Socioeconomic status:** This is one of the most effective data points you can use to help identify your audience. Are they wealthy? Are they working 9 to 5? Are they bringing up a young family? If your audience turns out to be office workers, a game that can be quickly played during a lunch break is perfect. If they have more spare time during the day, they'll enjoy a simulation or adventure game.

- **Interests:** What do your customers like to do, besides using your products or services? Do they express their interests on social media? If so, then a skill-based game would be perfect because they may be inclined to ask for help from their followers on a particularly difficult level. Alternatively, if they enjoy reading and learning, an interactive storytelling game may appeal to them.

- **Stage of life:** Are your customers new parents? Parents of teens? Retirees? Students? This information may be difficult to determine but it can be very effective for your final game options. Students are more likely to invest more time into your game than new parents are. Also, if your target is retirees, you'll most likely need to provide more guidance on how the user advances in the game.

TIP

If you're selling business-to-business (B2B) products or services, your data points will be slightly different. You may want to identify the size of the businesses and collect information about the titles of the people who are purchasing from you. Are they the CEO? The administrative staff? The social marketing manager? Understanding who within the company will be playing the game is a critical first step in crafting the ideal target market for the game.

Considering what the research is telling you

At this stage, it's a good idea to match the various criteria from the preceding section with the different game models. Table 7-2 lists which game options work best from example data points.

TABLE 7-2 **Examples of the Best Game Options Based on Audience Research**

Game Model	Age	Location/Language	Status	Stage of Life
Action	Under 45 years old	Any location, multiple languages	Does not require much time	All
Simulation	Over 30 years old	Any location, any language	Requires large amounts of free time	Wide range, including students, stay-at-home parents, and office-based workers
Interactive storytelling	Over 30 years old	Localized for one language	Requires large amounts of free time	Retirees or stay-at-home parents
Adventure	Over 20 years old	Localized for one language	Requires a certain amount of free time	Retirees or students
Puzzles	Over 10 years old	Any location, any language	Does not require much time	All
Skill based	Over 20 years old	Localized for one language	Does not require much time	All
Multi-player	Under 45 years old	Any location, any language	Requires a certain amount of free time	Students or office workers
Educational	Over 20 years old	Localized for one language	Requires a certain amount of free time	All
Role playing	Under 45 years old	Any location, any language	Requires a certain amount of free time	Students or office workers

Embedding Goals into the Game

The whole reason for creating a gamification marketing campaign is so that you can embed your marketing goals in the game. However, first you need to establish your goals. When you know what your goals for the campaign are, you'll be able to set your objectives for the game.

Creating SMART goals

A good way to create goals for an effective marketing plan is to use the SMART framework. Every goal you set should be: specific, measurable, achievable, realistic, and time-bound. If you develop your gamification marketing campaign's goals to meet these requirements, your marketing plan will have a very good chance of succeeding.

Defining a specific outcome

Your goal must be specific enough that it focuses on one clearly defined metric and must also define a specific outcome. The goal should contain enough detail so that the expected results are clearly understood. Generalities only create confusion within the campaign, which leads to poor results.

So, for example, just saying your object is to "raise more awareness" isn't helpful. However, say your business sells a product that has health benefits and the company's management wants to make sure customers are aware of these benefits. You can say that your goal is to ensure that you'll raise awareness of your product's health benefits. And you can do this by ensuring that the specific health benefits are highlighted throughout the gamification marketing campaign with goals embedded that specifically highlight these benefits.

Defining measurable results

In order for your goal to work, you need to have a way to measure the results. Imagine if you played a game of football but you didn't keep score. Keeping score matters! It's essential for keeping track of your progress, which will help you to define the expected outcome. You can't determine if you've reached a goal unless you can measure the progress.

If you take the previous example of increasing awareness of a product's health benefits to at least 5,000 customers every month, you can determine if your goals are being met by viewing the game's interaction statistics at the end of every month.

Achieving goals that are achievable

Is the goal even possible? How? Make sure you're able to take well-defined, measurable, small steps on the path to the goal.

One way you can tell if your goal is achievable is by asking yourself if you have the tools and skills needed to reach the goal. In the example, you should be confident that reaching 5,000 customers per month over the next six months is achievable. To do this confidently, you'll need to build a game-launch strategy (see Chapter 9).

Making your goals realistic

There's no point in setting a goal if it isn't realistic. Your goals must be formed in the context of the realities of your situation and climate. Although the goal can be set out in your game-launch marketing strategy, now you must measure whether the goals are within your means. This means you need to make sure you have the resources required to achieve the objective:

>> Do you have the right developers?

>> Is there enough budget to handle your campaign's objectives?

>> Can your servers handle the volume of traffic you need to achieve your goals?

In the example, it would be unrealistic to set the goal of increasing awareness of health benefits if your gamification marketing campaign is launched during a major holiday season. You'd be better off delaying and launching after the first of the year, when everyone suddenly becomes obsessed with being fit and healthy.

Meeting timely deadlines

You need to specify clear deadlines for your goals in order to reach them. Usually, I find all efforts made by your team will ramble aimlessly on, if a deadline doesn't exist.

In the example, I've specified a time period of six months, so it meets the requirement of establishing a deadline to meet the goal.

Devising your gamification objectives

Not all traditional marketing objectives can apply to gamification. However with a little creativity, you can usually find most objectives are achievable. Table 7-3 lists some potential marketing objectives for each game model.

TABLE 7-3

Matching Objectives with Game Models

Game Model	Potential Marketing Objective	Notes
Action	To increase website traffic	Aimed at the mass market and enjoyed by all. Most likely to go viral through sharing, which means all those players are coming to your site.
Simulation	To get more website engagement	Visitors are more likely to come back to the site to continue with their game. All that time spent on your site will create curiosity to find out what else is being offered on the site.
Interactive storytelling	To build brand awareness	With this type of game, your branding will sit in the center of the entire platform. This means that even if the game is embedded on other sites, the audience will be continuously exposed to your branding.
Adventure	To improve conversion rates	These type of games can be littered with discount codes, product benefits, and videos, which can all increase website conversion rates.
Puzzles	To gain more social media followers	By making your puzzles especially tricky, you'll force your audience to turn to their friends on social media for help.
Skill based	To increase sales	With skill-based games there does not necessarily need to be a right or wrong answer. In essence that means everyone is a winner, which allows the player to feel she deserves her reward. In this case, the reward may be a discount on your website, which helps increase sales.
Multi-player	To gain more social media followers	Multi-player games can be linked to most social media platforms, such as Facebook and Twitter. This forces your current audience to encourage their own followers and friends to join in and engage with your business.
Educational	To improve internal communications	Staff training can be automated and more fun when put into an educational game.
Role playing	To launch new products or services	If you're launching something new, an immersive 3D environment will be an ideal way to introduce it in a fun and modern platform.

TIP

Be sure to balance the campaign objectives with actual gameplay. If you lean too heavily on the campaign's message, you're in danger of creating a boring game that is filled with advertising. On the other hand, if you put too much emphasis on gameplay, the audience may enjoy your game but leave without remembering the campaign's core message. If you can cleverly balance the message with gameplay, the game will become a real asset to your business.

Building in Loyalty Rewards

After you've designed on the perfect game for your audience, you'll want to start thinking about how to keep them coming back and playing the game. You certainly want them to play your game more than once, and not just leave the campaign at the start of their gaming journey.

By designing desirable loyalty rewards into your game, you'll find that these players will be the ones who become your campaign's best advocates, who will fuel your word-of-mouth marketing and ultimately attract other loyal players to your game.

Deciding on your options

Rewards are the building blocks of all gamification marketing campaigns. Your audience will play your game so that they can win something, competing against themselves or others. Their naturally competitive game-playing instincts will be invoked, so you can motivate them further into your campaign using clever reward options, like the following:

>> **Points:** Your audience wins redeemable points in the game. You can award points for positive actions and experiences within the game, as well as for things like providing feedback and sharing the campaign on social media. Starbucks uses multiple options, including points, to motivate and award its audience (see Figure 7-2).

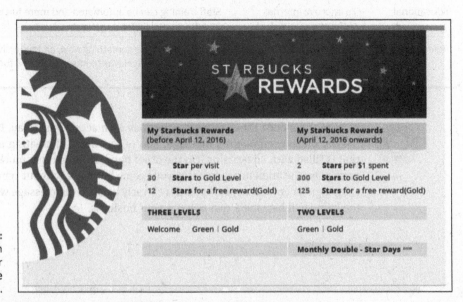

My Starbucks Rewards (before April 12, 2016)			My Starbucks Rewards (April 12, 2016 onwards)		
1	Star per visit		2	Stars per $1 spent	
30	Stars to Gold Level		300	Stars to Gold Level	
12	Stars for a free reward(Gold)		125	Stars for a free reward(Gold)	
THREE LEVELS			**TWO LEVELS**		
Welcome	Green	Gold	Green	Gold	
			Monthly Double - Star Days		

FIGURE 7-2: Using points can keep your audience motivated.

- **Badges:** Badges are visual representations that confirm your audience's achievements in the game. Think of badges as visual status symbols. Interestingly, badges can lead your audience to participate in certain challenges just so they can earn the associated badges. Makes sure the challenges are designed to fit your marketing objectives.

- **Leaderboards:** Allow your audience to see how their own success in the game ranks compared with everyone else with the use of leaderboards. Leaderboards can inspire more competition and show people which players have unlocked the most achievements. The desire to appear at the top, or even just be featured in the top ten, will drive your audience to earn more points, which will in turn drive them into deeper engagement.

- **Performance charts:** A performance chart is a graphical view of the audience's historical representation in the game. This will motivate a much longer playing term for each user because he'll be shown his performance over time. Your audience will be motivated to keep playing new levels as they look to improve their chart.

- **Avatars:** Avatars can be powerful for engagement. In more traditional platforms, users are encouraged to upload photo of themselves, but in gamification your audience will likely prefer to use an alter ego. Avatars are usually customizable cartoon models that represent a player in the game. Avatars can play a very critical role in the audience's overall engagement because they become a part of a community, which can trigger more interest.

Using rewards in your game

Think about interactive ways to use rewards for the game option you've selected so that your audience will have a positive experience while playing. Here are some rewards you'll want to consider:

- **Fun:** You want to introduce an element of fun into your gamification marketing campaign. This is especially true if your company or industry is not usually associated with fun and engaging campaigns. When done properly, your campaign can create a disruptive, fun, and engaging experience for your audience.

- **Competitiveness:** You can easily do this by adding a competitive element such as a leaderboard. Another way is to award badges that rank their audience's abilities. This is a great way to engage with your audience and provide good fun into your campaign.

- **Exclusivity:** Who doesn't love earning her way into an elite club? Giving a VIP experience as a reward makes your audience feel like they have a special relationship with your campaign and brand overall. This goes a long way toward building brand loyalty. A good way to achieve the goal of exclusivity is to encourage your audience to achieve particular goals (as in the Starbucks green or gold stars program; refer to Figure 7-2).

» **Rewarding experience:** Encouraging your audience to earn more rewards for a chance to redeem them against actual products or services can be a very powerful reason for them to keep coming back to your game. A lot of companies will, understandably, make scoring points difficult, which can potentially turn your audience off playing. However, you can counter this problem by making the process of *redeeming* rewards easy and attractive.

» **Added value:** One of the disincentives of a loyalty program is the difficulty in obtaining reward points. You may find that many of your players will abandon the game just because it takes too long to earn rewards. With this in mind, you need to be more creative and reward nearly everything in your game. This should be done on a sliding scale, matching the value of the points with the value of the audience's input. Also, keep in mind that with gamification, it's possible to have different types of rewards for each action, ensuring that everybody wins.

» **Giving random rewards:** By adding random rewards into your game, you'll delight your audience and keep them engaged in the anticipation of more. Because everyone likes to win something, the fact that your audience is present and participating in your gamification marketing campaign is valuable enough to be rewarded.

Chapter 8

Selecting the Right Components

When you know the right game to use in your gamification marketing campaign, the next step is to develop it. To do this properly, you need to make sure you plan every last detail before a line of code is written or a character is drawn. As with any development, having a master plan that everyone on your team will follow is essential.

There are a number of ways to plan and develop a game for your campaign. I recommend that you structure your project so that it not only fits your current objectives but also integrates easily with all future campaign goals. To do this, you need to look for scalability and versatility in your agreements with the team members and the technology you develop the game on.

In this chapter, I outline what you should include in your master plan, and warn you about areas you need to look out for. Ultimately, you want to ensure your game is developed on time, fulfills the marketing brief, and engages with your target audience.

Making Sense of the Game Development Process

Your master plan requires a tried-and-tested methodology to help you work out what happens when. After you've decided on your game development life cycle methodology, you can begin to put your master plan into action.

In this section, I explain the structure and requirements of a typical game development life cycle. I guide you through the steps required to develop your game and minimize the risks. Then I fill you in on the different methodologies you can utilize in your plan.

Understanding the stages of the game development life cycle

The game development process can be a highly complex process, but with a detailed and structured approach from the start, you'll find the entire process easy to navigate. Your plan needs to consist of the following stages:

1. The concept
2. Team building
3. Technical planning
4. Production
5. Testing
6. Deployment

REMEMBER

Don't stop the campaign process in your master plan just because your game has reached the deployment stage. This is the time to start planning for updates, patching any errors, expanding the game, redeveloping due to strong customer feedback, and performing general maintenance. For this reason, stay connected with your team. If your campaign is successful, you're most likely going to want to get started conceptualizing your next gamification marketing project!

Stage 1: The concept

This is the stage where you decide what kind of game option is right for you. Your campaign's objectives will help you select the game option that's right for you (see Chapter 7).

At this stage, you need to start asking the right questions:

>> What are the objectives and goals of the campaign?

>> How will we measure our goals?

>> Who is our potential player/user? What gender(s) are they? How old are they?

>> What game option is right for our audience?

>> What rewards will we employ?

>> Will there be a hero or protagonist?

>> What are the theme and overall branding guidelines?

Stage 2: Team building

Whether you're outsourcing the various roles to freelancers or other companies or you're using in-house talent, you still need to start by planning what each team member will be doing, and for how long, before you start hiring. When you have all the team members in place, you need to make sure the whole team shares the vision you've laid out in your master plan.

Apart from hiring your team, you need to think about the overall team schedule where each member has been delegated jobs at the various points of the project. In this way, they can schedule your project into their calendars.

Finally, be sure to assign a project manager (this could be you!). The project manager is responsible for the following:

>> Hiring staff

>> Creating the team schedule

>> Delegating jobs and ensuring they're completed

>> Continually synchronizing your campaign's goals with the team

Later in this chapter, in the "Assembling Your Team" section, I cover this subject in greater detail.

Stage 3: Technical planning

In many campaigns, teams tend to want to merge the technical planning stage with the production stage (see the next section), but that leads to confusion, delays, and in some cases a failed campaign. To avoid this, be sure that your overall technical strategy is planned and designed before any code is written.

Cover the following areas in your technical planning:

>> Designing the gameplay

>> Defining the art, style, and assets

>> Selecting the game engine or coding languages

>> Building a complete storyboard of the entire game

>> Documenting all this information to distribute to the team

I cover this subject in more detail in the "Preparing the Technical Strategy" section, later in this chapter.

Stage 4: Production

This stage is the longest of the entire game development life cycle. It deals with the design and development of your game. Time and sequencing are core parts of this stage. Things must happen in the right order and at the right time.

Depending on the life cycle model you select for your production, you may find your team revisiting this stage multiple times to ensure the game evolves with all the critical objectives you planned for in your campaign. Regardless of which life cycle model you select, be prepared to schedule enough time for this stage in your plans.

I cover life cycle models later in this chapter (see "Deciding which life cycle model is right for you").

TIP

Keep a close eye on your game's performance during this stage. You can do this during each version/prototype your developers deliver to you. Using bad coding techniques and not keeping a check on the overall memory performance on different devices can mean the difference between a well received, playable game and one that is unplayable and leads to angry reviewers.

Stage 5: Testing

Testing is a lot more than just playing your game. It's a repetitive process of running through the same input and recording the output of every scenario over all possible environments. The flow anomalies and bugs should be tracked on a bugs tracker report. Each entry within this report should be fixed and retested.

There are two stages of testing:

>> **Alpha:** When your game reaches the alpha stage of development, it should be playable but incomplete. Most of the core gameplay should be completed,

though. For example, when a game has one or more playable levels, it has reached its alpha version. However, the gameplay concept shouldn't change after your game enters its alpha stage.

>> **Beta:** The beta version is the phase where your game has been fully developed and ready to be tested by a third party. At this stage, it's important to pay attention to all the user feedback being collected. Commonly, beta testing is split into two phases:

- *Open beta,* where anyone and everyone in the world is free to participate

- *Closed beta,* where you send invitations to a select number of third-party testers

Stage 6: Deployment

At this stage, you're ready to launch your campaign to your audience! You need to be thinking of launch dates, generating pre-launch interest, and finalizing your game launch marketing strategy.

I look into this stage in more detail in Chapter 9.

Deciding which life cycle model is right for you

When you know the various stages involved in the life cycle, you can choose which life cycle model is right for you. These models are sometimes referred to as *process and development models.* No matter which model you end up with, it will follow a chain of steps in a circular formation, designed to ensure your development is a success.

In the following sections, I start by looking at some traditional models. Then I delve into a more adaptive model, which may be useful if you're looking to release a bigger gamification marketing campaign or lots of them.

Traditional life cycle models

Here are some of the most commonly used traditional life cycle models:

>> **Waterfall (see Figure 8-1):** Popular since the '90s, this model is ideal when requirements remain the same during development. The waterfall model follows a simple and straightforward methodology where every stage of the model depends on the information passed on from the previous stage. It's easy to understand and manage effectively.

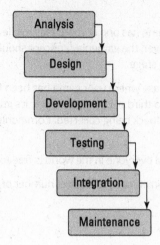

FIGURE 8-1:
The waterfall
model.

I prefer to use the waterfall model in my own projects with clients, but sometimes I use different models depending on the scope of the campaign.

» **Spiral (see Figure 8-2):** Unlike the waterfall model, where each step is rigidly followed by the next, the spiral model is more flexible. This model involves a repetitive approach, going forward in a circular manner, where the project passes through four phases over and over in the form of a spiral, until it reaches completion. This model ultimately allows your game to go through several rounds of refinement.

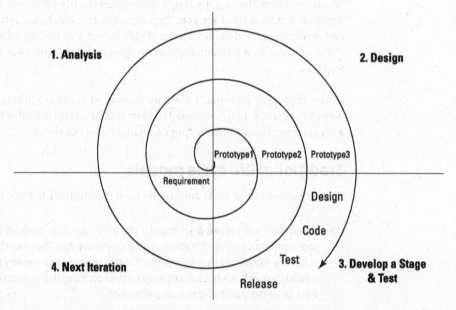

FIGURE 8-2:
The spiral model.

>> **Iterative (see Figure 8-3):** As the name suggests, in the iterative model a new game is produced during each cycle or iteration. Instead of beginning with a rigid set of plans and schedules, you can implement new requirements after each iteration. Essentially, you're doing a "rinse and repeat" of design, development, and testing until the game is ready.

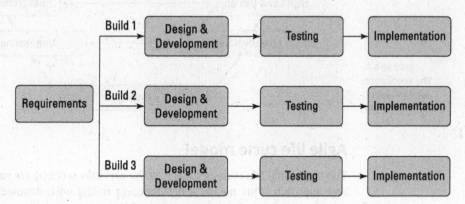

FIGURE 8-3:
The iterative model.

>> **Verification and validation (see Figure 8-4):** The verification and validation model is V-shaped. It's similar to the waterfall model, where you run parallel tests during each of the development stages. Each stage of V-shaped model is dependent on its previous stage. Here's the difference between verification and validation:

- *Verification:* Verification requires a static analysis review to be done without executing code. It's the process of evaluating the product development phase to find out whether specified requirements have been met.

- *Validation:* Validation involves dynamic analysis techniques, with testing done by executing code. Validation is the process of evaluating the software after the completion of the development phase to determine whether the software met the expectations and requirements.

WARNING

Be aware that all your requirements and schedules will need to be very clear at the start because it's very difficult to move backward in this model to make any changes. However, if done correctly, this model can work wonderfully for small gamification projects on a tight deadline due to the constant testing.

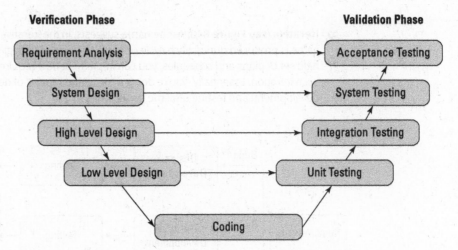

Verification Phase   **Validation Phase**

Requirement Analysis ──────────────→ Acceptance Testing

System Design ──────────────→ System Testing

High Level Design ──────────────→ Integration Testing

Low Level Design ──────────────→ Unit Testing

Coding

FIGURE 8-4:
The verification
and validation
model.

Agile life cycle model

The traditional life cycle models (see the previous section) are based on a predictive approach. This means a development model with detailed planning and a complete forecast of the exact tasks and features to be delivered during the game development's life cycle.

In contrast, Agile is based on an adaptive development methodology. With Agile there is no detailed planning involved, and the only future vision is the campaign's objectives that need to be developed. Whereas in predictive models, any changes go through a strict change control management system, with Agile, your team adapts to the changing requirements dynamically. This means that your game will be tested very frequently, through release iterations, which will minimize the risk of any major errors at release.

In the Agile model, your game is broken down into manageable sets, which means your game is delivered quickly in stages, each having small and incremental changes updated from the previous released version. At each cycle, the project is tested and then released.

Table 8-1 compares and contrasts the traditional life cycle models with the Agile model.

TIP

For much more information on Agile, check out *Agile Project Management For Dummies*, 2nd Edition, by Mark C. Layton and Steven J. Ostermiller (Wiley).

TABLE 8-1 Determining Which Model Is Right for You

Campaign/Development Feature	Better Suited Model	Notes
In-house staff	Agile	Agile promotes teamwork and cross training within the various teams.
Adding ongoing features	Traditional	Traditional models are more suited for sustainability and maintenance in the long term, as well as extending features beyond the development timeline.
Strict delivery management	Traditional	If your management dictates the functionality, scope, and date of delivery, a traditional model is better.
Early releases	Agile	Agile delivers early partial versions of your game. With traditional models, you have to wait until the cycle has reached testing.
No game development experience/no project manager	Agile	Realistically you need some form of project management, but if you only have yourself, then Agile requires little or no planning. With constant releases, you can easily spot any anomalies with your game and have them corrected for the next release.
Game sequels	Traditional	With Agile, the transfer of technology to a new team (if you want to change teams for a sequel) is challenging due to the lack of planning and documentation.

Assembling Your Team

Your game will be developed on time and within budget if you understand why the different skill sets required for the development of your game are used by the professional studios and agencies. When you work out which skills your gamification marketing campaign will need, you need to schedule them all efficiently. In this section, I look into alternative options, namely outsourcing the development to either fully fledged agencies or individual freelancers, so you can weigh the pros and cons to see which one will work best for your campaign.

Working out who does what

Here are some specifically defined roles in the gamification development process:

>> **Project manager:** The project manager acts as the central point of contact and information for all other members in your game development team. She coordinates and monitors the game development's progress from the start.

Her day-to-day job is to assign tasks, manage resources, and schedule priorities. She also ensures that your campaign's objectives and goals are being met.

» **Artist:** An artist creates the art for your game, including each screen with every element contained within it. He also works with the user experience (UX) designer to ensure the game art can be carried onto the website in which the game will be embedded. The artist works directly with the game developer to ensure the animations and graphics display at an optimal rate.

» **Game designer:** The game designer creates the gameplay, rules, and structure of the game. The game designer works closely with the project manager to ensure she fully understands the campaign's core objectives. The game designer is also responsible for the documentation, narration, content, and ultimate location of the game. As the development process takes shape, the game designer works with nearly all members of the team.

» **Level designer:** The level designer creates different levels for the game and designs them within the context of the overall game. He creates challenges and stages in the game. A level designer initially works closely with the game designer, to ensure he keeps to the game designer's overall concept and structure. Later, the level designer works closely with the game developer to ensure that each level's concept and uniqueness have been developed accurately according to the original concept.

» **Game developers:** Usually a team of game developers works on your game. They're responsible for coding the logic and flow of the game. In particular, some of the areas the game developer works on include:

- Game physics
- Artificial intelligence
- Graphics
- Gameplay
- User interface (UI)
- Input processing
- Network communications

» **Sound engineer:** Typically, the sound engineer is the person responsible for the sound effects and sound programming. This includes music, sound effects for actions, voice editing, and audio merging in the game.

TIP

Sound effects and music can now be searched for and purchased from royalty-free sites, such as Shutterstock (www.shutterstock.com). If your budget is tight, this might be a good option for you.

>> **Game testers:** The game testers are responsible for testing not only the gameplay, but also a variety of other areas, to ensure your game will be enjoyed by your audience. A tester is the final person to identify any errors or issues with the game flow before it goes to the end user. It takes a very experienced tester to not only find issues, but also possess a solid understanding of the game and your objectives.

>> **UX designer:** The UX designer is responsible for the final location of your game (the design and look of the web page). He needs to ensure the web page provides a meaningful and relevant space for your game to sit in. Before your audience plays the game, the web page will be the first impression they get of your gamification marketing campaign. So, it's important that your game is not just simply embedded into the first available blank space in your existing website.

Balancing everyone's role

Working out how each role fits into the game development timeline is essential to minimize delays and utilize your resources efficiently. Table 8-2 shows how each team member fits into the waterfall life cycle model (just as an example).

TABLE 8-2   **Determining Where Each Role Fits in the Project Life Cycle**

Stage Name	Primary Team Members Involved	Secondary Team Members Involved
Analysis	Project manager	Possibly the heads of each of the other roles toward the end of this stage.
Design	Game designer	When the gameplay and structure have been green-lit, the level designer will be brought in. The artist may be brought in as well, although in most cases the artist's brief will be ready at the end of this stage.
Development	Game developer	The artist will be heavily involved at this stage, working alongside the game developer. Similarly, the sound engineer will be brought in to create the sound effects and music.
Testing	Game tester	The game developer will be brought in to fix any bugs and issues found so they can be retested.
Integration	UX designer	Your company's web designer may be needed to integrate the UX designer's vision. Sometimes the UX designer is able to do the work himself.
Maintenance	Game developer	All work done by the game developer after the game has gone live will require the game to be tested by the game tester on a beta site.

Choosing freelancers, agencies, or in-house employees

You can develop a successful gamification marketing campaign with a pool of talent that is spread across the globe. With the ease of access to the growing number of freelancers and boutique agencies, game development can be outsourced worldwide to previously unfathomable locations and talent.

At this point, you're probably wondering whether it's better to invest in building an in-house team, hire an agency, or hire a pool of freelance talent. The truth is, there are pros and cons to each set of people; ultimately, the decision will depend on a few factors that you need to consider (see Table 8-3).

TABLE 8-3   **Comparing Freelancers, Agencies, and In-House**

Issue	Freelancers	Agencies	In-House Employees
Cost	Better	Good	Best
Availability	Good	Better	Best
Expertise and current trends knowledge	Best	Better	Good
Quality of work	Best	Better	Good
Reliability	Good	Better	Best
Intellectual property security	Good	Better	Best
Ease of communication	Good	Better	Best
Post-launch assistance	Good	Better	Best

In the following sections, I consider each of these three groups of people in greater detail.

Freelancers

The benefit of working with freelancers is that they're known for their flexibility and their hunger to keep abreast of the latest technologies and gaming techniques. However, freelancers can be costly and unreliable.

Before you hire a freelancer, ask to see her latest work. The games she presents to you will speak volumes about her abilities. If the game wasn't well received (via reviews) or is outdated, the freelancer probably doesn't have a progressive and innovative mindset.

When hiring a freelancer, make sure that your gamification marketing campaign's vision and objectives are translated thoroughly to the candidate. Because she works remotely, she won't be privy to your constant reminders of the campaign's goals, which you can easily give to in-house staff.

Freelancers are their own bosses. They run their own businesses, manage their own clients, and, usually, strive to turn in their absolute best every single time. The fact that their work directly depends on client satisfaction and referrals means they'll try to go above and beyond to keep you satisfied with superb results.

I always encourage project managers to outsource small and menial tasks to freelancers. Typically, a freelancer will work during the evenings and weekends, which means, if correctly time-managed, you can have an almost 24-hour development cycle.

A few websites, such as Guru (www.guru.com), are specifically geared towards matching freelancers with jobs. Some of these sites have escrow services to ensure that the freelancer is only paid when your job has been completed to your satisfaction. They also provide mediation services in case there are any disputes between your company and the freelancer.

Agencies

Working with design agencies can be a very positive experience because they're known for coming up with fresh and exciting ideas. Their staff — a mixture of developers and designers — will bring some interesting and innovative ideas and trends to the project. Usually, with an agency, you benefit from a team of developers, designers, and account managers.

On the downside, depending on the agency's workload, your development process can be long, laborious, and very costly. From the initial brief, when you hand over your gamification marketing campaign's master plan, to the final game, it can take several meetings. I also find that the team that you initially meet with won't necessarily be the team working on your game further down the line. So, your campaign's core objectives may get lost, which is not ideal.

An agency will expect the bulk of the work, if not all, to be awarded to them. They'll then go on to manage, plan, set goals, define standards, and take care of the day-to-day operations. Their job is to provide you with a rapid solution if for any reason your project is hindered by their team.

Another advantage is that agencies are responsible for any maintenance you require on your game (at a cost, of course). They're responsible for any future bug fixes and updates required on the development technology as well.

In-house employees

Due to disclosure or security concerns from your management, you may find it almost impossible to explain to an agency or freelancer your campaign's objectives. Working with external team members is also time consuming, especially if this is your first game where you may be constantly tweaking your objectives. On the other hand, working with in-house employees will alleviate all the security concerns. Plus, it'll be easy to constantly remind and update them on your campaign's objectives.

If you're working with in-house employees on the project, you may need to pay for new office space, new equipment, and training. Also, game designing software licenses tend to be very expensive. You'll also need to either project-manage the team or hire someone to do this.

Recruiting full-time top-tier marketing talent can be difficult, not only because they're not easy to find, but also because you need to be offering very competitive salaries and job security. When you're hiring in-house, you also have to factor in the turnover cost where an employee leaves after you've spent time and money training him and paying his salary and benefits.

Finally, unless you're looking to constantly create games for your gamification marketing campaign, this will be the most costly option. Managing a whole team isn't easy, and it's definitely not affordable unless you're getting viral results from all your campaigns. It will also require your constant involvement to keep campaigns going, to ensure you have future work to give them.

Preparing the Technical Strategy

You can avoid a lot of confusion in the development life cycle if, early on, you try to understand what lies underneath the hood of your gamification marketing campaign. By doing this, you can clearly identify the pros and cons of each tech option that will be suggested by your developers.

In this section, I look at the various platforms available to develop your game and then look at the reasons for choosing each.

Understanding the available choices

You need to decide what platforms your game can be developed in before hiring your game developers. Game developers typically specialize in just one of the platforms, so you need to choose the platform before you start building your team.

In this section, I look at three platforms for game development, each of which is unique and offers a different experience to your audience.

HTML5

HTML5, initially championed by Google and Apple, was developed to provide a lightweight solution to Adobe Flash Player (see the nearby sidebar for more on the history of Flash). The idea was to provide a much more compatible development platform for both mobile and desktop browsers. Since its inception, HTML5 has quickly turned into one of the most popular game development platforms.

HTML5 offers many advantages that allow game developers to build astonishing games for an interactive market:

>> HTML5 caters to many cutting-edge features like 3D graphics, quality audio, and offline data storage.

>> HTML5 allows games to be easily adapted to different resolutions, screen sizes, aspect ratios, and devices.

>> Compared to other technologies, such as Objective C (Apple's development language) or C# (a development language for Windows), HTML5 is much easier and more efficient for game development.

>> Games built with HTML5 work instantly on smartphones, tablets, PCs, and smart TVs.

>> HTML5 can improve your discoverability because you aren't limited to promoting your gamification marketing campaign on a third-party app store. Instead, you can promote your campaign all over the Internet, taking advantage of the web's inherent linking and sharing abilities to reach new customers.

>> Your audience can participate in your campaign anywhere, anytime. They can also check their progress on their phones, tablets, home laptops, and work desktops.

ALAS, POOR FLASH!

In the '90s, when the Internet was growing and becoming more accessible to the masses, there was a major stumbling block for all websites: media content. It could take 20 to 30 minutes to download a single song. Plus, due to very slow dial-up modems, web designers were heavily constrained when tasked with making websites with splashy content.

To solve this problem, FutureSplash Animator (eventually shortened to Flash) was born. Flash allowed designers to create animations using vector graphics and allow them to be viewed quickly on a dedicated player. By the end of the '90s, almost all online computers ran Flash. Very soon, Flash became the backbone for nearly every major video player and website, including YouTube.

It was around this time that programmers took this software, which was initially built for graphic designers, and started developing online games with it. Flash games became a billion-dollar business. It wasn't long before Flash became one of the most important programming languages and sparked the indie game revolution.

Unfortunately, by 2010, the demise of Flash began. Steve Jobs, founder and CEO of Apple, thought the use of Flash Player would limit the iOS experience, so he pushed for the use of HTML5, which is a combination of HTML, CSS, and JavaScript. He also said that Flash Player caused crashes with Apple machines, and he banned Flash-developed apps from the App Store.

In April 2010, Steve Jobs wrote an open letter (www.apple.com/hotnews/thoughts-on-flash), where he explained the reasons why he felt that Flash shouldn't continue. These reasons included lack of openness, reliability, and security, as well as reduced battery life. Most damning was the explanation of touch, which meant that Flash had no purpose in the post-mouse era where devices were operated by touch screens.

In July 2017, Adobe announced that it would end support for Flash at the end of 2020. Instead, it would continue to encourage the use of open HTML5 standards in place of Flash. This announcement was coordinated with Apple, Facebook, Google, Microsoft, and Mozilla. Finally, in September 2019, Microsoft announced that on December 31, 2020, Flash would be removed entirely from all browsers via the Windows Update system.

Unity

Unity is a game engine platform with a built-in integrated development environment (IDE) for developers. This means that it can be used to develop video games for the web and mobile devices. Unity is a complete package, letting you simultaneously play your game, edit it, and test it.

Unity also allows your developers to create environments, add physics and lighting, manage audio and video, handle animation, and develop for multiplayer. Although most of these features were inherently designed for console and mobile gaming platforms, many budding web game developers have been taking advantage of Unity's features to create exciting, viral web games. These features include the following:

>> Unity is a game engine designed specifically for developers who want to make games.

>> Unity contains a robust asset store where game assets, functional extensions, and ready-made solutions can be easily downloaded and integrated into your game. The store is a collection of asset packages, including 3D models, textures, materials, music and sound effects, editor extensions, and online services.

>> Although you're developing your game for the web, with Unity the same game can be quickly and easily ported to Android and iOS stores.

>> Unity is completely free and royalty free as a development tool. However, there is a Pro version, which offers more features and isn't free.

Mobile

If you want to keep your gamification marketing campaign accessible and online, your team will urge you to either select HTML5 or a platform like Unity to develop on. However, some campaigns are designed for mobile devices and as such require the native features and capabilities that come with developing an app. Here are some things to keep in mind:

>> Native apps are mobile platform specific (Android or iOS).

>> Each of the two mobile platforms has its own specific development environment (XCode for iOS and Android Studio for Android). A few alternative options, such as Xamarin, exist.

» Native apps provide a simplified environment for development functions such as debugging and project management.

» Native apps can easily integrate with mobile device features such as the camera, location, and address book.

» You can integrate with other apps to benefit from their features.

» Because each of the two app platforms requires specialist developers, it generally costs more to design, develop, and maintain your gamification marketing campaign as an app.

Comparing the platforms

In Table 8-4, I compare the highly popular HTML5 platform with the game-development-centric Unity platform.

TABLE 8-4   **HTML5 versus Unity for Game Development**

Development Feature	HTML5	Unity
Hiring developers	High availability of developers to choose from. This is due to the fact that the platform is based on JavaScript, which is very easy for any developer to pick up.	You'll need to look for specialist C# developers. The platform is designed for game development, so it only attracts developers who want to specialize in this niche.
Custom or complex game development ideas	Not good. Developers need to search for and, in some cases, install certain compilers and tools from unregulated third-party developers.	The platform has built-in game development features, including physics, engines, and renderers.
Publishing the game	This platform is web based, so it's very easy to get your game published.	Not as easy as HTML5. Requires plug-ins, and there is a cost to publish to certain platforms.
Centralized asset library	There is no centralized asset library; instead, assets are available from third-party providers, usually for free. However, with no regulation, these assets do not come tested, optimized, or license checked.	Unity features a vast asset library for game development, which includes textures, materials, music, and sound effects.

Table 8-5 compares HTML5 with mobile apps for game development. They both have pros and cons, and they also bring vastly different experiences to your audience.

TABLE 8-5 **HTML5 versus Mobile Apps for Game Development**

Development Feature	HTML5	Mobile Apps
Deployment and launch	Instant. You have control where it matters because you can update your game whenever you want.	You're at the mercy of the app store's approval team. Typically, you could be waiting days to see if your game has been approved.
Statistics and analytics	You're in complete control. You can collect your own data; there are even third-party solutions that gather information about your campaign.	You need to rely on the app store to make all the decisions about what analytics you need and can download for your campaign.
User feedback	You can engage directly with your audience without the fear that you're violating the app store's policies. You get to manage the customer relationship more closely, in your own way.	Nearly all your audience feedback will be filtered through the app store's limited mechanisms.
Mobile device features	HTML5 has limited access to some popular device-centric features such as GPS and the accelerometer. Also, because the game will basically run on the mobile device's browser, there are data storage limitations and game speed performance issues.	You have access to all the mobile device's native features. This can result in a more rewarding experience for your audience.

Chapter **9**

Launching and Promoting Your Game

Your audience can't play your awesome game if they don't know it exists! And you can't expect your marketing campaign to be successful if you rush to launch or don't plan enough time to reach out to your audience. By using a combination of a planned successful launch, a targeted email campaign, social media promotions, and a researched media outreach, you can ensure your game reaches all the people who would love to play it.

In this chapter, I explore simple yet powerful techniques to jump-start your gamification marketing journey.

Scheduling the Right Time to Launch

Many marketing campaigns fail not because the campaigns weren't creative or compelling, but because their launches were poorly planned. A well-planned and properly executed launch can be critical for your overall game's marketing success. And a key part of planning your launch is deciding on the right time to do it!

The actual launch date for your game can determine whether your campaign will be successful. For this reason, you need to apply an almost scientific thought process to determine the right launch date for your game. Unfortunately, over the years, I've found contradictory statistical data on this, which on further scrutiny is due to factors such as geographical, cultural, and industry-specific differences. I've compiled my own statistics based on the gamification campaigns I've been involved with.

TIP

I find that launching on a Tuesday or a Wednesday leads to a more successful campaign because people are far more engaged with their email early in the week. Plus, launching at the start of the week helps your initial campaign gain momentum in the following days.

Table 9-1 shows how launching on each day of the week can impact your launch.

TABLE 9-1   Determining the Best Day to Launch

Day	Quality	Why
Monday	Good	Your audience will be refreshed from a rested weekend and will be looking forward to the whole week ahead. However, their attention may be more focused on their to-do lists than on playing your game.
Tuesday	Very good	Having had a full day in the office to work on their to-do lists, your audience will be more receptive to your launch.
Wednesday	Excellent	Midweek messages get more attention due to the lack of urgency of people's to-do lists. Plus, there are still two full weekdays ahead in which to potentially maintain momentum for your campaign.
Thursday	Good	Your audience will be receptive because they should be available to view your message, but this only leaves one full day to build any momentum for your campaign before the weekend.
Friday	Not good	The end of a hard week is not a good time to message a launch to your audience. Even if your message *does* get received, there are no days left to build and maintain your campaign.
Saturday or Sunday	Bad	Your audience will be in a constant state of nonwork mode, which means your message will be lost among all the other unread messages.

TIP

Avoid launching on a major holiday as well. If your audience is international, check to find the dates of any major holidays in the countries you're hoping to target. If your target audience is in China, and you launch your campaign on the Chinese New Year, odds are, your message will go unread. In general, your audience is far more likely to participate when they're at their computers during a regular workweek.

Perfecting Your Landing Page

First impressions matter — especially because a high percentage of first-time visitors will leave without playing if they don't immediately find what they have been promised. Your visitors will be coming to play the game you've developed, so they should arrive at a stand-alone page centered around your whole gamification campaign. This *landing page* should be clearly distinct from your home page or any other page on your site, because it serves a single and focused purpose: to serve the traffic your gamification marketing will be generating.

A well-designed and focused landing page has a better chance of capturing your audience's attention for a longer period of time. Good landing pages must do several things at the same time:

REMEMBER

>> **It should focus on your game, not your company.** Your future audience is clicking through for a reason, and offering them content other than what you've promised (that is, the game) will result in an immediate bounce.

The landing page should still be tied to your company brand. In fact, your gamification marketing campaign should be an *extension* of your brand.

>> **It should be concise and free of distractions.** A good example of a distraction-free landing page is the one from Chipotle's A Love Story Game (shown in Figure 9-1); the landing page clearly presents whose game it is and how to play it, giving people the option to watch the film. Your content should have the end goal of delivering the audience your game, including an invitation to play it and share it, and instructions on how to play.

FIGURE 9-1:
Chipotle's landing page for A Love Story Game.

>> **It should introduce your audience to your other marketing channels.** You need to provide links to other offers, your social media profiles, or an email list to sign up, in case the people playing the game want to connect with your brand.

>> **It should have a clear call to action (CTA).** The CTA should be the core feature your users are drawn to when they arrive. The most obvious will be to invite the user to start playing. However, if your game is complex, you may want to invite the user to watch a video or tutorial on how to play. Make sure you're telling your visitors what you want them to do, and what they'll get out of it if they do.

USING A CONTENT DELIVERY NETWORK FOR YOUR LANDING PAGE

If you use the techniques in this chapter, you may end up with a tsunami of users streaming to your page all at once. Although this situation sounds like a dream, a sudden spike in traffic can cause serious issues with your server's bandwidth, which will result in your company's website running extremely slow and may eventually even cause it to crash. If that happens, your gamification marketing campaign will have caused harm to your company — and no one wants that.

That's where having a content delivery network (CDN) helps. A CDN provides alternative server nodes for users to access your site. These nodes are spread throughout the world, so a user requesting your landing page will be offered the node closest to him. This node then delivers a cached version of your landing page, ensuring a faster response and download time due to reduced latency and increased stability.

Many companies erroneously assume that a CDN is only for those who expect a constant, huge volume of traffic to their websites. But a CDN is essential for any website that's prone to intermittent spikes of traffic caused by marketing campaigns.

There are plenty of CDN providers, so research the options and find the one that's most suitable for your campaign and required points of presence around the world. Here are the top five global CDN providers to give you a place to start:

- **Amazon Web Services (AWS;** https://aws.amazon.com): AWS is the biggest cloud computing and services provider in the world. It offers a large scale of cloud services, such as distributed denial-of-service (DDoS) protection, CDN, storage, analytics, and online database services.

- **Google Cloud CDN** (https://cloud.google.com/cdn): Google Cloud CDN uses Google's global infrastructure (the same infrastructure that Google uses to deliver its end-user products like Google Search and YouTube) to cache and deliver content for its clients. You have to be a user of the Google Cloud Platform (https://cloud.google.com) to sign up for Google Cloud CDN.

- **Microsoft Azure CDN** (https://azure.microsoft.com/en-us/services/cdn/): This CDN is one of 600 services that are a part of Microsoft Azure, a cloud computing provider established in 2010 by Microsoft. Microsoft Azure has a much wider reach in developing markets than AWS and Google Cloud have.

- **Cloudflare** (www.cloudflare.com): Cloudflare is one of the fastest-growing companies in the security and performance space encompassing Domain Name System (DNS), CDN, web application firewall (WAF), and DDoS mitigation. Cloudflare has offices in San Francisco, London, and Singapore, and is backed by Google, Baidu, Microsoft, and Qualcomm. It offers self-service and enterprise plans to suit small, medium, and very large customers.

- **Rackspace** (www.rackspace.com): Rackspace is a cloud-computing company founded in 1998. Its main focus from the start was to support its customers with services like web hosting, but it has shifted to supplying CDN among other services.

TIP

You should aim to have *multiple* landing pages, not just one. Each landing page should speak to a specific segment of your target audience. Segmenting your audience helps you to target specific consumers through customized links in your campaigns. A general rule of thumb is to create one landing page for current customers and another landing page for your new users. New users should be presented with a more minimal landing page, whereas current customers who are already familiar with your website can be presented with a landing page that has some product or company content featured around the game's content.

Leading Up to T Minus Zero

No matter who your audience is, you can bet they're inundated with all forms of digital messages these days, and it can be difficult to stand out from all that noise. That puts a lot of pressure on you to reach your audience on launch day.

That's where a pre-launch marketing strategy comes into play. The goal of a pre-launch marketing strategy is to generate and build some excitement around your launch so that when you finally do launch your game, your audience will be scrambling to click Play Now.

Your pre-launch marketing will prime your audience to keep their eyes and ears open for your big launch. As you market during pre-launch, you'll increase curiosity around your new game, thereby increasing the likelihood of reaching your audience when you do launch.

Building pre-launch interest

To have a successful game launch, you need to build interest for the game via a pre-launch marketing campaign. Building pre-launch interest takes time — it should start at least a month before your launch. The steps you take leading up to your launch will determine whether your launch is a hit or a miss.

Here are two of the most important pre-launch strategies to include in your pre-launch plan:

>> **Collect email addresses through a Coming Soon page.** The people who sign up are the ones who will be the most engaged and excited about your game. After all, they want you to let them know when they can start playing the game. Also, a signup page allows you to gauge the amount of interest your pre-marketing campaign is generating.

>> **Create content to build buzz.** Another way to grow your pre-launch email list is by creating exciting news and content about the game that will create buzz. Share your experiences and excitement via social media so that others in your industry can follow your journey.

TIP

Search engine optimization (SEO) will be a useless endeavor unless you start over a year before your product launch. However, that doesn't mean you can't create SEO building viral articles and epic content to post on media sites. Your input will be shared by people interested in game development and viral marketing.

REMEMBER

Decide on the exact date you want to launch, so you can begin counting down (see the "Scheduling the Right Time to Launch" section, earlier in this chapter). Remember to consult with your colleagues before deciding on the launch date. For instance, you'll want to make sure your development team is comfortable with handing over the game for user acceptance testing (UAT), which is the last phase of the testing process. During UAT, actual software users test the campaign to make sure it can handle required tasks in real-world scenarios, according to your original specifications and objectives. The last thing you want is to have to push back the release date after you spent weeks generating hype around the game.

TIP

One week before launch day, cross the following goals off your list:

» **Start optimizing your landing page for speed.** Your audience won't be patient enough for the site to load if it takes too long. Use Google's PageSpeed Insights (`https://developers.google.com/speed/pagespeed/insights/`), which can help your web team to further optimize your landing page, especially for mobile devices.

» **Set up a separate Google Analytics for your landing page.** Monitor these analytics independently from your main website stats.

» **Set up tracking pixels on your landing page to start gathering information on your traffic.** Be sure to set up Facebook Pixel (`www.facebook.com/business/help/742478679120153?id=1205376682832142`) as well. Facebook pixel is code that you place on your landing page that collects data that helps you track conversions from Facebook ads and remarket to people who have already taken some kind of action on your website.

» **Test your game repeatedly.** Do this as much as you can. Your audience won't give the game a second chance, so make sure it's working perfectly before you launch.

» **Prepare a blog post for your launch.** Talk about why you're building the game, what marketing targets you've set, and what it was like making it. People love to see the behind-the-scenes of game development.

» **Tease your followers with posts that give them a preview of the game in a fun and entertaining way on social media.** See the next section for more on this subject.

» **Create a competition on social media where one person can win the chance to win a small prize and play the game one day before the launch.** All the person has to do is like and share your post.

» **Write personally to bloggers (give exclusives for the big ones) and give them a compelling story about the game.** Bloggers like to write interesting content, so make your story a coherent and a powerful one. Request them not to leak the story until your launch day. See "Giving influencers and bloggers a sneak peek," later in this chapter, for more information.

» **Start sorting your existing audience email list.** See "Reaching out to your current audience," later in this chapter, for more.

» **Prepare a video demo of your game and record interviews with yourself and colleagues having fun playing it.** Post the videos on your YouTube channel. Keep it short and fun!

Devising a game-launch marketing strategy through social media

If you're thinking you'll just make the game "available to play" on a certain date and that's it, you're not building excitement. Why should your audience believe that your product is a big deal? One excellent method I find very effective is to keep them guessing.

If you execute this method carefully, you can achieve a snowball effect where your audience will be excited about your game because they want to know more. Use social media to drop clues about your game with high-resolution screenshots and intriguing copy. Be sure not to disclose complete spoilers of the game, though. Give them just enough information to want more.

Employ your company's existing social media channels, including the following:

>> **Facebook:** You can't hope to generate a big pre-launch buzz about your game online without Facebook, which boasts an audience of over a billion people. Here's how to use Facebook to your advantage:

- *Facebook ads:* These ads appear in users' newsfeeds as though they were content posted by friends. There will be a "Sponsored" message on the ad, but it won't be too obvious. Your ad should include an attention-grabbing image of your game's content along with teasing content about your upcoming launch.

- *Call-to-action content:* The whole point of your content is to compel the audience to "like" your marketing campaign's Facebook page as soon as they read your headline. One of the best approaches is to ask people to click Like if they want to be alerted about the game's release date.

- *Market segment:* Make sure that you target the right types of people with your ads. Fortunately, Facebook allows you to craft an ad campaign with laserlike precision to users based on demographics and interests.

TIP

If you wish to learn more about using Facebook in your marketing campaigns, I highly recommend *Facebook Marketing For Dummies,* 6th Edition, by Stephanie Diamond and John Haydon (Wiley).

>> **Instagram:** With Instagram, you can cross-post images and text you've used on Pinterest, but you can also take advantage of posting more content via the Stories feature. Instagram Stories differ from regular Instagram posts because they come in a slideshow format and they are only available for 24 hours, but Stories can be saved to any of your devices and reused at a later point.

I recommend using Stories to capture behind-the-scenes insider posts that may not be as high-quality as regular posts.

>> **LinkedIn:** LinkedIn offers a few great ways to build buzz about your game, especially if your game falls into the business-to-business (B2B) space:

- *LinkedIn sponsored updates:* Use your company's LinkedIn page to create some intriguing content; then promote that content so people in your target market see it even if they're not connected to you on LinkedIn. Be sure to create compelling text with a fascinating image.

- *Existing LinkedIn groups:* Groups are a great way to tap into an existing community built around a shared interest. You can easily find groups for interests related to your brand and game by using the search bar at the top of the page. From the drop-down menu on the left of the search box, select Groups, then type in the keyword you want to find groups for.

- *Your own LinkedIn group:* This technique works especially well for promoting marketing campaigns. Creating a LinkedIn group for your launch can help connect audiences before and after the event, providing a central place for them to ask questions and create a real buzz around the game.

  As admin of your own LinkedIn group, you'll be able to share company updates about the game and other information about the launch. An often-overlooked benefit is being able to ask for live feedback as you plan your game-launch marketing strategy using group polls and discussion topics.

>> **Pinterest:** Image-driven social media apps such as Pinterest will ensure that your screenshots really are worth a thousand words. Create a clever image that reflects aspects of your game, include an intriguing text description, and then pin it to Pinterest.

TIP

Pinterest allows you to promote your pins so that they appear to users who don't follow your company's brand. Schedule at least a few promoted pins to roll out in the weeks leading up to the launch. If your images look great, you'll have people liking and re-pinning your pins.

>> **Twitter:** Twitter is a very effective social media channel for gamification. You can tweet a brief text message, an image, or a video. Then you can promote the tweet so that even people who don't follow you will see it.

Twitter ads allow you to target your tweet to people based on interests and demographics, so be sure to promote the tweet to people who are in your target market.

REMEMBER

Twitter ads don't just appear on individuals' timelines. Your promoted tweet can also appear at the top of relevant search results pages on Twitter as well as in search results for a promoted trend. This means your promoted tweet appears in the search results when people click a promoted trend.

Launch Day: Aiming the Spotlight on Your Game

Your entire audience can be initially split into two groups:

>> People who already know about your brand and products or services

>> The rest of the world

It is important to split your audience into these two groups early on in your marketing journey. The message you send to each group, and the method of delivery that works best for each group, will be different. If you don't target these two groups separately, you'll be in danger of alienating your loyal ambassadors and miss out on their actively promoting your game.

REMEMBER

Your game's marketing campaign will produce a massive return in value as it generates a buzz for your company. The more people talk about your game, the more you create awareness among people who may not have heard of your brand before.

Reaching out to your current audience

In marketing, I've seen only one strategy that can't miss: to market to your best customers first.

— JOHN ROMERO

I always like to tell my clients that the first way to market your game is to think about how you behave when a positive moment happens in your life. For example, you might think of that time when you got an A on a really tough test or the moment when you landed your first job. In both scenarios, you were probably bursting with pride and excited to tell someone! Odds are, you reached out to your family and friends rather than a complete stranger.

For your company, your "family and friends" are your current clients and subscribers — people who know you, some possibly very well, and who have purchased or just simply engaged with your company in the past. The game offers a new, fun, exciting side to your company. You should be bursting with excitement to email them and tell them the news!

Shooting for specific goals

Creating and executing specific goals is a powerful technique for smart marketing, and it can usually return a much higher level of success. However, first you need to apply segmentation to your current audience. *Segmentation* is simply the process of dividing your current audience into meaningful and manageable groups, or segments. In this way, you can tailor your emails to ensure specific goals are met within each group. Table 9-2 shows audience segments matched to goals.

TABLE 9-2   **Current Audience Segmentation Goals**

Audience Segment	Specific Goal
Those who have purchased your products multiple times and reviewed them positively	Share and promote the game to this group. They already trust and like you.
Those who have purchased your products at least once	Get them back onto the site where they may see another reason to buy again.
Those who have inquired about your products but not yet purchased them	Get them to make a purchase with an enticing offer within or around the game.
Those who have only subscribed to your mailing list	Get them to make an inquiry or just interact with your company.

TIP

If you don't already have a method to store and segment your current audience, it may be worth starting now. You could use one of the following methods:

>> **Customer relationship management (CRM) software such as Salesforce** (www.salesforce.com): Although these systems boast extremely useful and powerful features, they can be very pricey.

>> **Mail systems such as Mailchimp** (www.mailchimp.com): Mail systems aren't as costly as CRM systems, and you can use them to easily segment your audience. Just keep in mind that the mechanics of these systems are geared toward emailing and nothing else.

>> **Spreadsheets such as Microsoft Excel or Google Sheets:** These are extremely low cost (free, in the case of Google Sheets), but you need to input, segment, archive, and update everything manually.

Customizing emails

Your current clients and subscribers may not associate your company with producing games, so your email should promote the entire campaign as an event. With any event, there should be a pre-launch email, which should give your audience notice that a big announcement is happening soon.

TIP

Before I delve into email-writing techniques, it's worth exploring the frequency of your email campaign. Every email in your campaign should be able to answer the question "Why should they care?" The reason for a pre-launch email would be "to alert our audience that a big and exciting event is coming up." For this reason, sending a *second* pre-launch email may not satisfactorily answer the question "Why should they care?" because you aren't giving any new information to your audience.

Although the pre-launch email can be one generic email for everyone in your audience, all subsequent emails should be tailored for your segmented groups. The two main areas you should concentrate on customizing for each email are the subject and the call to action (CTA) buttons.

CRAFTING PERSUASIVE SUBJECT LINES

Although it may seem like a small part of your message, the subject line is one of the very first impressions you have on your email recipients. You want your email to be opened, read, and clicked, and this all starts with the subject line. Table 9-3 offers a subject-line strategy for each of your audience segments.

TABLE 9-3   **Subject-Line Goals for Your Segmented Audience**

Audience Segment	Subject Line Goal	Example
Those who have purchased your products multiple times and reviewed them positively	Urgency. Communicating urgency works well in an email subject line and can help compel readers to act immediately.	"We need your help today, [Name]."
Those who have purchased your products at least once	Curiosity. You're looking to pique the audience's natural curiosity and interest. Because they'll want to get more information, this strategy will result in a higher open rate.	"Hi [Name], are you free to join us for a game?"
Those who have inquired about your products but not yet purchased them	Offers. Everyone loves offers — whether they're free or discounted. Open with that by including the offer in your subject line.	"[Name], don't miss our free launch today (plus one-day-only special offers)."
Those who have only subscribed to your mailing list	Recognition. This audience wants to be kept informed of any news events your company may have. Similar to piquing your audience's curiosity, you'll want to tie your brand or product to the subject to compel them to click and read.	"[Name of your company] invites you to our new event."

WARNING

Be sure to avoid techniques that can result in your audience not opening the email or, worse, condemning your company to the spam folder:

>> **Don't use all caps and exclamation points.** Using all caps and too many exclamation points kills open rates.

>> **Avoid spam words such as** *free.* The game may well be free, but there's no need to announce this in the subject (or anywhere in the email).

>> **Keep it brief.** You have only seconds to capture their attention. Long subject lines get lost in the inbox especially on mobile devices.

>> **Make sure you don't have any spelling or grammatical errors.** This might seem obvious, but check your subject line for typos. They may not cause your email to end up in the spam folder, but they look unprofessional.

ADDING SMARTER BUTTONS

After you've have perfected your subject and the bulk of your email content, you're ready to consider your CTA button (see Figure 9-2). Your email should include at least one CTA to spur some kind of interactivity. If your email has *too* many CTAs, your audience could be overwhelmed. Aim to use a maximum of four CTA buttons in your email.

FIGURE 9-2:
This launch email has three CTA buttons, so users can clearly see their choices for action.

TIP

Make sure your CTA buttons stand out. Use action-inducing words, like "Play Now." Readers shouldn't have to hunt for the link that lets them play the game.

TIP

I recommend you use one or two of the following effective CTA buttons for your email campaigns:

>> **Play Now:** This button is the most important one for your launch and subsequent emails. Clicking it should take the reader to the predetermined landing page (see "Perfecting Your Landing Page," earlier in this chapter).

>> **Reserve Your Pre-Launch Seat:** This button can be used in a pre-launch email campaign. Clicking the button should add the person to a pre-launch list. This is a great way to inject early interaction by offering your audience a chance to play the game before the official launch.

>> **Watch <Icon>:** Clicking this button should lead to a YouTube video. The video could be a "how to play" video, a trailer for the game, or even just a blogger playing and commenting about the game.

>> **Share Our Game:** This button is an effective and easy way for your audience to share your game. A simple way to do this is to take them to a specific Facebook post where you share the game's link or to a dedicated Facebook page for the game.

>> **Complete our 5-Min Survey:** This button is a very helpful CTA for one of your post-launch emails. Getting honest feedback can help you gauge the real success of the game and also the mistakes to correct for your next one.

>> **Make Me a VIP:** Offer to give your audience a red-carpet treatment for future games. This level of interaction really is the holy grail of marketing where your audience is actively seeking to learn more about your company's games. Offer them exclusive access and news on future games. Have fun with this and even send a VIP ticket to them!

Grabbing media attention

Getting your company's name in the media is a powerful way to boost your online presence and reach prospects who would normally never have heard about you. The usual drawback for companies is finding an interesting story to share. However, with news that your company is about to launch a game, you can now grab their attention with an unusual angle for them to report and share.

Posting a press release on your website

In many ways public relations (PR) is far easier today than it was 20 years ago. Small businesses can reach out to journalists on Twitter, instead of paying a PR firm.

STEPS TO MINIMIZE BEING IDENTIFIED AS A SPAMMER

In the simplest terms, *spam* is unsolicited email sent to a large list of people. Unfortunately, there is not one main body to determine who is a spammer; it's left to individual Internet service providers (ISPs) to decide. If you do run afoul of one or two ISPs, you'll need to convince them you aren't a spammer, which can take time (and a lot of patience).

However, there are some steps you can take to ensure you remain in the clear:

- **Ensure your email deliverability is set correctly.** Free sites like Mail-Tester (www. mail-tester.com) allow you to send them an email, and they'll check your email message in real time.

- **Make sure you give the recipient an easy and identifiable way to unsubscribe.** If they do unsubscribe, make sure you take steps to ensure they've been properly removed from all lists.

- **Use your company name as the From name rather than the name of an employee.**

- **Use a real reply-to address.** I recommend creating an email such as hello@your companyname.com, which you can monitor after you finish your campaign. When checking your hello@yourcompanyname.com inbox, make sure you remove any emails bounced back from an ISP from your mailing list.

- **Check to see if your company is a blacklisted sender.** Free sites, like MultiRBL. Valli (http://multirbl.valli.org) or MxToolbox (https://mxtoolbox.com) allow you to check if you're a blacklisted sender.

TIP

Before approaching anyone in the media, take the time to post a press release on your website detailing the major points of the game and your company. The press release should contain the following:

- **The date of the release:** This is especially helpful if it means they can publish the story before the launch.

- **A catchy title that announces the new game**

- **Key facts:** Answer the who, what, when, where, why, and how about the game. Why did your company take the gamification marketing route? Remember this is less about the actual game and more about your company and its decision to develop and market a game.

>> **Contact information for follow-up enquiries:** Be sure to include your email address and phone number.

>> **A brief summary of your business history**

>> **Statistics:** Statistics are useful especially after the launch. At a minimum, you want to include data gathered from at least one month after the game goes live. Positive key performance indicator (KPI) metrics give meaningful and real-time statistics to the media.

Make sure the press release can easily be printed (it should be sized on a standard 8½-x-11-inch page). Use short sentences (no more than 20 to 25 words) and paragraphs, with sensible line spacing. Aim to have your release no longer than two sides of a letter-size document.

WARNING

Don't link the press release from your game's landing page — it should only be accessed by the journalists you hand the link over to, not discoverable by search engines or people just coming to play your game.

Getting your press release in front of journalists

When you have your press release ready, you're ready to share it with journalists. Journalists welcome stories from businesses because they need to satisfy their visitors' 24/7 appetite for interesting news stories. For this reason, they're very competitive. Reaching out to an individual reporter instead of going straight to the news desk can work well, because reporters like to be able to report something before the story becomes public (in other words, before you game launches).

When you're getting ready to approach journalists, follow these steps:

1. **Make a list of all the media sites you want to target.**

This list should contain not only the obvious sites (such as HuffPost) that are known to post stories about viral games, but also media sites from the following categories:

● *Local news sites:* This includes online and offline media outlets.

● *News or websites that cover your industry:* The story that a relevant company is offering a unique game other than a special offer would be welcomed.

● *Digital news sites:* Examples include The Next Web and Buzzfeed.

● *Game review sites:* Although they mostly cover AAA Xbox-type games, most do cover online games as well.

2. **Understand how individual journalists like to be pitched to.**

Many journalists are happy to be approached on Twitter. If you can't find their Twitter profiles just by searching for them there, you should be able to find them on their bio pages on the websites of the publications they work for. Twitter is a great platform to connect with journalists directly, and it should form part of your overall PR strategy.

3. **Take time to build relationships with the journalists before you start bombarding them with your press release.**

REMEMBER

For example, you might start a conversation by replying to one of their tweets. This process takes time, so I recommend starting this relationship building in the early stages of the development of your game.

4. **Start pitching your game and press release link to them.**

Summarize the essence of your press release link in the tweet and only include a link when asked for more information.

Avoid sending the same tweet to all the journalists; instead, customize the tweet to each one. You might also want to consider using direct messaging. This strategy will help make your story seem a little more exclusive.

5. **If a journalist uses your story, make sure to thank him publicly and tweet a link to the story.**

TIP

Consider more traditional media journalists — they can produce surprisingly amazing results for gamification models. My consultancy was approached by a local radio station to discuss one of the games we had developed. At first, I was a little reluctant — it meant taking a whole morning out of my day to travel to the studio, and wait around for my time slot, all for just 15 minutes of airtime. My colleagues were also reluctant — they couldn't fathom anyone remembering the website URL or our company name after hearing it on the radio. Turns out, we aired later during the midday slot, which ended up producing a very healthy and lively debate on air with people on their lunch break.

Giving influencers and bloggers a sneak peek

Times have changed and marketing campaigns cannot solely rely on press releases and traditional media relationships. In this social-media-obsessed era, companies need to also build strong ties to influential bloggers and digital influencers.

Incorporating influencers and bloggers can have a very steep learning curve compared to some other marketing activities, but you should try to incorporate it into your marketing strategy. This is especially true if your business has limited reach — for example, if you operate in a niche industry/sector or if you operate a local business focused on building a local customer base.

By using the techniques in this section for your game, you'll start to expose your company to an audience it would normally never be able to speak to. Consider that people who would never even know your company existed will now actively share and discuss it via your game.

Finding social media influencers

Leveraging influencers to play your game is an extremely effective technique — their recommendations will be regarded as more trustworthy to their followers. With the increasing popularity of social influencers, there's no denying that influencer marketing is a great way to enhance your game's marketing efforts.

Influencers usually have a large reach and a loyal following. They have attained this status by detailing their lifestyles through digital storytelling. Their followers observe the trends that they promote and often try the products that they suggest. Encouraging influencers to play your game on social media can be a fun and effective way to successfully reach their audience.

Here's how to do it:

1. **Find relevant influencers who have an audience that aligns with your target market.**

   The right influencer can reach your target audience, build trust, and drive engagement in your game. So, it's critical to work only with social media influencers whose vision aligns with your own.

2. **Contact an influencer initially via a direct message on their social media channel.**

   If you can find an email address, try that, too. However, don't send a mass email or generic message. It may take a little longer to write a personal message to each influencer, but it'll show that you're serious about working with them. This will, in turn, increase your chances of striking a deal.

3. **Provide as much information about your game and company as possible to help influencers trust you.**

   Tell them what you hope to accomplish with your social media campaign. Make it clear how the influencer will benefit, beyond the paycheck.

4. **Establish a unique and relevant hashtag the influencers can use to promote your game.**

TIP

With the use of a hashtag, your marketing campaign will be easily identifiable to your audience and all those searching for your game. If you opt for a generic hashtag such as #game, then yours and your influencer's posts will most likely be lost among thousands of other generic posts using the same hashtag.

5. Include influencer fees in your budget.

Influencers with extensive reach expect to be paid (and rightly so) for their work. A free product from your inventory may work with new and upcoming influencers, but a larger influencer campaign requires a budget. Think about what kind of payment structure makes the most sense for your campaign while considering the influencers' needs, too.

Reaching into the blogosphere

Bloggers, who are trusted voices in their communities, can expose your game and help get a real buzz started. Blogger outreach is one of my preferred modes of influencer outreach for gamification marketing because bloggers keep active on many social channels to stay relevant and to promote themselves. Ultimately, their influence can be used as a springboard for the "one-to-one-to-many" approach.

Unfortunately reaching out to potential bloggers is a far more difficult process nowadays than it was just a few years ago. The best bloggers are constantly getting pitched by marketers, making it all the more important for you to stand out from the crowd if you want them to pay attention.

Despite this challenge, I still find it well worth the time to invest in building connections with high-quality bloggers who can become great advocates for your game and, more important, will be willing to help you out over and over again on subsequent games that you develop for your company.

Look for bloggers who are in your industry or in an industry that somewhat relates to your product/service. Their audience should be similar to what you're expecting. Encourage the blogger to play the game; in this way, you'll find their readers will trust the blogger's message more when they talk about your game while playing it.

A few online tools can help you find the perfect bloggers. My favorite is the website GroupHigh (www.grouphigh.com), which boasts a dedicated database to find bloggers. However, it can be very pricey, especially on your first campaign. Alternatively, you can find bloggers by Googling for *blogrolls* (lists of blogs) on your industry. Finally, a very useful online tool I like to use is Tweepi (www.tweepi.com), which allows you to tap into bloggers on Twitter.

TIP

The larger the blogger's audience is, the better the posts will be for your brand awareness. Chances are, you won't be able to see their traffic or follower numbers directly on their blog pages, so keep a close eye on their following and their post comments. By doing this, you'll be able to distinguish how many fans they have and how engaged their audience is with their content.

Here are a few tips for reaching out to bloggers effectively:

» **Send a frank email or social media message.** The message should explain that you would like to give them a sneak peek at a major event for your company.

» **The message should originate from your company email address** (yourname@yourcompany.com). The bloggers should be able to Google you and reach your bio easily via LinkedIn or your company's website.

» **Don't be discouraged if at first they don't reply.** Good bloggers get hundreds of pitches a day. Send a follow-up, but don't go overboard. It may also be worth trying to find another means to contact them (for example, via a shared connection on LinkedIn or Twitter).

» **Learn about the bloggers and their content.** Actually, read a couple of their blog posts to get a feel of their style, attitude, and overall voice. Include this in your message as the reason why you chose them. This is a far more effective way to appeal to a blogger than to simply say, "I'm a fan."

» **Don't expect them to do this for free.** They may, but the majority need to make a living through this competitive medium. Offer a token amount with the clear indication that you're open to negotiation. You could also sweeten the pot by offering one of your products or services.

» **Select by fit not followers.** It may seem natural to simply go for the bloggers who have the largest following. This strategy makes sense in theory, but if you don't have the right fit, your game will likely go unnoticed.

Using your existing social media channels (or not)

Your company's current online social media accounts may not be appropriate for this gamification marketing campaign. This is especially true when your business has nothing to do with games and/or technology. Those channels will be the right fit for your company, but you need to make sure your gamification message is not lost and confused with your company's main accounts.

REMEMBER

Your main social media accounts should continue to do their jobs. For this reason, the overall message given by these accounts may become confused when mixing normal business messages with your gamification marketing ones. I recommend that you cross-post, but not too frequently.

TIP

Open a secondary account dedicated to your gamification campaign, ensuring that both accounts are easily distinguishable to their respective audiences. This strategy will allow you to maximize your reach on social media, engage with the right people, and achieve your specific social media goals for your campaign.

Looking at the top social media sites for gamification marketing

Today, there are more than 30 social media sites that I would rate as most important. However not all 30 are the right fit for a gamification campaign. To make things easier, here are the top seven must-have social media sites that are vital for gamification marketing. Some will be familiar to you; others you may not have heard of.

>> **Facebook:** Facebook is the biggest social media site around, with billions of people using it every month.

>> **Instagram:** Instagram is a very popular photo and video sharing social media app. It allows you to share photos and videos of your game quickly. As long as you use the right hashtags, your posts can reach a significant number of your intended audience in seconds.

>> **Twitter:** Twitter is a social media site for news, entertainment, sports, politics, and more. Whatever your goals for your game, there's no question that Twitter can be a powerful tool to help you achieve them.

>> **Reddit:** Known as "the front page of the Internet," Reddit is a platform where users can submit almost anything (video, images, and so on) so that other people can discuss and vote. More important, you can search for a subreddit (dedicated forums) that is most relevant to your campaign.

>> **LinkedIn:** LinkedIn has evolved into a professional social media site where industry experts share content, network with one another, and build their personal brands.

>> **Snapchat:** On Snapchat, users create billions of videos a day, spending an average of 30 minutes per day on the platform. This, coupled with its extensive audience-targeting capabilities, means big opportunities for your game's campaign.

>> **TikTok:** TikTok is a Chinese social network that puts video first. It allows you to record, edit, and share short, looping 15- or 60-second videos with musical overlays, sound effects, and visual effects. Some of the most popular genres include short skits, lip singing, cringe videos, and cooking tutorials.

Avoiding this one social media mistake

WARNING

Whatever you do, don't post the same message across all social media accounts. You may be tempted to do it, because it keeps your accounts active, saves time, and makes it easy to share your content widely. But your message and overall campaign will get lost in translation.

Each social media platform has its own way of helping you to express yourself. By using one universal language, you come across as weird and unprofessional — the last thing you want to be doing.

A prime example is when posting on Instagram and then copying that post onto Facebook. Instagram allows (and encourages) you to use a plethora of hashtags. These hashtags make it easy to find relevant images and connect with people with similar interests. However, hashtags aren't something people expect to see on Facebook, so if you include them, your post will genuinely look alien to Facebook users.

TIP

Take the time to learn each site's language and become fluent in it. As you post regularly across all your social media accounts, instead of repeating messages word for word, you should be writing a new post each time. Crafting a new message may sound like a lot of work, so consider optimizing each of your posts so it fits the platform.

Writing unique posts for each platform requires more time and effort upfront, but the results I've collected over the years show that it's definitely worth it. Your social media posts will show that you care about your message, and your audience will notice this.

TIP

In every post, make sure you have a clear CTA. Each of your posts should not only share information but also initiate some form of interaction. Look at what stage you're on in your marketing campaign and come up with appropriate CTAs that will take the audience to the next step. For instance, at your pre-launch stage, your CTA should be to get as many signups for the launch as you can. Your post should make it clear that the launch is imminent and tell people why they need to be signing up.

Getting your game onto other sites

Although it would be ideal to have everyone be on your website when playing the game, but you may lose a potential audience share if you don't allow the game to be played on other websites as well. Media sites and bloggers would rather their visitors remain on *their* sites and play your game there (as opposed to physically sending them away to your site). This also means that when their visitors want to share the game, they'll use their URL rather than yours, resulting in more traffic and revenue for them, which ultimately means your game will be more attractive for them to post.

Giving permission to embed

You've probably seen embedded videos on web pages before. Embedding a game works the same way. The game is still being hosted on your servers, though, so no one can change or control your game mechanics and design. Also, when you're ready to shut down the campaign, your game will disappear from all other websites as well.

TIP

Prepare a Terms of Service for website owners to read and agree to. In this way, you'll protect your brand and game if you find a website doesn't follow your terms. Here are a few terms you should add to your Terms of Service:

>> Do not change the appearance or content inside the embedded games' boundaries.

>> Do not use any other technology or means to modify, build on, or impair any of the embed functionality.

>> Do not claim ownership of the game.

>> Do not charge a fee to play the game. Similarly, do not force users to view an advertisement before playing the game.

>> Do not place this game on a site with illegal, pornographic, or gambling content.

Getting your game onto Facebook

Facebook offers you a way to upload your game's client code directly to its servers. It's free and an extremely easy way to reach millions of people using the Facebook platform. Even better, your game will be on the same fast and reliable infrastructure that powers Facebook photos and videos.

Currently, there are two methods to share your HTML5 game on Facebook. The first is to use Web Hosting by Facebook, where your game appears in an iframe within a Facebook page (see Figure 9-3). An *iframe* is an HTML document embedded inside another HTML document on a website. HTML5 game hosting was introduced in 2015 and remains the most popular method to share games on social media.

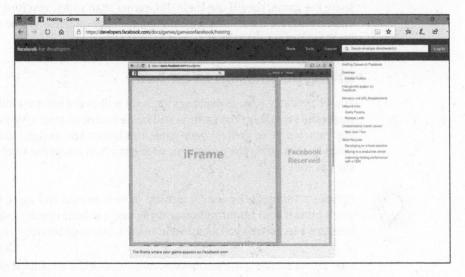

FIGURE 9-3:
The iframe where your game appears on Facebook.

TIP

I recommend getting your IT team or game developers to help you with this step. Facebook will require your files and code to be provided in a certain way. It'll also ask you to create a developer account for your Facebook account. A developer account will extend access to Facebook developer tools including Facebook application management. You may not want to hand over control for your primary Facebook account to your developers, so I recommend that you open a secondary Facebook account for your game's campaign and hand that account over to the developers.

The second method to share your game on Facebook is with its new Instant Games platform. When you integrate your game into Facebook Instant Games, people can play it directly in their news feeds or in their Messenger conversations on both desktop and mobile devices.

Instant Games requires more work for your developer to integrate, including a tricky software development kit (SDK), which must be imported into your game. It's worth discussing and negotiating this step at the start to ensure the developer keeps the overall code compatible with Facebook's guidelines.

4

Monitoring Real-Time Events and Data after You Go Live

Chapter 10

Capturing All the Data

D ata capture can help you better understand your audience's experience of and behavior surrounding your gamification marketing campaign. The data insights you gain from your campaign will help you to improve and tailor future campaigns to increase overall audience engagement. The data can also help drive engagement for your company's overall digital campaign. Fortunately, gamification marketing is an ideal platform for collecting audience-driven data.

Thanks to audiences being able to connect to your campaign 24/7 along with the versatility of cloud storage, you should be aiming to capture as much user data as possible during your campaign.

In this chapter, I look into the various methods and techniques you can use to successfully capture your audience's behavior and trends. First, I explore the development of an administration portal site, which helps you easily process all the data that you'll be collecting. Then I explain how to visually outline your audience's experience to learn more about their engagement behaviors. Finally, I discuss how to gain valuable feedback from your audiences — feedback that can be used to perfect your next campaign.

Establishing a Portal to Your Data

An *admin portal* is a web-based platform that provides you and your management team with a single access point to your gamification marketing campaign's data. The portal presents all the information collected from your audience's interaction on various platforms in one secure location. If developed correctly, it can be used to enhance and improve the way your company engages with your clients in the future.

With an admin portal, you don't need to log into multiple primary business applications to manually gather all that information. For this reason, an admin portal can significantly improve the productivity and performance of your current and future gamification marketing campaigns.

Developing your portal

The interface for your portal should be intuitive and easy for you and your team to work with. So, the first step is for your development team to find the right template for your portal.

Fortunately, a huge range of off-the-shelf portal sites are available for your development team to purchase online. These sites typically offer prebuilt and highly customizable admin portal templates. All your team has to do is download them and code them.

Here are some admin portal sites worth checking out:

>> **ThemeForest** (https://themeforest.net)**:** Contains a huge library of HTML5 and WordPress templates

>> **Colorlib** (https://colorlib.com)**:** Only offers WordPress themes

>> **aThemes** (https://athemes.com)**:** Not as big as ThemeForest, but offers high-end themes

HTML5 is typically the simplest and easiest technology for your developers to work with. It can be used with all types of server technologies (for example, Windows or Unix).

If your campaign is already using WordPress, you'll probably want to use a WordPress-themed admin portal template. The template will have key features built in. All you'll need to do is connect it with your WordPress credentials.

REMEMBER

Develop your portal for more than your current gamification marketing campaign. Ask your developers to assume that there will be multiple campaigns. They should design the database structure so that you can select which campaign you want to see the results for. If you don't tell them you want this upfront, you may face a cumbersome and costly process when you request it later on.

Securing access

As your gamification marketing campaign starts storing masses of data on a daily basis, you need to ensure that your company doesn't become a victim of a data breach. Unfortunately, as beneficial as a portal is for your campaign, it can also become a magnet for breaches and hacks.

Data security can be a complex and confusing topic in an ever-evolving technological landscape. Here are some methods I recommend you discuss with your development team:

>> **Renaming your login URL:** Hackers can only brute force their way into your portal if they manage to find out the direct URL of your login page. (A login page is a web entry page to your portal that requires user identification and authentication, usually performed by entering a username and password combination.) For this reason, you should avoid page names such as login, default, and so on. Choose something obscure — maybe a combination of your company's name and random letters.

Place some type of web stats counter, such as Google Analytics (http://analytics.google.com), just on the login page. If you ever see any third-party hits coming to the page, you can ask your developers to change your login page name again. Luckily, changing your login URL is an easy task.

>> **Requiring email addresses to log in:** People should use their email addresses instead of usernames to log in to your portal. Usernames tend to be easy to predict; because email addresses are unique, they're a safer and far more valid identifier for logging in.

REMEMBER

Put in place a policy to ensure that anyone who doesn't need access anymore (for example, anyone who has left the company) has his email address login access automatically revoked.

>> **Adjusting your passwords:** As with any secure website, make sure all users change their passwords regularly. Also, encourage them to improve their strength by adding uppercase and lowercase letters, numbers, and special characters.

Long passwords are nearly impossible for hackers to predict, but they're harder for users to remember, which means most users will opt to use a short password if you allow it. Your developers should all be using a password manager such as 1Password (www.1password.com), which keeps passwords safe and doesn't require them to remember their passwords.

» **Logging out idle users automatically:** Any users leaving the portal site open on their screens or devices can pose a serious security threat. Idle sessions make session hijacking easier, and sometimes they can create other problems, especially if there are a number of simultaneous active user sessions.

You can avoid this situation by ensuring that your portal site's code logs users out after they've been idle for a certain period of time. Ideally, get your developers to log out any session that has been idle for 15 minutes or longer.

» **Using SSL to encrypt data:** Implementing a Secure Sockets Layer (SSL) certificate is absolutely imperative to securing your portal website. SSL ensures a secure data transfer between user browsers and your data server, making it difficult for hackers to breach or spoof any logged-in connection session.

Getting an SSL certificate for your server website is simple and can be installed by your developers in a matter of minutes.

TIP

Although you can purchase an SSL from a third-party company, I recommend using one from Let's Encrypt (https://letsencrypt.org). Let's Encrypt is a nonprofit certificate authority that provides SSL certificates at no charge. The certificate is valid for 90 days, during which renewal can take place at any time.

» **Adding user accounts with care:** If multiple departments or external contractors are working with your team on the campaign, multiple people will be accessing your portal, which could make your admin portal more vulnerable to security threats.

Here are a few precautionary steps you can take to minimize the threats from having multiple users:

- **Work with your developers to create multi-tiered access control accounts.** In this way, you don't have to reveal all the portal's functionality to all users. Try to only give each user the information and functionality she requires.

- **Give each user a small window of time in which he can use the portal.** If the user requires access after his time has expired, grant him an extension. Have a clear policy for removing users as soon as possible if, for instance, any staff member or contractor no longer requires access within his time window.

- **Limit one session per user.** With multiple users, it's nearly impossible to ensure that all users keep their credentials safe. If a user has had his password compromised, by limiting all users to just one session, he'll quickly realize the password has been compromised when he keeps getting logged out.

- **Apply IP intelligence.** Get your developers to log all users' IP addresses when they use your portal. The system can then use an IP address lookup to determine the geolocation of all users. If a user logs in from a different country, you can have this flagged — both for yourself and for the user. *Note:* This information won't be 100 percent accurate, because some users may use a virtual private network (VPN), which allows them to access your campaign from another country's IP address.

- **Introduce a lockdown feature for failed login attempts.** If there is a hacking attempt with repetitive wrong passwords on an account, that user's access will be disabled, and you should be notified of this unauthorized activity. If this happens to multiple accounts at the same time, the entire website will be locked down until your server admins can deal with the threat.

REMEMBER

Data security is a continuous process that requires constant assessment to reduce the overall risk. Revisit the steps in this section both during your campaign and for any future campaigns.

TOKENIZING YOUR DATA

You need a clear digital security and privacy strategy to protect your company. Like any other digital campaign, your gamification marketing campaign must be secure enough to keep the data protected.

Unfortunately, security breaches and high-profile hacks are very common these days. Even with appropriate measures in place, it's still important that all your data is handled, stored, and processed in a secure, protected way.

Work with your developers to employ an advanced form of encryption called tokenization from the very start. This will essentially hide your data behind an encryption key. Without this key, the data cannot be read even if it's compromised or stolen.

Your actual data, such as your users' email addresses, are converted into a string of random characters called a *token*. This token is the same length and size as the actual data, but it has no meaningful information whatsoever. So, even when the data is breached, the hackers can't make sense of it.

Building your reports

Your portal's real benefit comes with the reports it will produce for you. I'm always obsessed with ensuring that the reports built by the developers focus on the relevant goals for the campaign. With a series of good reports, you can condense huge amounts of user data into efficient blocks, which can be quickly digested.

REMEMBER

Reports should help you make a decision, whether that decision is to modify your current campaign or adjust for future campaigns.

Setting your goals

It all starts with three steps that will help you create effective reports:

1. **Set goals.**

   When you set goals, your gamification marketing campaign can be better geared toward delivering measurable results. By continually monitoring your reports throughout the campaign, your focus will remain on your end goals, which means your campaigns progress will be better optimized in the long run.

2. **Make sure you're gathering *all* the data.**

   All your data should be available for reporting within one central platform. Most of this raw data will usually come from your own campaign (your database and website). However, make sure your developers are connecting the various platforms' data sets into your reporting, whether this be from other departments within your company, social media platform data, or third-party analytics data.

3. **Interpret your data.**

   Your reports should be providing you with powerful and actionable insights. Your campaign will be in a far better position to adapt to, say, emerging trends if your reports are keeping you continuously better informed. Good reports will be a powerful tool to help you find better answers about your campaign.

Designing a marketing report

The reports you'll develop will inform and benefit both yourself and your team, which will probably include management and members in other departments. Typically, your marketing reports should contain the following elements:

>> **Title:** What was the purpose of this report? Whether you're running a report on campaign performance or user behavior, make sure the intent of your report is clear in the title. This becomes important when you start sharing your report with people outside of your team.

>> **Reporting period:** Your report should be relevant to a certain time period in your campaign. This period can be a few hours, days, or months. By analyzing user data within a set time period, you can effectively compare engagement metrics with past periods.

>> **Summarize:** Your report summary should reflect the key points of your report. The summary should concentrate on the metric results on specific campaign goals for a specific time period.

Knowing Which Data You Should Be Capturing

One of the greatest benefits of gamification marketing is the ability to collect useful insights about your target audience and about the performance of your campaign overall.

Marketing campaigns needs to be data driven to be effective. With gamification marketing, by learning your target user's behavior, goals, exit points, and challenges, your company can develop far more effective future marketing campaigns. As your audience engage with your games, you should aim to collect as much information about your target market as much as you can.

Your gamification marketing campaign is that much more fun and engaging when you incentivize and reward user participation. As a result, your audience will be more involved with a particular process or operation within your game, which results in more accurate, relevant, and meaningful data for your campaign.

Progress tracker

By setting goals and milestones within your game, you can measure the progress of your audience during the campaign. (I explore the benefits of this metric in "Following the User Journey," later in this chapter.)

Although your game will have obvious visual goals that the user will be aware of, you should also be looking to install goals that work in the background. For instance, what time of the day or day of the week do most users complete a certain goal?

Keeping an eye on your audience's progress will give your team invaluable feedback on your campaign. This data can answer questions such as, "Was the game too difficult for my audience?" or "Was there enough help and guidance given?"

Interaction

Throughout your landing page and game you should have several call-to-action (CTA) buttons, like the following:

>> Play Now

>> Learn More

>> View Our Latest Products

>> How to Play

By measuring each user's interaction with your CTA buttons, you can track the success of each button. I find that this metric is far more beneficial at the start of your campaign. If you find, for instance, that there is a low percentage of clicks to a certain CTA, you can look at reasons why that has happened and correct it while the campaign is still going on.

Duration

Duration is a metric that reports the average amount of time your audience spends on your campaign. When a user lands on your campaign, the session timer doesn't necessarily start right away. It starts when that user clicks on one of your CTA buttons. Unless the user takes an action on your campaign, the time spent on the landing page shouldn't be counted as part of the session duration.

Percentage of new sessions

Percentage of new sessions refers to the number of first-time visits. This is essentially the number of sessions that are created by new visitors, which indicates the efficiency of your efforts to drive new traffic to your campaign.

A good campaign will have a healthy mix of new and returning visitors, and this mix will vary depending on your campaign goals. For instance, if your goal is to generate new leads for your sales team, you'll want a healthy number of returning visits because it often takes multiple interactions with your site for users to convert.

Goal completions

Marketing goals will measure how well your campaign fulfills your intended objectives. A goal represents a completed activity, called a *conversion*, that contributes to the overall success of your campaign. Examples of goals include the following:

>> Completing the first game level

>> Completing all game levels

>> Making a purchase

>> Submitting a query

>> Subscribing to your newsletter, YouTube channel, or Facebook page

TIP

Defining clear and meaningful marketing goals is fundamental to your digital analytics measurement plan. If you set clear goals, your portal will provide your team with critical information, such as the overall conversion rate for your campaign, allowing them to evaluate the effectiveness of your gamification marketing campaign.

Views versus sessions

Views measure the number of times your campaign was loaded. By contrast, sessions take into account your visitor's actual interaction with the campaign.

The most immediate difference is that sessions conveys the amount of time a user spends on your campaign, whereas views just shows the number of times they loaded your campaign.

If your gamification marketing campaign was an advertisement in a print newspaper, your views would be like the number of papers sold that day. Sessions would be how many people read your ad, possibly cut it out, or even called the number advertised.

TIP

Session data gives you a much better idea of your audience's experience with your campaign than views data does.

Bounces

Bounces measures the percentage of people who land on your gamification marketing campaign and do not engage with your game. This means they don't click the Play Now button or any other menu items (such as a Read More link or any other internal links on the page).

This portion of visitors to your campaign have no engagement with the landing page, and the visit ends with a single-page visit. You can use this bounce rate as a metric to measure against other data points. An example is to see if you can spot a pattern such as the user's browser or device. If a high percentage of these users are using a particular browser or device, your game may not have been optimized for it.

Location

Location data can be useful to check that your campaign has, indeed, targeted your intended geographical location. Your developers can now capture a very high level of detail on where your users are coming from. By using this data, you can measure the success of your campaign's popularity in intended cities or countries.

However, with gamification marketing, due to the viral nature of games, campaigns can reach a high percentage of unintended localities. For instance, one campaign my company ran was supposed to be targeted for audiences in the United Kingdom. Although the campaign's location data showed a successful pickup from the three major U.K. cities (London, Birmingham, and Edinburgh), there was also a spike of users coming from other cities in Europe.

Returning versus new

A key audience demographic is your proportion of new and returning visitors to your campaign. New visitors are those navigating to your campaign for the first time on a specific device. Returning visitors have visited your campaign before and are back to play again.

Keep these two sets in mind when studying the following metrics:

>> **Sessions:** You'll want to know which of the two sets spends longer on the game. For instance, are you finding new visitors spend more time as opposed to returning visitors? If you begin to see a disproportionate amount of time spent on first visits, this means your audience isn't being engaged on your campaign as much on their second and subsequent visits. In this case, you should be looking at the frequency of your rewards and goals to ensure you give a compelling reason for your audience to return and play.

>> **Behavior:** This section breaks down how returning users and new users behave after they're on the game. Are they engaging with your CTA buttons on their first visit? Also, after returning to the campaign, are they engaging in other aspects of your campaign and company site or are they just focused on the game?

>> **Goals:** Goals can ensure your audience keep returning to your campaign. But are new visitors "completing" those goals too quickly? If so, this could be a reason that your audience doesn't return.

Referrals

In Google Analytics, referrals show you sites that "referred" visitors to your campaign by clicking a link. In a way, a referral is like a recommendation from one website to another. This metric helps you view these referrals, which then add to your understanding of how your audience found their way to your campaign.

Referral traffic can be a strong indicator of which external sources are most valuable to your campaign. Some examples of referrers you may see are:

>> The link in your email campaigns

>> Tweets on Twitter

>> Pins on Pinterest

>> Links on blog posts

>> Threads on web forums such as specialist subreddits dedicated to your industry or the gamification model selected

Following the User Journey

Following the user journey is a method used to visually outline your customer's experience with your gamification marketing campaign. This journey can be from the first interaction with the landing page, playing the game, to returning and referring their friends and family.

Ideally, you should be looking to use the data your portal provides you so that you can ultimately motivate your audience to reach the last point of your game. Here are some advantages to following the user journey:

>> It gives valuable insights into your audience's expectations of your campaign.

>> It allows you to understand the channels your customers are likely to use to reach your campaigns.

>> It tells you what expectations your audience has for your campaign, as well as what their possible frustrations could be.

>> It helps you predict and change audience behavior, which optimizes the overall conversion process.

Watching all their moves

Your audiences will provide you with more than enough data on their behavior throughout your campaign. You need to use this data, gathered safely in your portal, to understand what motivates and engages your audience.

Table 10-1 lists the typically expected data metrics you should be aiming to collect for each game model (turn to Chapter 7 for more on game models).

TABLE 10-1   **Expected Data Metrics for Each Game Model**

Game Model	Interaction	Returning versus New	Duration
Action	High interaction to play, beat their high scores, and share.	Higher proportion of new sessions, which means you should be looking to minimize the number of CTA buttons to one or two.	Low
Simulation	Medium. Users will be more focused on one CTA (to build their activity).	Very high proportion of returning, which means you shouldn't inundate the user with your rewards and CTAs on the first session. Instead, you should distribute them through several sessions.	Very high
Interactive storytelling	Multiple CTA options means you should expect very high user interaction.	Higher proportion of returning because most users will want to reach the end of their game within a few sessions. This means your CTAs should be available from earlier sessions.	Medium
Adventure	High. Users will be highly invested in the gameplay, which means they'll be more susceptible to other CTA buttons you offer on their way.	Expect an even proportion of new and returning. Ideally, you want to equally distribute your rewards and CTAs throughout an average few sessions.	High
Puzzles	Variable depending on the levels and difficulty. On average, you'll find a high interaction with users looking to succeed further in the game.	Higher proportion of returning, depending on the number of levels and difficulty. You should aim to reward the user at the initial sessions. Similarly, present your CTAs initially to ensure the users are aware of them.	Medium

Game Model	Interaction	Returning versus New	Duration
Skill based	High, because the campaigns tend to hinge on the audience's mental abilities and persistence. Audiences tend to be more willing to explore all other CTA buttons on offer.	Higher proportion of new sessions. Most users will have completed the game within the first session and will return to see if their skill has beaten other users. Ideally, you want to present your CTAs initially to guarantee engagement.	Low
Multi-player	Medium because users will not only have the ability to play against a computer, but they'll also actively respond to social CTAs that you provide to encourage an increase in the pool of human opponents.	Equal proportion of new and returning. Due to the highly competitive nature, you'll find your CTAs lost, so ideally you'll want to continually distribute your CTAs throughout all sessions.	Exceptional
Educational	High due to the fact that the users are being led by your game, so they're more open to interacting with other CTA options you offer.	Higher proportion of new. A higher level of goals at the initial levels is required to encourage a higher returning rate. Depending on the value the user places on the content, you'll see varying engagement on your CTAs.	Low
Role playing	Low, because users will be entrenched in the deep gameplay. This means they're less likely to be distracted by the other CTAs you'll be offering.	Very high proportion of returning. You shouldn't inundate the user with your rewards and CTAs on the first session; instead, distribute them through several sessions.	Very high

It may take a few gamification marketing campaigns to understand the user journey. During your first campaign, try to keep track of your bounces and duration. If these two are not ideal (if the bounce rate is high and the duration is low), you may need to make adjustments to your campaign's landing page.

Learning what the users don't tell you

Although your portal data will collect an impressive amount of user journey information automatically, there is more you can learn to gain deeper insights into your audience. The only way to get this information is by requesting feedback from your audience. By conducting surveys and simply reaching out on social media, you can learn the following:

>> **Audience stages:** In addition to learning how your user journeys through your campaign, you should figure out the stages your audience goes through

to come to your landing page. These stages usually come in the following order:

1. Awareness: Usually social media channels, word of mouth, or referrals.

2. Consideration: What made them think this campaign was worth their time? Was it the game itself, the information the campaign provided, or your brand releasing a gamification marketing campaign that piqued their interest?

3. Retention: What held their interest once they arrived at your campaign? Were there enough goals and rewards to make them come back? Finally, was there any incentive or interest to get them to actively promote your campaign to their friends and family?

>> **Audience goals:** Finding out what it will take to get your audience to spend more time on your campaign is invaluable. This means working out the actual goals and rewards your users would like to achieve in your game. When you have this information, you'll be able to shape more engaging user journey maps in future campaigns.

>> **Audience emotions:** One thing no amount of data in your portal will be able to tell you is how your gamification marketing campaign left the audience feeling emotionally. Whatever their emotion, whether happiness or frustration, how your audience reacted emotionally will help you understand your campaign's success overall. An easy way to do this is to use a feedback widget, like the one from Surveyapp (www.surveyapp.io), shown in Figure 10-1.

FIGURE 10-1:
Feedback widgets offered by companies such as Surveyapp can be easily integrated into your campaign.

TIP

One way to collect this audience insight information is to offer your audience in-game surveys. These surveys should cover all three areas (stages, goals, and emotions). Also, encourage your audience by offering rewards if they complete the whole survey.

Gaining Valuable User Feedback

Audience feedback is an excellent way to improve the overall user engagement in your gamification marketing campaign. If you manage and develop this aspect from the start, you'll gain this feedback data from day 1. This means you can fix any issues identified through this feedback process at the beginning of your campaign.

Focus on getting users of the campaign to share feedback about:

>> Any device- or software-specific issues that stopped them from engaging with the game or campaign

>> Whether enough help was provided

>> Whether they understood how to play the game

>> How their experience did or did not meet their expectations

By giving your users a feedback channel to your team, your audience will feel satisfied that their concerns are being heard. With the growing use of social media, it's not uncommon for a positive feedback experience to go viral and strengthen the credibility of your brand.

Providing a dedicated feedback form

You can place a feedback form on your landing page or link to it from there. Or you can take this one step further and integrate the feedback form into your game. Regardless of where the form is located, it will provide your audience with a means to express their issues and grievances to your team.

As a best practice, the form should include all relevant questions related to the campaign bearing in mind that it shouldn't be too long. Whenever possible, provide customers with multiple options. For greater impact, the email address for feedback or the feedback form should be highly visible on the website.

Installing live chat support

Live chat through a company like Zendesk (www.zendesk.com) can address many immediate issues such as problems understanding the gameplay. These issues can usually be answered quickly and allow your company to get closer to the audience.

REMEMBER

Log all issues so that your team can review and action the needs and challenges posed through the chats. It also helps identify patterns if there are any recurring issues. Your goal here should be to work with your developers to find long-term solutions for those issues.

As with other types of feedback, your team's response plays a critical role in achieving optimum feedback data. You should do your best to make sure all audience feedback is promptly addressed and logged.

Rating your campaign's performance

Prepare a very short survey and send this out after your gamification marketing campaign has ended. The aim of the survey is to determine whether the campaign's goals were met.

Such surveys work well when there are only a few questions, so aim to make them short — I recommend presenting your users with just one option: to rate their experience on a scale of 1 to 5. These options can be icon-based buttons or even emoji-type buttons such as those shown in Figure 10-1. Another example is a series of questions that just allow yes or no answers.

Over time, these ratings can reveal valuable trends on your campaign and can help shape your next gamification marketing campaign.

Creating an online forum

A forum or community for your campaign can produce excellent feedback data. Although this method is quite easy to implement, it requires continuous monitoring and possibly a full-time moderator.

This method greatly increases and strengthens user engagement with your campaign. It can also provide some new ideas that you can look to implement into your game. Many sites can help you quickly create your own online forum. One worth checking out is Get Satisfaction (https://getsatisfaction.com).

Displaying positive customer feedback

Displaying customer feedback not only shows recognition from those who have shared feedback, but also encourages other users to provide feedback. In this way, your campaign will see more and more people sharing feedback and experiences.

TIP

Make sure that the reviews you post appear genuine. A good way to do this is to display the customer's full name and location, if available. Stay away from fake reviews — your audience will spot them from a mile away.

Using polls

Polls can be very effective in getting feedback due to their user-friendliness. Polls can be conducted:

>> On your landing page

>> In a newsletter

>> Via online tools such as SurveyMonkey (www.surveymonkey.com)

>> Via social media polls such as those on Twitter

Polls can play an important role in identifying trends in your campaign. The results of the polls can help you make informed decisions for future campaigns.

Monitoring social channels

Social media sites can be an invaluable source for audience feedback. Go one step further and propose a hashtag that people should use when posting on social media. Citroën actively used this method in its gamification marketing campaign, Game of Scroll, which used the hashtag #GameOfScroll.

Keeping an eye on your hashtag provides a simple and effective opportunity for you to improve user experience and quickly respond to any issues.

WARNING

Time is of the essence when it comes to handling complaints or issues. Negative comments will spread rapidly, so be sure to address them promptly.

Chapter **11**

Analyzing and Applying Data

Data analysis is a technique in which you use data from your current campaign to help your team create more efficient and engaging campaigns in the future. (Chapter 10 covers all the types of data you can capture.)

REMEMBER

Your campaign will generate and store a lot of data every single day. But what happens with this data after it's stored? Instead of allowing it to just sit in a database, never to be looked at again, you should be analyzing and applying the data.

In this chapter, I fill you in on what data analysis can do for you, explain how to source your campaign data, show you how to apply all the information you've gathered into coherent and intelligent reports (a process commonly referred to as big data), explain the benefits of predictive analysis, and finally, tell you how to control your data.

By using the techniques in this chapter, you can make substantial improvements in your customer engagement in the future.

Understanding the Why and How of Data Analysis

Data analysis gives your team an insight into the market and audience your campaign was engaged with. Data analysis can benefit all the departments in your company, giving them a report on how your campaign has done. For management, it can identify any room for improvement for your company as a whole.

When you initially embarked on your gamification marketing journey, you noticed a problem or opportunity and you set the goals you wanted to achieve with your campaign. After the campaign launched, you collected data about the users.

After the campaign ends, the real work with data begins — this is where you begin to analyze the data you've gathered. By using data analysis you can answer the following questions:

>> What impact did the gamification marketing campaign have for your company?

>> How well did the campaign do in the long run?

>> Is there any room for improvement?

>> What steps can you take to improve the performance and engagement for the next campaign?

>> Is there something different you could try for the next campaign?

>> Were all your resources efficiently used in the campaign?

>> Was the campaign received well by the majority of your audience?

>> Did the campaign provide the audience with what they were promised?

>> Did your campaign struggle to communicate its objectives to the audience?

>> What put the audience off?

>> What kept the audience coming back for more?

>> What made the audience click that all-important Share button?

>> Was the game option you chose right for your audience and company's image?

>> Did your audience struggle with the game?

>> Were there enough levels and content to keep your audience coming back?

>> Was there enough help?

» Did your campaign gain significant interest on all social media channels?

» Was your campaign's hashtag (see Chapter 10) adopted by your audience?

» What percentage of your new audience came from social media platforms?

» Were the overall messages expressed on social media positive for your company?

With the answers to these questions, you'll be able to make your *next* campaign even better.

Extracting Your Campaign Data

In this section, I fill you in on the different forms of raw data your gamification marketing campaign produces.

Sourcing your data

Raw data is all the information that has been collected from your gamification marketing campaign. The majority of your raw data will come directly into your portal from your own platform (the landing page and your game). But there is a wealth of information that can be pulled from other sources as well. I cover those sources in the following sections.

Web analytics

A variety of web analytics tools are available, such as Google Analytics (http://analytics.google.com) and the Facebook pixel (www.facebook.com/business/learn/facebook-ads-pixel). The web analytics data is presented on the provider's dashboard. From here, you can customize the data and break it down into categories:

» **Audience:**

- The total number of visits to your landing page

- The ratio of new visitors to returning visitors

- Location data, such as which country your audience originated from

- Device and software data, such as what browser and mobile device your audience used

>> **Audience behavior:**

- The most common landing page and exit page, as well as the most frequently visited pages (if your campaign has more than one page)

- The average length of time your audience spent on your campaign

- The *bounce rate* (the percentage of people who didn't engage with your campaign after coming to your landing page)

>> **Landing page:**

- Which websites and marketing channels drove the most traffic to your campaign

- The top keyword searches that resulted in visits to your landing page

Social media analytics

Each of the major social media providers provides you with a comprehensive analytics package:

>> **Facebook** (https://analytics.facebook.com): The Facebook Analytics dashboard is available via your Facebook Business page. From here, you have access to the following features:

- **Page Insights:** The Insights tab gives you an in-depth view of your Facebook Analytics. The overview section offers a summary of your campaign's performance.

- **Reach:** Reach measures the number of people who had any posts from your campaign appear on their session. If someone decided to hide posts from your campaign, you can find that information here, too.

- **Posts:** This shows you how your campaign's posts are performing and offers insights on the best times to post and the types of posts that are most successful.

- **Videos:** You can track the top-performing videos in your campaign. The videos are ranked by how long they were viewed, usually in minutes. You can also drill down to see how many minutes of each video were viewed.

- **Followers and Likes:** An extremely useful feature that allows you to check the number of people who follow or like your campaign. You can also analyze your campaign's popularity over time, and see when and where the new Follows and Likes are originating from.

- **Page Views:** This is where you will find out where your campaign traffic originated from. You can also measure the views for each section or page, including About, Photos, and so on, which will help you understand what areas are most popular.

- **People:** Learn about your fans and follower demographics, including location, gender, and language information.

- **Promotions:** If you want to boost one of your campaign's posts, but you can't decide which one, this section helps you identify the posts that may be worth boosting. You can also choose which audience segments to target your posts at.

» **Twitter** (`https://analytics.twitter.com`): Twitter Analytics offers a summary of your campaign's performance. You get a breakdown of your follower count, tweet impressions, profile visits, and mentions. Here's what you can find in Twitter Analytics:

- **Monthly Summary:** Highlights from each month include your campaign's top tweet, top follower, and top mention.

- **Tweets:** Here you can track the engagements and impressions on your tweets over a selected period. If you've promoted any tweets, you can track those analytics, too.

- **Audiences:** This is where you can learn about your audience's demographics and interests. You can also add a comparison audience to see how your followers differ from other users.

» **Instagram:** Instagram Insights are available for accounts with business profiles. In addition to analytics on your content, Instagram Insights also provides information about who your followers are, when they're online, and more. To access Instagram Insights, go to your profile, tap the menu button in the upper-right corner, tap Insights, and select the posts or stories you want to get information on. Here's the kind of information you can find:

- **Impressions:** The number of times your campaign's posts were shown.

- **Reach:** The number of unique post views your campaign received overall.

- **Website Clicks:** The number of times your campaign's website link, as shown on your profile, was clicked.

- **Profile Visits:** The number of times your campaign's Instagram page was accessed.

- **Posts:** Analyze the likes and comments on each post your campaign makes. You can also view the number of people who saved your post.

- **Actions:** See which posts inspired users to visit your profile, follow you, and click your web address.

- **Discovery:** The percentage of accounts that saw your posts but aren't following your campaign's Instagram page yet.

>> **Pinterest** (`https://analytics.pinterest.com`): The Pinterest Analytics tool monitors what pins people like, how much traffic goes to your campaign, and what people are pinning from your landing page. Here's what you can find:

- **Pin Stats:** Which pins are gaining the most traction, with an overview of your pin performance.

- **Impressions:** How many times your pin has shown up across Pinterest.

- **Closeups:** How many users have tapped your pin to have a closer look at your content.

- **Clicks:** How many people looking at your pin have clicked through to your campaign's landing page.

- **Saves:** How many pinners have plans to reengage with your content at a later date.

>> **LinkedIn:** LinkedIn company page analytics allow campaigns to monitor metrics and trends across specified time periods. To access LinkedIn analytics, navigate to your company page, click Manage Page, click the Analytics tab, and choose what you want to focus on. Here's what you can find:

- **Visitors:** Monitor traffic to and from your page and learn more about your visitor demographics in this section.

- **Updates:** Track the reach of each post and analyze engagement. You can also track actions on each post, such as how many followers or profile visits you gained.

- **Followers:** Monitor follower trends over periods of time, and investigate whether followers were acquired organically or through paid content.

Audience feedback

In Chapter 10, I explore the various methods you can use to receive your audience's feedback. Here's what you can do with this information:

>> **Feedback form:** Typically, all this valuable data is simply emailed to your team. Unfortunately, there isn't much data analysis can do with it in this form, though. So, you can either get the data fed directly into your database or do it manually via your portal.

>> **Live chat:** All chats can be downloaded from your chat supplier's interface. Aim to tag any issues or feedback straight into your admin portal. Work with your developers to ensure that they accommodate for this in your database and give you this functionality in your portal.

>> **Campaign ratings:** These surveys contain extremely valuable data that needs to be stored in your database as soon as they come in from your audience. Make sure that the results are tagged properly, along with any audience information you may already have.

>> **Polls:** All poll data can be downloaded from your poll supplier's interface. Most poll interfaces allow you to refine your data by selecting dates, audience segments, and responses. You can then download these reports in CSV format, which your developers can upload to your database.

Locating your data

Before you can do anything with your data, you need to know where the raw data is located and how you intend to integrate it all into one database.

Table 11-1 identifies where all this data is located and how you can connect it to your data storage.

TABLE 11-1 **Types and Location of Your Campaign's Raw Data**

Data Source	Type of Data	Typical Storage Location
Campaign stats	Campaign goal and objective data. All data displayed in your admin portal.	This data should be stored in your own company database or cloud-based service. All data should belong to your company and be available 24/7.
Web analytics	Data from online tracking services such as Google Analytics or the Facebook pixel.	Stored on the software provider's servers. The data is available on their admin panel, where you can download the data as a CSV file. The data from the CSV file can then be uploaded to your company's database or cloud.
Social media analytics	Data collected and offered to you by each of the social media channels.	Stored on the social media provider's servers. This data is available on their admin panels, where you can download the data as a CSV file. The data from the CSV file can then be uploaded to your company's database or cloud.
Audience feedback	Feedback you've proactively collected from your audience.	This data could be stored on your own company database or cloud-based service. It may also be in the form of emails. All data should belong to your company and be available 24/7.

Applying Intelligent Big Data

Earlier in this chapter, I explore a number of methods for collecting your campaign's day-to-day raw data. *Big data* is essentially a term to describe all this unstructured data. However, all this data isn't particularly important or useful to your company. It's what you *do* with the data that matters. Intelligent big data can be analyzed for insights that lead to better decisions and strategic business moves.

Deconstructing big data

Around 2005, analysts began to realize just how much data was being generated through sites such as Facebook, YouTube, and other online services. Specialist open-source frameworks, like Hadoop, started to spring up. This was the catalyst for the growth of big data, as huge databases of raw data suddenly became easier to work with and cheaper to store.

In the years since, the application of big data has skyrocketed. Although companies are still generating huge amounts of data, it's not just human beings who are doing it. With the advent of the Internet of Things (IoT), more objects and devices are connected to the Internet, gathering data on customer usage patterns and product performance.

In the early 2000s, industry analysts articulated the now-mainstream definition of big data as the "three Vs." Recently, two additional dimensions, or Vs, have come into play when it comes to big data. Here are all five Vs:

» **Volume:** The amount, or volume, of data matters to organizations that collect it from a variety of sources, including business transactions, smart devices, industrial equipment, videos, social media, and more. This data can be of unknown value, such as Twitter data feeds, clickstreams on a webpage or a mobile app, or sensor-enabled equipment. For some organizations, this may be tens of terabytes of data. For others, it may be hundreds of petabytes. In the past, storing this data would have been a problem, but cheaper storage on platforms like data lakes and Hadoop has eased the burden.

» **Velocity:** Velocity is the rate at which data is received and (perhaps) acted on. Normally, the highest velocity of data streams directly into memory instead of being written to disk. With the growth of the IoT, data streams into organization databases at an unprecedented speed and must be handled in a timely manner. Some Internet-enabled smart products operate in real time or near real time and require real-time evaluation and action. Radio frequency identification (RFID) tags, sensors, and smart meters are driving the need to deal with these torrents of data in near real time.

» **Variety:** Variety refers to the many types of data that are available. Traditional data types were structured and fit neatly in a relational database. Data comes in all types of formats — from structured, numeric data in traditional databases to unstructured text documents, emails, videos, audios, stock ticker data, and financial transactions. All of this requires additional preprocessing to derive meaning and support metadata.

>> **Variability:** Variability refers to both the variable number of inconsistencies in the data and the variable speed at which big data is loaded into your database. These need to be found by anomaly and outlier detection methods in order for any meaningful analytics to occur. Big data is also variable because of the multitude of data dimensions resulting from multiple disparate data types and sources. It's challenging, but businesses need to know variable data such as trending topics in social media, or how to manage daily, seasonal, and event-triggered peak data loads.

>> **Veracity:** Veracity refers to the quality of data. Because data comes from so many different sources, it's difficult to link, match, cleanse, and transform data across systems. Businesses need to connect and correlate relationships, hierarchies, and multiple data linkages. Otherwise, their data can quickly spiral out of control. This is one of the unfortunate characteristics of big data. As any or all of the above properties increase, the veracity decreases.

Benefiting from big data and data analysis

Simply put, big data makes it possible for you to gain more complete answers because you have more information about your gamification marketing campaign. More complete answers means more confidence in the data, which in turn means a more productive post–campaign data analysis.

Here are some ways you can benefit from the analysis of big data:

>> **Designing better marketing campaigns:** Big data enables you to better target the core needs of your audience. This results in better designed campaigns, which are engaging and informative. For example, think about how you'll collect data on your users' activities while they're on your landing page. This information can help your team understand your audience's behavior and create a more personalized and informative experience.

Gamification marketing campaigns that use big data are more effective than the aggregative advertising campaigns of the past. This is because it takes the guesswork out of determining what your audience wants. You can confidently develop different audience personas using data like audience session behavior data.

>> **Designing better products:** You can use big data to model new products and services by classifying key attributes of past and current products or services. You can also use data analysis from polls, social media, and feedback forms to plan, produce, and launch new products.

For example, Netflix has used big data to anticipate customer demand (see Chapter 15). Netflix developed Black Mirror: Bandersnatch and proved that its audience welcomes a more immersive and interactive product. Bandersnatch was completely different from Netflix's usual offerings.

>> **Providing a better customer experience:** With big data, you can get a clearer view of your customers' experience. Big data enables you to gather data from social media, landing page visits, feedback logs, and other sources (see "Sourcing your data," earlier in this chapter) to improve the interaction experience and maximize the value delivered.

When your campaign ends, your company should be delivering more personalized offerings, reducing customer loss, and handling issues proactively. You can easily achieve these goals by applying data analysis to the big data you'll collect during the campaign.

>> **Improving your operational efficiency:** Marketing teams aren't tasked with a company's operational efficiency, but this is an area in which big data has a big impact. With the big data from your campaign, you can analyze and assess customer feedback to improve decision-making in line with current market demand, as well as anticipating future demands.

>> **Driving innovation:** By using big data, you can examine trends and what your audience wants. This data can be used to deliver new products and services. Big data can help you innovate by determining new ways of using the insights from your data analysis. Data analysis can also help improve decisions about financial and planning considerations.

>> **Showing appropriate web content:** Big data has gained considerable attention as an effective tool for digital marketers to gain insight into what their customers need and want. You can serve customized content to your website visitors by tapping into the data analysis from your campaign to determine which content will be more engaging to each visitor.

For example, look at *duration* data (the time spent on your landing page) to determine what your audience is interested in. The next time that particular visitor comes to your website, you can show him relevant content based on his browsing history.

Just as Google returns different results when you search for a term in different locations, your website can look different depending on who's looking at it. Showing customized content is a technical challenge, but an increasing number of consumers are demanding personalized experiences.

Getting Help from Predictive Analysis

Predictive analysis can enable your big data to forecast future probabilities. Your team can move from focusing on a historical view to a forward-looking perspective when analyzing your campaign.

When applied to your campaigns, predictive models analyze current data and historical facts in order to better understand your audience and help identify risks and opportunities for your next campaign. Predictive analysis uses a number of techniques, including data mining, statistical modeling, and machine learning, to help you make future marketing forecasts.

A good example is using predictive analysis to better design a landing page, based on browsing behaviors, which will deliver a far more engaging and personalized website experience for your audience.

Installing a predictive analytics tool

Predictive analytics solutions are currently available from a number of companies, including SAS's Predictive Analytics Suite (www.sas.com), IBM's SPSS Statistics (www.ibm.com/products/spss-statistics), and Microsoft's Dynamics CRM Analytics Foundation (https://news.microsoft.com/2007/02/12/microsoft-announces-microsoft-dynamics-crm-analytics-foundation-to-drive-business-intelligence-for-customers-and-partners/).

TIP

If you aren't ready for expensive and complex enterprise-class solutions, there are alternatives such as Marketo (www.marketo.com), GoodData (www.gooddata.com), Tableau (www.tableau.com), and a host of others. These solutions are better for gamification marketing campaigns because the data gets deployed in the cloud, which means you can share the results with members of your team and management.

Using predictive analysis

Until recently, predictive intelligence was very straightforward, but with the advent of big data, it has taken a much more sophisticated turn. Advanced computer *algorithms* (a set of computer instructions to accomplish a given task) have made the science of prediction through data more accurate and more far-reaching than ever before.

Predictive analysis helps decode audience behavior, which you can then use in marketing to make better decisions. Any process or tool that helps marketers discern the habits of their audience can be helpful for their future campaigns, as well as for other departments in your business.

For instance if you can decode the past call-to-action (CTA) habits of your audience, you can project the future buying habits, and then make decisions based on those projections. Predictive analysis also helps ensure that these predictions are accurate.

EXEMPLIFYING PREDICTIVE ANALYSIS

One of my clients, a property management campaign, used a skill-based game for its gamification marketing campaign. The main issue the campaign faced was the fact that the audience was busy and didn't always have the time to complete a level, which meant they weren't getting rewarded.

Our team realized we could use predictive analysis to reach out to each user when they could be free. To play the game, the audience had to be invited, which meant every time the game was played, our system could identify each user. When a user entered the campaign, our system would log this into the database.

The predictive analysis algorithm was then instructed to reach out to users who hadn't logged in for more than 48 hours. However, the email was to be actually sent at the exact time the user most frequently had been logged in to play.

Taking it a step further, this information was then used after the campaign had ended. When the sales team sent their monthly emails, they tailored the trigger to each user's email at the most frequently logged time.

Maintaining Control of Your Data

Your team needs to be in control of your data. Having data is important, but ensuring that private information remains secure is vital to your business.

In this section, I explore key areas to help you plan and prepare for threats and attacks against your data. With the right knowledge and preparation you can control:

>> Which systems and what data you want to protect

>> Where your backup copies are stored

>> How you access the data

WARNING

Marketing data can offer a more attractive target for hackers than data from other departments because marketing departments usually don't invest as many resources in cyber security. It's important for marketing departments to be mindful of what kind of sensitive information they have that a hacker might want.

Keeping your audience's trust

When your audience trusts you, they'll follow your company, engage with your gamification marketing campaigns, recommend you to friends, advocate for you, and eventually buy from your company.

Trust is especially important when you're asking your audience to engage fully with your marketing campaigns. This is why protecting your audience's data is one of the most important things you can do to build their trust and encourage them to fully commit to your campaigns.

Here are some ways you can retain your audience's trust:

>> **Be open.** Be upfront about what data you're collecting and why you need it. Being open and honest about the data you collect is a way to show your audience you respect them. Explain your data policy in plain English. If you're working with a third-party software provider, your audience has a right to know.

>> **Allow people to opt out.** Your audience will probably be willing to share personal information in exchange for something, such as a personalized user experience. If you do collect personal data, explain the benefits to your audience. This information can be communicated via a pop-up on your site or in an email.

If your audience is uncomfortable with how their data will be used, they should be able to opt out with the simple click of a button.

>> **Use Secure Sockets Layer (SSL) certificates.** SSL certificates are digital certificates that authenticate the identity of a website and encrypt information sent to the server. They're used to ensure a secure connection and protect user data.

SSL certificates are particularly important when users need to share confidential information, such as a mailing address or credit card number. Consumers can easily recognize these sites as secure because they begin with `https://` instead of `http://`.

SSL certified websites gain better search engine ranking than websites with no security certificates. Also, most browsers, including Google Chrome, flag sites that don't use SSL certificates as unsafe. If people receive this notification upon trying to visit a site, it will deter them from sharing personal data.

Protecting your data

If your audience is trusting you with their personal details, you need to employ reasonable security measures to ensure that data is protected from inappropriate and unauthorized access. Providing better data security doesn't have to break the budget. Here are some suggestions for keeping the information of customers protected:

>> **Implement a strong privacy policy.** Your audience needs to feel confident that you're protecting their information. Make sure you have a policy they can refer to, explaining how you're keeping their personal information safe. A strong privacy policy will help you build consumer trust and show that you value their data and are working to protect it.

>> **Know what you're protecting.** Be aware of all the personal information you have, where you're storing it, how you're using it, and who has access to it.

>> **Don't collect what you don't need.** The more valuable the information you have, the bigger a target you may be. Also, periodically cull your database by deleting personal information that you don't really need.

>> **Keep your data and server clean.** Cleanse your database of old data that isn't relevant to your marketing team. Be sure to update your security software, web browser, and operating system whenever updates are available; this strategy will help defend against viruses, malware, and other online threats.

>> **Employ multiple layers of security.** Spam filters weed out malware and phishing scams. In addition, use a firewall to keep criminals out and sensitive data in.

>> **Educate your employees on the importance of these issues.** They're the ones who will have all access to your customer data, so they need to be kept up to date on how to protect that information to make sure it doesn't accidentally land in the wrong hands. They should also employ best practices, such as not opening attachments or clicking suspicious links in unsolicited email messages.

Securing your database

Even some of the largest tech companies have found themselves exposed to hackers, so ensuring the security of your company's information is vital. Even though you may have an IT team that looks after your database, you should at least be aware of the basics in database security.

Here are some ways you can make sure your database is secure:

>> **Encrypt it.** Encryption means converting your data to a format such that, were it to be intercepted, it would appear as a string of letters and numbers with no tangible meaning. Make sure that your database is encrypted with up-to-date encryption software.

>> **Make sure you're using secure passwords.** Hackers have increasingly sophisticated tools at their disposal that can make passwords increasingly vulnerable. Fortunately, there are some good password management tools that will help you such as Dashlane (www.dashlane.com), Keeper (www.keepersecurity.com), and NordPass (https://nordpass.com).

Set rules that make admins change passwords on a revolving basis. If the password isn't changed after, say, 90 days, lock out that account until the password has been changed.

>> **Monitor and audit.** One way to prevent database breaches is to keep an eye on the database itself. This can include the following:

- **Monitoring access and behaviors:** Keep an eye out for anyone using an employee password who should not be. Monitor any odd behaviors that may imply a leak. Check for unfamiliar IP addresses.

- **Conducting audits:** Regular audits of your database can help find inactive accounts. If you remove inactive accounts, you can prevent problems that may arise when someone obtains old employee information.

>> **Perform timely checks on your database.** The following areas should be covered each time:

- **Permissions:** If you find any change in permissions, there may be a high chance of compromise or misconfiguration.

- **Database configuration and settings:** If security configurations or settings are changed (possibly due to a third-party patch), your database could be open to attacks.

- **Any changes:** If you detect any sort of change in the system that has not been applied by your team, chances are, a malicious software program is present.

- **Web applications:** Audit your web applications for SQL injection (where malicious code is placed into your database via website inputs), misconfiguration, or weak permissions.

- **Logging:** Log as much as you can, such as failed login attempts, incorrect SQL syntax, permission errors, and so on.

- **IP addresses:** Only allow connections from IP addresses that require access to it. When an admin leaves your company, make sure her IP address is removed as well.

CREATING A HONEYPOT

A *honeypot* is a network-attached database server that is set up as a decoy. The idea is to lure cyber attackers to detect the server and fool them into thinking they've hacked a high-value target. After they've attempted to hack the honeypot server, your system will gather information on the hackers and notify your team of the attempt.

In this way, you can detect database attacks in your organizations at an early stage. Typically, you need to do the following to set up a honeypot server:

1. **Base the honeypot on a real asset.**

2. **Reference the honeypot anywhere you reference real assets.**

3. **Have a procedure in place to rapidly investigate alerts generated by the honeypot.**

4. **Make the server looks interesting. Create databases with names like Credit Cards and Customers Info, with fake data that seems real.**

Honeypots are a highly effective and efficient way of alerting your company to attackers. However, to be effective, your honeypot needs to be well implemented, well maintained, and closely monitored. Talk to your server administrators about setting up a honeypot for your campaign.

Chapter **12**

Avoiding Data Overload

Not preparing for viral traffic can be a horrible mistake. If your company's website already has a healthy number of visitors and your servers do a great job handling their needs, you may think you're fine. But the viral nature of gamification may bring an exponential increase of visitors all at once to your servers — and they may not be able to handle that sudden spike in traffic.

In this chapter, I help you prepare for this very exciting possibility!

Watching Out for Maximum Capacity

Campaigns with unresponsive and crashed landing pages due to heavy traffic can be the worst. If people can't get through to your campaign the first time they try, not many of them will be willing to give your campaign a second chance. Plus, if they do come back, they'll only face the same issue again and again, due to the heavy traffic.

Your team should prepare your campaign for handling several times the current traffic level your company's website receives. In this section, I explain how you can do this, as well as look at the effects your campaign will see if you *don't* prepare.

Identifying the effects of crashing

Whether it's through review websites or their own social media channels, disgruntled users have plenty of ways to vent their frustration to anyone who will listen. Complaints are an inevitable part of life, but the complaints about campaign if your website crashes will border on the brink of downright insulting. There's nothing like the anonymity of the Internet to unleash some people's inner hatemonger.

If your campaign isn't prepared for viral traffic and your website loads too slowly or completely crashes, your company may experience the following:

>> **Loss of business:** Unfortunately, there will be a severe lack of audience-to-client conversions, resulting in a loss of business for your company.

>> **Reduced ranking in search engines:** Your campaign's search engine ranking will suffer because search engines will see a huge spike in your bounce rate (see Chapter 10 for more on bounce rates).

>> **Loss of analytical data:** You'll have inaccurate and/or incomplete data for your campaign's data analysis (see Chapter 11). Because the insights produced by data analysis are only as good as the data they have to work with, any service outage can cripple your ability to make the best possible decisions. Also, much of this analysis takes place in cloud-based applications, where scalability and economies of scale make powerful analytics resources practical for companies of all sizes. But when the cloud servers go down, the data processing goes down with it.

>> **Loss of sales:** If your gamification campaign sits on the same server as your online store, your online store will be affected, too, which means a loss of sales.

>> **Reduced productivity:** If your business depends upon employees using cloud-based applications and software to carry out their day-to-day job functions, the immediate impact of server downtime is reduced productivity. Employees won't be able to access the tools they need for their day-to-day duties and could end up sitting around with nothing to do while they wait for service to be restored. These fluctuations in workflow can disrupt supply chains or project schedules, both of which can have long-term impacts on a company.

>> **Damage to your brand's reputation:** In today's fast-paced online world, your campaign may never get a second chance to make a first impression. Audiences expect speed and efficiency more than ever, and they're quick to abandon campaigns that don't work. Crashing landing pages or slow loading times will cause lasting damage to your brand reputation. This can be very difficult to correct.

Preparing for increased traffic

In the preceding section, I warn you of everything that can go wrong if your campaign is slow to load or crashes. In this section, I let you know how you can *avoid* these problems and ensure your campaign has the most sustainable uptime assurance possible.

Using a content delivery network

One of the most effective ways to ensure that your campaign stays online, even when you're dealing with viral levels of traffic, is by using a content delivery network (CDN). CDNs store cached versions of your campaign on multiple servers around the world. CDNs minimize the distance between your audience's device and your campaign's server, so each of the caching servers is responsible for delivering your campaign to visitors nearby.

In essence, a CDN puts your campaign in many places at once, providing instant coverage to your users. For example, when someone in Australia accesses your U.S.-hosted campaign, she's accessing it through a cached server in, say, Melbourne. This is much quicker than having the visitor's requests travel the full span of the Pacific to a server in San Francisco. These servers around the world, called *points of presence*, cache the campaign's content, removing the load from your server.

IDENTIFYING THE DIFFERENT TYPES OF CONTENT DELIVERY NETWORKS

There are different types of CDNs offering different kinds of services:

>> **Content oriented:** Content-oriented CDNs cache your campaign's last updated state. This means if your server goes down, the CDN server's content will still be accessible to users.

>> **Security oriented:** Security-oriented CDNs can detect distributed denial-of-service (DDoS) attacks early and block them with special DDoS protection servers called *scrubbers.* This means any attack with the intent to crash your server will never reach it.

TECHNICAL STUFF

A DDoS is a malicious attempt to disrupt normal traffic to your campaign by overwhelming your server with a flood of online traffic. It's like causing a deliberate traffic jam on a highway in order to prevent regular traffic from passing through. DDoS attacks achieve effectiveness by using multiple compromised computer systems as sources of attack traffic.

>> **Knowledge oriented:** By using knowledge crowdsourced from its many clients, a knowledge-oriented CDN can learn about suspicious IP addresses, spammers, and spammers' behavior. Any offender identified on any server will stop working on all other sites protected by the same CDN.

SELECTING A CONTENT DELIVERY NETWORK PROVIDER

Many CDN providers are available, including some that are free, but you'll want to opt for a premium CDN provider for your gamification marketing campaign. Here are five CDN providers I recommend:

>> **Amazon Web Services (AWS;** https://aws.amazon.com**):** AWS is the biggest cloud computing and services provider in the world. It offers large-scale cloud services, such as DDoS protection, a CDN, storage, analytics, and online database services.

>> **Google Cloud CDN** (https://cloud.google.com/cdn): Google Cloud CDN uses Google's global infrastructure (the same infrastructure that Google uses to deliver its end-user products like Google Search and YouTube) to cache and deliver content for its clients. You have to also be a user of Google Cloud Platform (GCP; https://cloud.google.com) in order to use the Google Cloud CDN.

>> **Microsoft Azure CDN** (https://azure.microsoft.com/en-us/services/cdn/)**:** This is one of 600 services that's part of Microsoft Azure, a cloud computing provider established by Microsoft. Microsoft Azure CDN has a much wider reach in global developing markets than AWS and Google Cloud CDN do, so if you're launching on a global scale or an entire continent, I recommend using Microsoft Azure CDN.

>> **Cloudflare CDN** (https://www.cloudflare.com/cdn/)**:** Cloudflare is one of the fastest-growing companies in the security and performance space. Cloudflare has offices in San Francisco, London, and Singapore, and is backed by Google, Baidu, Microsoft, and Qualcomm. It offers self-service and enterprise plans to suit small, medium, and very large customers.

>> **Rackspace CDN** (www.rackspace.com/openstack/public/cdn-content-delivery-network)**:** Rackspace is a cloud computing company based in Windcrest, Texas. Its main focus is providing superior service and support. Although Rackspace started with web hosting, it now supplies virtually any service imaginable, including CDN services.

IMPLEMENTING A CONTENT DELIVERY NETWORK

Implementing a CDN typically entails changing DNS records with your domain name registrar, the company holding your domain name. This results in all traffic going to the CDN first. Because it all happens behind the scenes, the user isn't even aware it's happening.

Installing a CDN can be a relatively easy process. In most situations, you can stick to the simplest settings and tailor things to suit your specific needs. If you have specific needs, you may have to contact your CDN provider for additional assistance.

Before you begin adding a CDN to your campaign, you'll need administrative access to your domain's dashboard (known as the CPanel). Don't worry about handling this yourself — the IT manager or server administrator at your company can handle it for you.

Checking your server

Make sure the server your campaign will run on is equipped to handle a sudden spike in web traffic. Here are a few server checks you can do before you start your campaign:

TIP

>> **Bandwidth:** All hosting providers impose limits on your server's bandwidth. Bandwidth is consumed when data is retrieved from the server and delivered to your visitors. All data sent from the site to the client (and vice versa) counts toward bandwidth usage.

Check with your host to see if you can upgrade your bandwidth for the duration of your campaign.

>> **Timeout:** Server timeouts prevent your visitors from endlessly waiting for your sever to respond. When timeouts are lower, the connections to your server will be released sooner, so your server will be able to handle more connections. The timeout duration varies depending on which program makes the data request from the server and can range from a few seconds to a few hours.

Reduce server timeout values by consulting your hosting provider. They'll be able to advise you on the optimal number based on your server configuration and your needs.

>> **Hardware:** When it comes to your server's hardware, more is usually better and faster. Upgrade your server hardware before your campaign begins. This includes upgrading both your physical and virtual memory. Work with your hosting provider on what options it provides.

>> **Load balancing:** Load balancing is used to improve the performance and reliability of your campaign by distributing the workload of your server. This is done by introducing a load balancer and at least one extra web server on the backend.

Updating your software

WARNING

Updating your server software isn't just a way to protect against cyberattacks. Software updates also help to ensure that your server can continue to handle the traffic your campaign will be getting. If you don't update your server software often, your server may crash, even with a low volume of visitors.

Outsourcing your media storage

All *rich media* (advanced features like video, audio, or other elements that encourage viewers to interact and engage with the content) should be delivered through an outsourced media distribution service or on a dedicated media server. By utilizing external file delivery for your rich media, you reduce the burden on your server's bandwidth and push the weight onto external servers. This way, your campaign should load faster even during spikes in traffic.

Here are the two main services you should consider:

>> **Image-hosting services:** Sites such as Flickr (www.flickr.com) and Photobucket (https://photobucket.com) provide this service, but I strongly suggest that you consider more robust solutions such as a dedicated server or CDN.

>> **Video-streaming service:** Hosting videos on the same server as your website can drain your bandwidth relatively fast. For this reason, you may want to consider offloading your media onto a third-party service such as YouTube (www.youtube.com) or Vimeo (www.vimeo.com).

Dealing with Data Failure

If your server goes down, you could lose valuable data and compromise your whole gamification marketing campaign. That's why you need to know how to identify the cause of a crashed server, find a solution, and take steps to make sure it doesn't happen again.

Identifying the cause

The first step is to see if you can discover what happened. The most obvious cause is a power failure. Storms, natural disasters, and citywide power outages can shut down your server.

Here are some other less obvious causes of server failures:

>> **Configuration issues:** Both automated and manual configuration mistakes can cause permanent issues, including missed data backups.

>> **System overload issues:** A spike in traffic due to your campaign going viral is good news. But it can also be a nightmare. Your server may no longer be able to handle the growing attention of users, ultimately leading to a system overload.

>> **Hardware problems:** Unfortunately, server hardware sometimes fails, and when it does, it can cause your server to go slow and, in some cases, fail. Make sure to update your servers regularly.

>> **Network-related issues:** If your campaign suffers from a slow network, your server may be suffering a bandwidth bottleneck. It could also be that the server's hard drive is starting to fill up or it has become fragmented.

>> **Service issues:** Your servers run multiple services, such as File Transfer Protocol (FTP), in the background. Periodically, these services need to be maintained; for example, they need to be updated and sometimes manually restarted by your administrator. Make sure a member of your IT team is responsible for this.

Fixing the problem

If your server has crashed or is running too slowly, your IT team will determine the cause of the issue and get your campaign up and running again.

TIP

If your issues only affect certain users, IT should be able to troubleshoot the problem quickly and fix it. On the other hand, if you're under a DDoS attack, it can take a lot longer. Your IT team will need to shut down your campaign while they deal with the attack. They'll also want to secure all data before the server is brought back online.

Preventing problems from happening again and minimizing the damage

Many server crashes can be prevented if you follow some key safety guidelines:

>> **Conduct regular audits so that you catch problems as soon as possible.** A regular audit is done by IT teams to help automate the identification of certain patterns or anomalies an organization may be looking for. It can

include control and risk assessments, for example. You may choose to perform them monthly, quarterly, or biannually, but they should be done at least twice a year. The length of time between audits depends on the level of complexity of your systems and the type of information you hold (for example, highly confidential data).

» **Limit the number of administrators.** One way to minimize overall security risk is to minimize the number of administrators you have and how often they need to log on. The specific number depends on the operational needs and business strategies of each environment, but as a best practice, two or three is probably a good amount.

Sadly, many organizations simply add everyone as an admin to make it easy for them to fix and configure the servers they need to administer. Unfortunately, this leaves them far more exposed to malicious hacks. Admin rights should be handed out with care and used with discretion.

» **Routinely check server logs for any anomalies.** Businesses must review their logs daily to search for errors, anomalies, or suspicious activity that deviates from the norm. From a security point of view, the purpose of a log is to act as a red flag when something bad is happening. Reviewing logs regularly could help identify malicious attacks on your system.

Given the large of amount of log data generated by systems, it's impractical to review all these logs manually every day. Log monitoring software takes care of that task by using rules to automate the review of these logs and only point out events that may represent problems or threats. Often, this is done using real-time reporting systems that alert you via email or text when something suspicious is detected.

» **Use firewalls and cryptographic keys to authenticate users.** A *firewall* is a piece of software that controls what services are exposed to the network. This means blocking or restricting access to every port, except for those that should be publicly available. Firewalls are an essential part of any server configuration. Even if your services themselves implement security features or are restricted to the interfaces you'd like them to run on, a firewall serves as an extra layer of protection.

A *cryptographic key* is a string of bits used by a cryptographic algorithm to transform plain text into cipher text or vice versa. This key remains private and ensures secure communication. In computer security, a key server is a computer that receives and then serves existing cryptographic keys to users or other programs.

» **Create a server failover.** A server failover can help prevent your campaign from going down in the event of a server crash. It works by performing automatic detections for any errors on your server. If an error is detected, all traffic will automatically be sent to a backup server.

A server failover is an easy solution for your IT team to set up. It works by installing two servers with identical content on both of them. They're referred to as the primary server and secondary server. A third server then monitors the primary server and looks for any issues. If the third server detects an issue, it automatically updates the DNS records for your website so that traffic will be diverted to your secondary server.

When IT has fixed the primary server and it's functioning again, the traffic will be routed back to your primary server. The best part of all this is that, apart from the people visiting your campaign at the exact moment the server fails, the rest of your audience won't notice a thing.

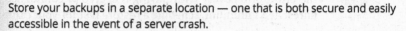 **Back up your campaign.** Make regular backups of your campaign and data in case your server goes offline. If you have a recent backup, IT team will then be able to get your campaign up and running again quickly.

REMEMBER

Store your backups in a separate location — one that is both secure and easily accessible in the event of a server crash.

There are many backup types available:

- **Full backup:** This is the most important type of backup, where a copy is made of your entire campaign, including all the data. A full backup is the most time-consuming one to perform. It also takes up the most amount of storage. However, it can be easier to restore data from a full backup than from the other types of backup, which is why it's the most important one to have. The average company will benefit from performing a full backup every 24 hours.

- **Incremental backup:** An incremental backup is ideal after a full backup has already been completed. With an incremental backup, only the data that has changed since the last backup is copied. This means it's the least time-consuming and storage-consuming backup method. However, to restore the data, you have to reconstruct it from the last full backup, plus all intervening incremental backups.

- **Differential backup:** Whereas an incremental backup only saves the data that has changed since the last backup, a differential backup makes a copy of all changed data since the last full backup. To restore, you need the last full backup plus the latest differential. The advantage of differential backups is that restores are easier than with a full-plus-incremental backup regime. However, each differential backup is more likely to be of greater size and more time consuming than incremental backups.

- **Synthetic full backup:** A synthetic backup takes a full backup and combines it with subsequent incremental backups to provide a full backup that is always up to date. Synthetic full backups have the advantage of being easy to restore. However, there is a processing overhead at the backup server in excess of the processing incurred by a simple incremental.

TIP

Have a strategy in place to ensure your team regularly tests the solutions for a server failure. Each of the solutions is akin to insurance coverage for your campaign, but you want to make sure they're working when you need to "make a claim." For example, you don't want to wait until you need to restore your campaign to find out whether your backups are any good.

Data recovery is an extremely stressful scenario — one that does not need the additional worry of your solutions failing when you need them most. The answer is to test your solutions in mock scenarios. Regular testing can show that your recovery strategies are successful and also that the entire process can be completed in time.

TIP

If possible, schedule a test straight after every backup to validate that the data has been successfully secured. This won't always be practical. So, you need to balance the effort of recovery with having a degree of confidence in your restore procedures. At a minimum, schedule a restore test for your campaign on a weekly basis.

Applying the Best Development Practices

Most server and data failures caused by viral traffic will be outside of your control until they happen. However, there are plenty of good development practices that can ensure the coding and data won't add to the pressure on the servers when a spike of traffic hits your campaign. These practices can help push additional visitors through your network without having to worry about exceeding your bandwidth.

Optimizing the gamification code

There are two areas in which your developers can greatly reduce the amount of bandwidth each visitor consumes. These strategies will result in many additional benefits, such as faster browsing speeds for your visitors and fewer page requests, considerably reducing the load on your server.

With these changes, you should enjoy faster delivery speeds and ultimately a huge reduction in bandwidth use.

Compressing images

Conserving the amount of bandwidth consumed will ensure your campaign is constantly delivered to visitors. One technique is to reduce the size of the images used on your campaign's landing page and in your gamification code. You can do this by running the images through a program that will reduce the image quality to an acceptable level, as well as by reducing the dimensions to the optimal requirements. This strategy also benefits other aspects of your server, such as disk space and usage. With the reduction of file sizes, you'll reduce your bandwidth use overall and give your visitors a faster browsing experience.

Make sure not to compress your images too much, or you'll reduce their overall quality. There are a variety of image compression algorithms that take different approaches to reducing file size. The following tools use a number of those to minimize the size of your images:

- >> JPEGmini (www.jpegmini.com)
- >> RIOT (https://riot-optimizer.com)
- >> Shrink O'Matic (http://toki-woki.net/p/Shrink-O-Matic)

Reducing the code

You can further reduce your bandwidth usage by encouraging your developers to adopt good standards with your gamifications code. All HTML5 games are coded using JavaScript and CSS. Although this optimization won't make much of a difference early on in your campaign, the benefits will be huge when your campaign starts reaching more than 100,000 daily visitors.

Combine all your CSS into one global `style.css` file and reduce comments and white space. Each character and white space amounts to bytes of data, so if you have dozens of CSS pages loaded up on every page refresh, you can easily save a few kilobytes of data transfer when a visitor comes to your campaign if you use one `style.css` file.

The same techniques can be applied to JavaScript files, but there can be serious ramifications for your game if the changes aren't properly utilized and tested. Avoid combining all code into one file. You're better off having specific files called only when needed on the pages that require that code. For example, you don't want to call `playgame.js` on every single page that doesn't have the gameplay featured. That would counter the purpose of combining your JavaScript files.

Finalizing the development

There are a few additional bandwidth saving tips that your developers should try to follow:

- >> Make sure your server is running some form of compression software for optimal file delivery.

>> Enable page caching. It will drastically reduce server resource use, as well as bandwidth usage.

>> Consider a dedicated rich media server or third-party media delivery service, so you're offloading some bandwidth to those servers.

>> Fix all missing images. Missing images increase the load times of your website and, on some JavaScript based pages, actually increase bandwidth usage.

Focusing on the purpose of the data

Although optimizing the web server will help reduce bandwidth usage, your campaign will most certainly be running a separate database server, which can also benefit from good coding standards.

If you don't work closely with your developers, your database is in danger of being designed incorrectly from a structural standpoint.

Data is stored to be consumed later, and the goal is always to store it and retrieve it in the most efficient manner. To achieve this, the database designer must know in advance what the data is going to represent, how it's going to be acquired and at what rate, what its operational volume will be (how much data is expected), and, finally, how it's going to be used.

Work with your developers so they know the purpose of the data system you want them to create:

>> Make sure the game developers and web developers have an open group discussion with the database developers.

>> Work out what data analysis and reports you'll want from the campaign early on in the development process, and share this information with the database developers.

>> Make sure all gamification goals and rewards are fully explained at an early stage in the development process.

>> Make sure that your database developers accommodate for new gamification goals and rewards that can be implemented after the campaign has launched.

>> Make sure the developers are aware that there will be future campaigns that will use the same database server.

5

Preparing for Your Next Gamification Quest

Chapter **13**

Failing Up: Learning from Your First Quest

> *"One thing is certain in business. You and everyone around you will make mistakes."*
>
> —RICHARD BRANSON

Every gamification marketing campaign makes mistakes. The ones that eventually become successful are typically run by marketing teams that can admit when they've gone wrong and learn from those experiences.

Making mistakes during any stage of your campaign is inevitable. The important things are to:

» Remain open to the possibility that your campaign will have major flaws.

» Train your team to spot any issues early. Actively encourage problematic feedback.

» Resolve the issue by taking action.

You need to be able to identify when your campaign is not delivering the results you want. Be prepared to adjust your strategy midway to ensure your campaign delivers to its maximum potential.

Taking a Hard Look at the Results

Every campaign you run will give you a wealth of information on how you can improve for your next one. However, you need to know where to look. The first place you should start looking is the data that you've collected.

The data will give you information not only on what has been collected but also on what has not. Analyzing your data will give you a better idea of what areas of your campaign you need to strengthen.

After you've identified these weaknesses, you can plan on improving future campaigns and ensuring that you put in place checks to ensure that you don't make the same mistakes again.

Using data to your advantage

You're infinitely more likely to find success in your gamification marketing campaign when you base your decisions on information analyzed from data.

WARNING

Here are some mistakes marketing teams often make when trying to get the most value out of their data:

>> **Relying on web traffic:** Many marketing teams think that looking at web analytics is enough to decide whether their campaign is a success. Sure, web traffic is the most obvious and easiest data to spot when assessing your campaign's analytics. But unless your sole goal for your campaign was to get traffic, you need to treat web traffic as just one metric among many.

Web stats don't tell you whether your audience liked your campaign's content, or if they enjoyed the gamified elements, or even if they earned points and badges. All it really shows is that your audience found your campaign — which is still important, but not a measure of your campaign's overall success.

TIP

If you want to get more out of your web analytics, analyze your campaign's bounce rate. The bounce rate will give you a clue whether your campaign was what your audience actually wanted to see. Use extra data from your analytics, and you'll be able to see real results and have a better idea of your campaign's successes.

>> **Failing to go big:** You need to go beyond the data you capture and use big data (see Chapter 11). Big data is great for finding out what went wrong with your campaign, and it'll give you a good idea of what was actually happening.

By using big data techniques, you'll be able to predict future trends within your industry, which will allow you to target certain topics and ensure your content marketing is relevant and influential.

REMEMBER

Your campaign, whether it was a success or not, will deliver you valuable user-sourced data. This data can then strengthen any assumptions you've made with your campaign and will help all your future efforts to be more effective.

>> **Leaving your personas alone:** Many marketing teams spend so much time building their target *personas* (types of people) that once they're done, they assume they're perfect and should be left alone.

With each of your gamification marketing campaigns, you'll gather more data directly related to your target markets. But it's important to realize that your target market will be filled with complex individuals. This is why the whole idea of creating personas in marketing exists — marketing directly to all these potential audiences is difficult, so you group them into personas. However, if you don't take the new information each campaign generates and use it to *update* your personas, they'll remain outdated and possibly wrong.

TIP

Try to update your personas after every campaign.

>> **Treating mobile and desktop data as one:** Treating data from both platforms as a single entity is a major mistake that can lead to incorrect data. Your audience will interact with your campaign differently on mobile devices than they will on computers. Your data has to be treated and analyzed separately so that you can discover insights into your target audience that you would normally dismiss if the data were all in one grouping.

REMEMBER

When launching a gamification marketing campaign, cross-platform marketing can be a major challenge. However, you can simplify your marketing strategy for your next campaign if you treat the analytics from previous campaigns from both platforms uniquely.

>> **Going broader and not deeper:** The metrics you generate day to day during your gamification marketing campaign are only beneficial for the duration of the campaign. When the campaign is over, you'll need to dig deeper into your analytics to find out how your audience interacted with your campaign.

For instance, analyze what your audience did when they reached the landing page:

- Did they click any of the calls to action (CTAs)? If so, which were the most popular and which were the least?

- Did they spend time learning how to play and interact with your gaming elements?

- What pages did they visit the most and least?

- On average, how long did the audience who did *not* interact with the game stay on the page before leaving?

While you're analyzing and going deeper into your analytics, you need to start finding answers to pertinent questions. For instance, why were certain pages not visited? Was there a barrier to getting to those pages (for example, not enough clear links)?

These types of insights can guide you to fine-tune your next campaign and streamline the audience journey.

>> **Failing to capture their attention:** It's very difficult to know whether your campaign's strategy captured your audience's attention. Looking at the bounce rate can help, but translating your landing site's bounce rate into a measure of audience attention isn't totally accurate.

You need to tie in other metrics to form a better picture of how well your campaign captured your audience's attention:

- Did your content deliver what your audience was expecting?

- Did your game spark their interest immediately?

- Did your game provide enough elements to convince your audience to return?

TIP

One of most helpful analytics is the length of time visitors spend on particular pages of your campaign. Analyze how long an average but engaged visitor spent on your entire campaign. This will include any help sections, videos, content areas, and the game itself. If there is a large deviation from what you expected the average times to be, you're losing your visitors' attention.

REMEMBER

Too much time spent on a page can be a sign of lost interest, too. Anything over the 30-minute mark could mean that your audience looked away from your campaign but left the browser tab open. Most analytics stop tracking the visit time after 30 minutes; if the user returns to the page and clicks something, it records it as a new visit.

If the times are short (for instance, only a few seconds long), either you audience was extremely put off by something on your campaign or it didn't deliver anything of value to them. Start working on the reasons for this and work this into the next campaign's pages. You're looking to retain interest and help your audience engage with your campaign.

Using analytics the right way

Analytics are a very powerful way to communicate your gamification marketing campaign's results to your team and your management. If you aren't already representing your data properly, then you aren't just confusing your analytics; you could be misrepresenting them entirely. Taking the time to understand how your analytics work will enable you to assess your campaign fairly and learn valuable lessons for the next one.

WARNING

Here are some common mistakes marketing teams make when it comes to analytics:

>> **Thinking low numbers equals bad news:** When you see a low number in your metrics, your first reaction may be to think the campaign failed. After all, high numbers for traffic can only mean a success. However, a low number isn't always bad.

For some metrics, low numbers are welcomed. For instance, you want to ensure the number of people unsubscribing to your emails has decreased. When this metric is low, it means your emails are welcome and your content is appealing to your audience! Did your customer acquisition cost go down? This means that your marketing efforts are becoming more efficient!

REMEMBER

Apart from the obvious low-seeking metrics, low numbers can sometimes be a good teaching moment for your team. Where they *aren't* welcome, low numbers can highlight a marketing channel that isn't working. Granted, this information is frustrating, but you can learn a lot from it, and that's what matters.

For instance, when you're analyzing how well your social media channels are performing, you may realize the conversion rates from Twitter are low. At the same time, the conversion rates from Facebook and LinkedIn may be quite good. Knowing this information can guide you to focus your efforts more efficiently by investing in the marketing channels that work for you on future campaigns.

>> **Confusing visits with views:** Visits and views may sound similar, but they're actually quite different. Here's what these two key terms mean:

- A *visit* is when a website visitor comes to your website from an external URL.

- A *view* (or *pageview* as it's known in Google Analytics) is counted when your page is loaded or reloaded by a web browser.

The key to understanding these two metrics is to appreciate their context. For instance, a blog post for your campaign that inspires a huge number of page views for your blog but results in a relatively low number of visitors to your campaign's landing page may not be as influential as it first appears.

Page views are a valuable piece of raw data, but without a deeper understanding of your site and your audience's behavioral patterns, they only represent a portion of your website's performance.

>> **Chucking all traffic together:** Not all traffic is created equal, and it certainly shouldn't be treated that way. Traffic to your campaign will come from multiple channels, including organic search, referrals from other websites, direct traffic, paid traffic, email marketing, social media, and possibly more.

TIP

You should always try to break up your traffic into smaller pieces representing the different marketing channels you're employing. From here, you can analyze the percentage each channel has increased or decreased month over month.

When you know these categorized numbers, you'll begin to understand where to invest your time and resources for your next campaign. If social media generated traffic to your website that converted, then this is a good indication that you should continue to invest in your social media efforts. However, if your email marketing generated few to no visits with a very low conversion rate, then you may want to slow down on email and invest more in the channels that are generating traffic and conversions.

>> **Comparing unrelated data points:** You need to compare related data points, not unrelated ones. The hard part is knowing which data points are related and which ones aren't. For instance, comparing the performance of CTAs may sound obvious, but it doesn't always make sense to compare them. One data point may be about encouraging your audience to engage with your game whereas another may offer help on how to play.

Comparing unrelated data points can lead you to invest your budget in the wrong way. For instance, while looking at the sources of visits to your campaign, you may notice a higher number of visits came from email clicks than from, say, mobile devices. You shouldn't invest more in email marketing and not as much in mobile marketing. Email marketing and mobile marketing are completely different — email marketing is used to *deliver* a message, whereas mobile marketing is the device used to *receive* that message.

>> **Equating engagement with time:** The fact that a person spent a long time on your campaign doesn't mean he was more engaged. For instance, it could mean that he was having trouble finding what he was looking for. And if that's the case, you have a user experience (UX) issue that you need to address in the next campaign.

If you see visitors spending long periods of time on your campaign, don't just assume they loved the content and experience. Conduct user testing to see if people were actually engaged with your content, or if they were having trouble finding what they were looking for.

Researching for the Future

Each gamification marketing campaign has a different target audience. If you don't know who your audience will be, you can't possibly hope to reach them. Plus, you may be creating a campaign that won't appeal to or resonate with your audience.

You can refine your target market in many ways (see Chapter 7). For instance, market research can give you an excellent insight into the personas that will engage with what your campaign has to offer. When you identify these personas, you can concentrate on ways of reaching them. In the following sections, I show you how.

Branding trust

Branding your campaign will create a trustworthy and clear message you can convey to your audience. Your audience will be wary and skeptical of any campaign that they don't instantly recognize. The best way to minimize this possibility is to ensure that your brand message and imagery are consistent.

However, branding alone doesn't always gain trust, especially if your company is smaller or newer. In the modern digital playground, more and more people are turning to reviews to decide whether they can trust a brand or product. This means you need to monitor your campaigns on review sites and social media channels. Your audience will want to see other reviews or comments that show the quality of the campaign, so they aren't going in blind.

One way to boost your reviews is to proactively ask your current audiences to review your previous campaigns. You could go as far as to incentivize existing audiences to leave honest reviews of previous campaigns in exchange for rewards for future campaigns.

Many independent review sites are available for your audience to leave their experiences, such as Reviews.io (www.reviews.io). Here are some of the top review sites:

>> **Google My Business** (www.google.com/business): Google My Business is a free tool for businesses to manage their online presence across all Google's products, including their Search and Maps. It works well for all types of businesses.

>> **Tripadvisor** (www.tripadvisor.com): Tripadvisor is a travel website company where users can leave reviews of hotels, restaurants, and so on. Tripadvisor operates websites internationally in more than 25 countries. It works well for campaigns related to travel, restaurants, and food-related businesses.

>> **Angie's List** (www.angieslist.com): Angie's List is a service listing and review website that offers user-based rankings and reviews of service professionals in local areas. Angie's List reviews are from members, who grade companies using a report-card scale from A to F on price, quality, responsiveness, punctuality, and professionalism. It works best for service businesses.

>> **Yelp** (www.yelp.com): Yelp is one of the largest review sites for online customer where users can publish reviews about local businesses. Yelp also encourages businesses to respond to reviews. It works well for all types of businesses.

>> **Facebook** (www.facebook.com): Due to the sheer size of the user base of Facebook, it's gaining momentum as one of the most popular business review sites. Facebook is mostly good for restaurant-related reviews, but it's open to all types of businesses.

Sticking to your budget

You need a budget for your gamification marketing campaign, and your team can err by spending too much or too little. If you spend too little, your campaign won't reach your target audience and it will fail before it begins. If you spend too much, you can be capturing uninterested audiences who won't engage.

Manage your campaign proactively. For instance, ensure that you budget for each marketing campaign's setup costs. Your campaigns will take time and resources to set up in order to be effective. So plan how your budget will be spent at each stage of your campaign's duration. In this way, you'll make sure that you won't overspend or underspend overall.

Handling your expectations

You need to be clear from the start on your desired outcomes for your gamification marketing campaign. Clearly communicate the goals of your campaign to your team (see Chapter 7).

Ideally, you need to understand what your marketing campaign aims to achieve. From here, you'll need to analyze which of these aims are possible with the resources and budget you have.

TIP

Don't restrict your goals to just increasing sales. Gamification is perfect for creating brand awareness and recognition. Sure, those won't deliver instant results, but they'll deliver huge results in the long run.

Paying attention to detail

Everyone can make mistakes, but by creating layers of proofreading and testing, you'll drastically reduce the likelihood of mistakes happening in your campaign.

A lack of attention could unwittingly lead to broken links or spelling mistakes, which will have huge impacts on your conversion rates (and you could end up wasting your campaign's budget).

WARNING

Mistakes such as wrongly linked CTAs can lead to frustration. Frustrated audiences usually air their unhappiness on their social media accounts. And if that happens, your campaign can actually *damage* your brand image rather than support it.

Being consistent with your brand identity

If your audience notices a lack of branding or even conflicting messages, they'll most likely be put off from engaging with your campaign. For this reason, you need to start defining how your company's overall brand will be represented within your campaign.

Look to shape your branding into your campaign's awareness strategy. Also, set your company's tone and message into the campaign so that it will appeal to potential audiences. By doing this kind of planning, your campaign will be instantly engaging and you'll create a better connection with your audience.

TIP

Start by creating a guidance document that outlines your overall branding, including the tone and messaging your company wants to promote. This will help reduce any inconsistencies in all future campaigns. Ideally, everyone on your team will understand the way they're supposed to communicate your brand.

Learning to attribute traffic

Analyze your previous campaigns' analytics and try to identify any sudden spikes in engagement. Figure out what caused this success so that you can replicate it in all future campaigns.

For instance, was it a well-performing Facebook ad? Or was it a mention in a blogger's post? Without careful analytical attribution, you'll never know where the spikes have come from. This is why traffic attribution is so important, so that you can assess what's working.

When you realize the high-performing channels, you can ensure that all future campaigns divert resources away from the platforms that aren't bringing in the audiences.

Set up Urchin Tracking Modules (UTMs) within your Google Analytics platform. This will centralize all your traffic reporting in one place. UTMs are designed to tell Google Analytics (and other analytics tools) a little bit more information about each link and which marketing campaign it relates to. This allows you to break down traffic and segment customers, to refine your marketing efforts to the platforms that work better for you.

Explaining your unique selling proposition

Your audience needs to understand what makes your campaign unique straight away. If they don't understand this, they'll swiftly move on to the next distracting campaign they find on the Internet.

Your next campaign may have an amazing unique selling proposition (USP), but if your landing page and content don't communicate this effectively, audiences won't stick around. Your audience will tend to move at breakneck speed, and if they don't find a connection with your campaign, they'll look elsewhere.

Make sure that your next campaign is based around the USP. This means planning your USP strategy well before you spend time and money on the later stages. One way you can quickly explain your USP is to create an effective strapline. This will ensure your USP is communicated in a few seconds and will let your audience know why they should stick around and engage with your campaign.

Finding out what's new

Many marketing teams sticking to a "copy paste" mentality when it comes to developing their next gamification marketing campaign. Although it feels comfortable and makes financial sense, it can also be a dangerous attitude in gamification marketing.

Social platforms and mobile technology are constantly evolving. Before you know it, there are new platforms and marketing methods to explore. If you don't take the time to evaluate them for your next campaign, you may end up being seen as dated when compared to your competitors' campaigns.

Ensuring that your team is continually aware of new platforms and keeping an eye on technology will keep your next campaign ahead of the curve and relevant.

Evaluating and improving

Try to spend time evaluating the outcomes of your completed campaigns in the hope that you and your team can hope to improve on the next one. With regular reviews and improvements, you can refine your future campaigns to get more.

After every campaign, there will always be areas for you to improve on the next one. By doing this, you will ensure your campaigns will create value to your company.

Shaping the Future

Gamification marketing is constantly changing as innovative marketing teams continue to push the boundaries of engagement. For the most part, new technologies dictate the new limits marketers can go to with their campaigns.

You can improve your marketing strategies by exploring your valuable data analytics. This includes using analytics to understand how current and potential customers behave. This can then help you make better decisions and analyze the design of your next campaigns.

Cleaning your data

Big data is a fantastic and effective way to plan for your next campaign (see Chapter 11). However, big data itself can leave you overwhelmed by the unprecedented volume and variety of unstructured information. After you've gathered the data, working out how to separate the useful insights from the noisy data can seem impossible.

TIP

Here are some useful techniques you can employ to ensure you get what you need from big data:

>> **Develop a plan for ensuring the health of your data.** The plan's sole purpose is to ensure that your data remains clean. Identify where most data quality errors occur, and try to give more guidance on the campaign's page to minimize this. Also, identify incorrect data and build a system to eliminate this from the source.

>> **Check important data at the point of entry.** This ensures that all information is standardized when it enters your database and will make it easier to catch duplicates. Install a system of intelligent validation on all forms.

>> **Try to validate the accuracy of your data in real-time.** For instance, you can use data hygiene tools that offer email verification, which lets the user know if he hasn't entered a valid email address.

>> **Make sure that you identify duplicate records before they infiltrate your database.** Duplicate entries can cost more in campaign spending and will cause inaccurate reporting.

Using artificial intelligence

You can't have failed to notice the impact artificial intelligence (AI) is having on the world around us. AI is already being used in ad exchanges and for campaign optimization. If you want your campaigns to remain competitive and relevant, then you need to explore ways to integrate AI.

For instance, for customer experience, you could think about using chatbots to automate customer engagement efforts. These tools not only help save you time and money, but also give you more time to attend to other matters and help you to grow your audience.

Here are some applicable AI uses:

>> **AI has the potential to both curate and generate content, and then place it in front of the right people on the right platforms.** This means your campaign will have newer content generated more frequently, leaving your team free to work on other areas of the campaign.

>> **AI will change the way you advertise your campaigns.** For instance, electronic billboards can be powered by AI to deliver the right kinds of ads in front of the right kinds of people based on complex algorithms and big data. Google and Facebook ads are already using powerful algorithms to ensure you have the right tools to maximize your ad spend.

>> **The future lies in smart chatbots, as opposed to the simple ones you regularly see now.** These are AI-powered systems that communicate with humans using real-time, creating responses based on their experiences. Some very complex chatbots are available for you to implement into your campaign.

Chapter 14

Relaunching Your Gamification Marketing Campaign

Whether your campaign was a success or not, start thinking about investing time, money, and resources toward relaunching it. Each new campaign (including relaunches of previous campaigns) should be seen as a stepping stone to your overall gamification marketing journey.

In today's fast-moving digital age, running multiple successful gamification marketing campaigns is extremely difficult. New campaigns need to be constantly visible in order to capitalize on your earlier brand awareness. The good news is, you don't need to rush out new campaigns all the time. If you did that, you'd be sacrificing the innovation and the overall look and feel your first campaign was based on. Instead, you can tweak your previous campaign — fix what didn't work, try new things — and relaunch, saving yourself lots of time and money in the process.

When you relaunch a new campaign, you need to learn from your past mistakes and consider how your audience perceives your brand. You can revamp your campaign's branding by adapting a completely new gamification model, if you want.

But you should try to (subtly) reuse and remind audiences of your earlier campaigns. Correct positioning and appropriate application of earlier campaigns will *enhance* the value of your new one.

Launching another campaign may seem like something to think about a long time after you've ended your first one. But the earlier you start thinking of your next campaign, the more time you can give to how you can improve the user experience.

When you start thinking about your second, third, and fourth campaign, you'll start to think about building on top of the existing relationship you have with your target audience. This will then enable you to create an image of professionalism and reliability, which will, in turn, get your audience to respond by trusting your company's messages.

In this chapter, I start by explain why you may want to relaunch a campaign. Then I explain how you can tweak that previous campaign to prepare for relaunching it. Finally, I end by helping you decide when it's time to call a campaign quits.

Understanding Why You May Want to Relaunch Your Campaign

With all the hard work and effort you put in the first campaign, you can't be blamed for wanting to delay thinking about relaunching it. But this is precisely what you *should* be doing. Here are some reasons you may want to do exactly that:

>> **To continue building your brand awareness:** Your audience's first gamification experience with your company will have left them curious and excited about what's coming next. You've done well to create brand awareness and educate your audience on the gamification model of your last campaign.

Don't let all that education and engagement go to waste! Instead, capitalize on it through revised and varied options and designs. This way, you're giving your audience a reason to not only engage even more with your brand but also use their own social media channels to highlight it.

>> **To give your team another chance:** You'll make lots of mistakes in your first campaign — that's only natural. Use a relaunch to make an even better impression on your audience. Show them you've listened and improved your offering. Maybe you can improve the overall design, the landing page, the incentives you're offering, and the content. Focus on improving the gamification model's quality, design, and formulation. When you do this, you'll begin to

create a more premium gamification marketing campaign — one your audience will appreciate even more.

>> **To acquire a bigger audience:** The real key to getting a bigger audience for your campaigns is to *know your audience.* Luckily, your first campaign will have given you an immensely rich database of analytics about your audience. You know what they liked, what they didn't like, and what challenges they faced. With this data, you can better target your content and gamification model options to deliver an experience the next time around that you *know* your audience will love and engage with.

>> **To clear up any confusion:** Sometimes a gamification component can confuse or event distract audiences from the campaign's main goal and objectives. *Remember:* Engagement isn't your only goal. A clear product positioning strategy can help solve this problem in your next campaign. Brand identity should be a very important factor when designing your gamification model. If possible, your brand identity should be visible at all times.

>> **To go for bigger data:** The thing about big data is that you continually need more, fresh data. Luckily, with each new campaign, you'll generate more analytical and behavioral data. This is what will keep your marketing campaigns profitable. Launch your campaigns, get as much data as possible, and analyze them over time. When you've got the data, you're in a powerful position to grow your audience and increase engagement in future campaigns.

>> **To increase trust:** You'll increase the trust your audience has in your message as you launch more gamification marketing campaigns. The more your audience trusts you, the more they'll engage with your campaigns, and the more likely they are to buy your products and services.

TIP

Building trust is not something that can be achieved with one campaign. Generally, the campaigns your audience will trust the most will be the ones they've seen multiple times.

>> **To figure out what works:** With each new campaign, your team will learn which types of advertisements and marketing tactics were most effective and which ones weren't. There are hundreds of marketing strategies that you can use for your marketing campaigns. Experimenting with different marketing methods over several campaigns will help you find the ones that work best for your company.

>> **To improve your ideal audience profile:** At some point, you will have created the ideal audience profile that you want to be targeting in your campaigns. You'll have included variables, such as their age group, income levels, and locations. After you've launched several marketing campaigns, your data will reveal patterns and characteristics to help you better refine your audience.

Tweaking Your Gamification Campaign

Tweaking your gamification concept for your relaunch should start at the end of your current campaign. If you don't take the time to think about what you should do differently next time, you may end up with the same issues and problems that prevented your original campaign from delivering on all your marketing goals.

After your first campaign, you'll have all the data available to analyze. Your next campaign's chances of success will be greatly increased if you can start identifying and planning the changes right away.

Checking your exit points

The success of your gamification marketing campaign will depend on whether the gamification model you selected appealed to your core audience (see Chapter 7).

Using the analytical data you've collected, check your campaign metrics to see which parts of your campaign caused the most number of exits. Also, look at the audience data to see at what level you see the highest level of people not progressing further.

For instance, if you find the highest saturation of audiences reached a certain badge or level, you can analyze the reasons for that. Maybe you didn't offer enough incentives for them to progress further. Maybe the next level was too difficult to play or understand. Or maybe some technical error or issue prevented them from moving on.

TIP

There are two metrics you want to pay close attention to:

>> **Bounce rate:** This is the percentage of single interaction visits to your campaign's entry page. This metric lets you know that your audience left your campaign from the entrance page (your landing page) without interacting with the campaign.

>> **Exit rate:** The percentage of people who exited from a specific page in your campaign, regardless of how many pages they visited. In a way, your exit rate is the metric that reveals the performance of all the pages in your campaign.

Start with the page in your campaign that has the highest exit rate, because this is the first place you need to fix for your next campaign. Essentially, you know that this part of your campaign provoked you audience to exit your campaign, and your job is to figure out what that is.

Your campaign's bounce rate and exit rate are the best metrics for gauging whether your campaign was successful. Your aim for the next campaign should be to reduce these two as much as you can. If you can put in place measures to reduce your bounce rate and exit rate, you should see significant improvement in audience engagement.

TECHNICAL STUFF

Google will likely reward your campaign's website with a better search engine optimization (SEO) ranking if it sees a reduced bounce rate and exit rate. Search engines always favor user experience more than other analytical metrics. For this reason, the greater amount of time your audience spends on your campaign, the higher Google will rank your site.

REMEMBER

All campaign websites have exit rates — the audience has to exit at *some* point. You just want to ensure the highest concentration of exits is around the end of levels so you can be sure people have at least spent enough time to understand the campaign and successfully engage with it. For bounce rates, you want to ensure your audience remains on your campaign for a significant amount of time and doesn't "bounce" after less than ten seconds.

Assessing whether the gamification option you chose was right for you

In Chapter 7, I cover the strengths and weaknesses of the various gamification options. Now that your campaign has been run, you can assess if the option you selected was right for your brand. In the following sections, I walk you through what to look for depending on the option you chose.

Action

If you ran an action game, it's quite normal to see a high volume of new visitors as opposed to returning visitors. Action games generally run for a short time, but they attract a high volume of traffic over the duration of the campaign.

The key factor is to work on your exit rates and pinpoint where in the game you found your audience losing interest and disengaging from your campaign. Here are the key areas to cover:

>> **Gameplay:** Was the difficulty too high? Or was the level too long? Are the controls intuitive enough for your audience to quickly pick up on them?

>> **Badges/points:** Were the criteria to reach the next stage too hard for the average person?

>> **Leaderboard:** Was the leaderboard lacking useful content? Although the leaderboard is there to provide a competitive environment and, thus, lower bounce rates, it can also work against you if the campaign was too successful. If people find themselves way down in the ranks where there can be no possible way to reach a visible spot, they'll be turned off. To counter this problem, consider creating mini leaderboards that show the top ten positions for each audience member where they can see a snapshot of their current position with just the nine members above their score.

Simulation

If you ran a simulation game, you should have seen audiences spending a long time engaging with the various objectives of the game. The niche virtual world you created for your campaign should now have a dedicated army of players.

If you find that you *didn't* achieve all this, then your analytical data will help pinpoint where your campaign went wrong. The data should show where you're failing to convince your audience to invest a lot of time in the game. Here are a few key areas to consider:

>> Is your audience constantly collecting rewards? Can you pinpoint the saturation point for most users?

>> Is there a big discrepancy among the devices used in the metrics? If you find an overall low mobile screen usage, this will indicate that your simulation game wasn't responsive enough for all devices.

>> Were the objectives at each stage made clear to the audience? To sustain your audience's interest, your campaign should be supplying them with constant objectives to complete. If the metrics indicate low objective completions, you need to look at redeveloping these in your next campaign.

Interactive storytelling

For interactive storytelling, the only metric you need to worry about is whether the audiences completed the full story experience. Unlike other gamification options, this type of game has a finite end for all audiences. Typically, you find audiences completing the campaign more than once, opting for different choices to engage in a wholly different experience.

Here are a few key areas you may need to look at:

>> Was the story interesting enough? Send questionnaires to registered users and get feedback. Did they find it interesting? What put them off? With this valuable data, you can work to correct the experience.

>> Is there a big discrepancy among the devices used in the metrics? If you find an overall low mobile screen usage, this indicates that your simulation game wasn't responsive enough for all devices.

Adventure

Adventure games are typically a hybrid of action, simulation, and interactive storytelling, so you need to look at a broad range of metrics. If your audience failed to invest their time in the campaign, try to figure out why.

Apart from the key areas I explore in the previous three sections, for adventure games you should also investigate the level of help that was being offered. Did you provide your audience with enough FAQs, help pages, and how-to videos to aid them in their journey through your campaign's objectives?

Puzzles

In my experience, this type of game can be hit or miss with audiences. When they miss, it's usually because they're too hard or too easy. Unless you can hit that sweet spot when it comes to level of difficulty, your audience won't be engaged.

Make sure you've provided enough content. Were there enough levels, objectives, and rewards being offered? Also, are you giving a realistic amount of time or attempts to solve the puzzles? Take the time to match your metrics with these potential problem areas, and identify the main cause for any lack of engagement.

Skill-based

I find that skill-based games have a better success rate than other game types, but there are some areas you should keep an eye on here. The main problem is that skill-based games are not always intuitive to your audience. Aim to provide as much help documentation as possible for the user.

Also, with skill-based games, the outcome is determined by the audience's reactions, mental abilities, strategic thinking, or trivia knowledge. This means that not everyone will engage because they just won't understand the concept. However, if your metrics indicate a large portion of your audience not engaging, you need to review the "skill" element of your campaign.

Multi-player

Because multi-player games allow your audience to compete not only against one or more human contestants, but also against an artificial intelligence (AI), you should see a lot of engagement within the campaign.

However, there is one key area to explore if you find your campaign didn't generate the right amount of engagement: your server. Did the server's bandwidth let your campaign down? For the multi-player component, the server needs active sockets available for your audience to play with. Also, the amount of information being recorded every second could lead to points in the day where your database is overloaded with commands. Have your server administrator analyze the server and database logs and check for any warnings or anomalies for the duration of the campaign.

Educational

Because an educational game provides a useful way for your audience to learn something valuable, you should see an increase in the awareness of your product or service. Also as this information has been given an entertaining platform, so you should see a much more engaged campaign.

If you haven't seen increased awareness and engagement, check that the game was educating your audience while they were playing it. At the end of the game or campaign, the audience should have left more educated on your business or product.

Role playing

Because role-playing games are the least common type of game selected for gamification marketing campaigns, they leave a more lasting impression on your audience.

Your audience will have been immersed in your branded gamified world, so they should have a good understanding of your campaign's objectives. If they don't, try to balance the gamification elements to have more information and data about your business and fewer gamified elements.

Redefining your target audience

Your analytics will show, over the duration of the campaign, the average statistics of your audience. You need to match these statistics with the criteria you set when deciding which gamification options to develop into your campaign.

At this stage, it's a good idea to reevaluate the different game models and see if you should possibly change your model depending on the data. Chapter 7 outlines which game options will work best for various categories, based on age, location/language, how much free time they have, and stage of life.

Building a seasonal version of your campaign

Your campaign may not appeal to your audience year-round. Consider having a rebranded version of your campaign with a seasonal theme, such as for the holiday period. Holiday marketing is an exciting experience, but it's also incredibly competitive. As other marketing teams around the world are scrambling to think of how they're going to celebrate the festive season, you'll have a campaign locked and loaded and ready to go.

Think about rolling out holiday marketing slogans into your campaign that tap into the warm and happy feelings your audience will have at that time of the year. Your gamification options don't need to change, but your designs can be instantly transformed to create the seasonal theme, as shown in Figure 14-1. For instance, your badges can have a very simple holiday makeover during the festive period.

FIGURE 14-1: Holiday-themed campaigns can be easily integrated into existing gamification marketing campaigns such as Starbucks did with its Starbucks Rewards campaign.

REMEMBER

Whatever seasonal strategy you decide on, you need to keep in mind that your campaign will be facing a lot of competition for your audience's attention. Your audience will be distracted with family, celebrations, and every other company launching its own holiday campaign. That means that almost every one of your competitors will be looking for a way to distract your audience and grab their attention.

TIP

The key to success is to separate yourself from the rest of the noise. Try to avoid simply becoming part of the holiday collections, and instead find a way for your holiday gamification marketing campaign to connect with your audience through emotion, excitement, and experience. You can do this by connecting the festive feelings into a road map for the user's journey (see Chapter 10). Your company will have a different experience to showcase during the holiday season than everyone else. Translate this to your team to build into the gamification model so that this uniqueness will differentiate your campaign.

In the following sections, I look into some strategies you should consider when developing your holiday-themed gamification marketing campaign.

Creating anticipation

Building up to the event is what the holidays are all about. When you make your audience anticipate the launch of your holiday campaign, they'll naturally feel happier when they finally get to engage with the campaign. Some of the best holiday marketing ideas focus on the buildup of excitement.

The Google Santa Tracker, shown in Figure 14-2, is a great example of building excitement. By releasing new Santa content every day of December, Google got its audience noticing its brand.

REMEMBER

Building anticipation isn't just about building excitement for the big day; it's also about building excitement for your campaign.

Giving back

At the holidays, people feel compelled to give back. Your holiday gamification marketing campaign can take advantage of this feeling, by offering your audience an experience so valuable that they feel compelled to give you something back.

If your campaign delivers a rewarding and engaging experience, your audience will

FIGURE 14-2:
Make your audience anticipate the holiday launch like Google does with its Santa Tracker.

>> Come back next year because they'll feel a sense of loyalty to your holiday campaign

>> Share it on all their social media platforms and advocate for it personally in their posts

>> Feel compelled to engage with your company's products and services

Feeling festive

REMEMBER

When designing your holiday-themed campaign, make sure you leave your audience feeling happy and festive. If you do this, the audience will be more likely to engage with your campaign and go on to purchase your company's products or services.

TIP

Capitalize on the seasonal sentiment. For most people, the holiday season is a joyous time of year. After all, the end of December means more time off work, memories made with family, and of course, giving and receiving presents. People feel more uplifted and excited in general, so your campaign should amplify these feelings.

Creating urgency

Your holiday-themed campaign should leave your audience feeling as though they're missing out on something special if they don't immediately engage with it. You can do this by displaying a very visible countdown timer that displays when your campaign will come to an end. The timer will prompt people to stop dithering over decisions and start taking action.

If you can design your holiday strategy with a clear expiration date, you can appeal to your audience's sense of urgency, which will inspire them to engage and purchase. The best holiday-themed gamification marketing campaigns are the ones that recognize the finite state of the festive period and make sure the audience appreciates the urgency of engaging immediately.

Personalizing your content

When building your holiday-themed gamification campaign, think about how you can create content that your audience will want to share with their network. Typically, people will place a larger sense of value on things that they can personalize.

Office Depot/OfficeMax's ElfYourself, shown in Figure 14-3, is a great example of this. Office Depot/OfficeMax gave its audience the chance to create a completely customized experience, which could then be shared easily on all social media platforms.

FIGURE 14-3: Customizable seasonal experiences, like Office Depot/OfficeMax's ElfYourself, have a better chance of getting shared by your audience.

This helps your company to develop a stronger emotional connection between your brand and your audience. Another popular example is the Oreo Design a Pack campaign, which tweeted out an invitation to design and personalize a pack of Oreos for friends and family members.

Knowing When to Shut It All Down

A well-developed and well-executed gamification marketing campaign can be relaunched multiple times — effectively. Gamification marketing is an ongoing process that typically requires numerous iterations until success is achieved.

However, sometimes your post-marketing analysis indicates more negatives than positives. In these cases, it may be worth considering not continuing with the current gamification model and completely redeveloping your strategy. Here are some scenarios where you should stop and reevaluate your current gamification strategy:

>> **Your audience reacted negatively.** If your audience had real problems with your campaign, they may complain about it on social media. If enough people do this, it's time to stop using this game. Use the techniques I explore in this chapter to improve and change your strategy. If the changes you made will bring a positive reaction, consider sharing the fact that you listened to your valued audience. Reveal a message on social media letting them know their views and feedback are important and offer the revised campaign as proof.

>> **You're a bomb on social media.** Metrics such as volume, reach, and engagement are all important to see if the campaign fully engaged with your audience. Typically, you should see some engagement, especially if you've provided a unique hashtag for people to use. If you're hearing crickets on social media, that means your audience isn't willing to share the campaign's message with their friends and followers. Head back to the drawing board and come up with something new.

>> **You're not seeing enough growth.** At the start of your campaign, you may see a spike in engagement. But does this continue? More important, do the metrics indicate any form of positive growth? If your campaign's content isn't resulting in verifiable growth, then the gamification model you selected could be all wrong.

>> **No one shared your campaign.** One of the most obvious signs that your campaign is resonating with your audience is the generation of new inbound links. If your audience loves your content, they'll share it all over the place. If you aren't finding an influx of inbound links from social media and blog posts, you need to reevaluate your gamification model.

6

The Part of Tens

Chapter 15

Ten Best Gamification Marketing Examples

Throughout this book, I show you real-life examples of the techniques I describe. In this chapter, I highlight what I think are ten of the best gamification marketing campaigns ever produced. I walk you through why the company produced the campaign, how said company developed and promoted the campaign, and how successful the campaign was.

The companies in this chapter have been quite open with their success metrics. Plus, their campaigns were easy to track online. But the actual gamification techniques they used are no different from the techniques I cover in this book — and you don't need to be a huge multinational corporation to put them to work for you! Each of these gamification models is within the grasp of your company's marketing goals if you apply the techniques outlined in this book.

Starbucks: Starbucks Rewards

In my opinion, Starbucks Rewards is one of the most successful gamification marketing campaigns ever produced. It was intrinsically based around the reward and loyalty programs I discuss in Chapter 4.

Many people already buy coffee on a regular basis, often on their way to work. However, a higher price point and an ever-increasing number of competing coffee shops meant that Starbucks had to work harder to get people to keep coming back. Starbucks needed a campaign that would increase not only brand loyalty, but also repeat visits by customers.

To solve this problem, Starbucks created the Rewards app, which rewards members for coming in multiple times over a certain period of time. The brand used gamification tactics to enhance the Starbucks experience. This helped boost brand loyalty as well as sales.

For this campaign, Starbucks opted for a mobile and web app where customers would register for Starbucks Rewards. Then every time customers purchased Starbucks products, they earned rewards, which actually looked like cups that were graphically filled in.

The gamification marketing campaign didn't stop there. Starbucks introduced levels — progression through each of the three levels depended on customer loyalty. When customers visited Starbucks stores, they earned upgraded rewards. Examples of rewards included an extra cup of coffee, a birthday present, and even customized offers.

As of March 2019, Starbucks Rewards had a staggering 16 million active members, with an 11 percent growth of its user base in the second quarter of 2018.

Chipotle: A Love Story Game

Chipotle launched a memory game based on its animated short film called *A Love Story*. The film, which had more than 60 million views at the time of the game's launch, is a cautionary tale about two young entrepreneurs whose rivalry results in competing fast-food empires that sacrifice quality for quantity.

The gamification marketing campaign, called A Love Story Game, allowed customers to match real ingredients while avoiding the use of added colors and flavors. The game was consistent with the brand's overall image of making natural, healthy foods.

Chipotle's gamification marketing campaign cleverly rewarded winning audiences with a buy-one-get-one-free coupon for any food item. This is an excellent example of gamification marketing providing an opportunity for customers to interact with your brand while bringing attention to the company but also rewarding them at the same time. (In Chapter 4, I cover ways you can reward audiences so that they'll be encouraged to keep playing the game and stay engaged with your company.)

As opposed to the Starbucks example (see the preceding section), where the platform was a mobile app, Chipotle went with developing the campaign with HTML5. This meant that its customers could play the game and receive rewards on all their devices, including mobile phones, tablets, and computers. (I cover the differences between these platforms in Chapter 8.)

According to internal research, after Chipotle's gamification marketing campaign, over 70 percent of users reported that they believed the brand used high-quality, whole ingredients, and 65 percent said it made them more likely to trust the company. Also, according to the Brand Keys Customer Loyalty Engagement Index, Chipotle was number one in customer loyalty.

Chipotle went on to create another gamification marketing campaign after A Love Story Game called Cado Crusher. The campaign, which was launched two weeks before the Super Bowl, required players to collect ingredients to create guacamole for the big game. This concept was tied into Super Bowl parties that might feature guacamole.

Nike: Nike+ FuelBand

Incredibly, since Nike launched this gamification marketing campaign, it has developed into a worldwide popular gamified sport. The idea was simple: to encourage lifestyle changes by helping Nike's audience to keep themselves fit.

The campaign centers around the Nike+ FuelBand, which is a bracelet with technology that can monitor user movements. By implementing the campaign on a mobile app, Nike was able to take advantage of the mobile device's native features, which meant its audience could track their progress on a very personal level.

Statistics (like the number of calories burned) were displayed to provide feedback to users. The app also collected personal data from users and kept a close update on their physical activity, displaying their latest achievements and overall performance. Ultimately, the app converted the users' performance into points, rewarding them for their efforts. These rewards came in the form of trophies and badges after completing different levels.

Nike's gamification marketing campaign went one step further and introduced a social element to the game, which undoubtedly helped to expand awareness and demand. Audiences were given the opportunity to challenge friends, which provided a great incentive to share the campaign. Users' points accumulated based on the distance they traveled. This was then revealed to their community, where everyone could track who was ranked at the top of the leaderboard.

Furthermore, when rewards are won, consumers are encouraged to share their results on social media, increasing the brand's presence and visibility on all social platforms. As I explain in Chapter 9, encouraging and engaging users to promote your campaign will boost your campaign's momentum.

Within two years of launch, Nike had 11 million Nike+ FuelBand players. The gamification marketing campaign greatly boosted Nike's customer loyalty. More important, the campaign allowed Nike to collect lots of data over a long period of time (see Chapter 11); Nike could then use this data to market its products and services directly.

M&M's: Eye-Spy Pretzel

The M&M's Eye-Spy Pretzel app is a good example of how a simple gamification marketing campaign can create a huge impact. I always recommend that you keep your games simple and not make them too difficult or include too many elements. By doing so, you ensure your audience won't feel overwhelmed or frustrated, which means that they're more likely to share your campaign.

The idea for the campaign came when M&M's was about to launch a pretzel-flavored version of its popular candy. In order to promote M&M's pretzel products, the company launched this marketing campaign.

The idea was clever: The users had to find a pretzel hidden in an image full of M&M's. This straightforward puzzle game, which ran solely on Facebook, brought in tens of thousands of new likes for the company. More important, the campaign was shared by thousands of people in a very short period of time.

This gamification marketing campaign brought real-life, tangible benefits, including creating user engagement with the brand. At its high point, the campaign resulted in 25,000 new likes on the brand's Facebook page, as well as 6,000 shares and 10,000 comments.

Target: Wish List

Target's gamification marketing campaign was entirely focused on children. The campaign, a mobile app called Wish List, combined gamification with Target's registries technology to create an interactive shopping list. The campaign, which was presented as a fun way for kids to create their own wish lists, was also an easy way for parents to buy their children gifts. They could also, in turn, share these gift ideas with other relatives.

Designed for the holiday season, the users had to navigate through a 3D animated game that takes place in Target's Toy Factory. The audience would drag-and-drop the toys they wanted to build their holiday wish list and then send the completed list to Santa.

Target used a 3D animated gaming platform to create a highly successful gamification marketing campaign. The app was an instant success, with the initial launch generating approximately 75,000 downloads. Over the course of the holiday season, more than 100,000 wish lists were created, made up of 1.7 million total items, which represented a total sales potential of $92.3 million.

By analyzing its data using techniques I explain in Chapter 11, Target's research found that 61 percent of its audience used the app multiple times a week, including 31 percent who used the app multiple times a day, generating over a million page visits to Target.com via the app.

Citroën: Game of Scroll

For the launch of the new World Touring Car Championship (WTCC) season, Citroën unveiled its gamification marketing campaign, called Game of Scroll. This was an adventure-type game (see Chapter 2) that allowed the audience to participate in a car race. The purpose of the game was to scroll as fast as possible to keep your car ahead of the rest and set the best race time.

The game, which was designed and developed using HTML5 technology, was accessible on mobile phones, tablets, and computers. The campaign rewarded the top players with one of ten VIP passes for two people to the French leg of the WTCC at the Le Castellet racetrack in France.

The campaign also included a social element, where players were encouraged to share their scores and challenge their friends by using the hashtag #GameOfScroll.

During its limited run, the campaign enjoyed much international success for Citroën, notably in Morocco, Germany, and Argentina.

Coca-Cola: Shake It

Coca-Cola is known to be at the forefront of developing creative and innovative product promotions, and it has run several gamification marketing campaigns, all successfully. Shake It was run primarily in Hong Kong, where users were encouraged to download the campaign's app onto their mobile phones.

After they had downloaded the app, they were asked to shake their phones. Although this may sound like a strange choice for a game, the campaign was aimed at teenagers. At the time, the word *chok*, which means "rapid motion or shake," was a slang term used exclusively by teenagers in Hong Kong.

The campaign only worked while the TV ad aired, at which point the teens had to have the app running and then shake their phones. The players were rewarded with instant prizes and discounts, including real-life discounts at restaurants and also virtual prizes that could be redeemed on other apps.

The campaign was an instant success and proved to be hard to resist for the target audience. Coca-Cola aligned the campaign with its mission to bring happiness and optimism to the world.

Netflix: Black Mirror: Bandersnatch

Although Bandersnatch was not launched as a stand-alone marketing campaign, it was an incredibly innovative gamification campaign, hailed by many as the "gamification of television." Due to the arrival of Apple's and Disney's streaming services, Netflix had to be as innovative as possible if it wanted to maintain its dominance in the market. Black Mirror: Bandersnatch was the answer to Netflix's stronghold problem.

The premise of an interactive TV movie may sound wrong, because the whole idea is that viewers want to "switch off." But Bandersnatch proved that audiences wanted to become fully immersed in the world of an engaging story. In fact, the feedback received was that a gamified movie actually helped to *enhance* the viewers' experience.

This campaign, which is essentially a *Choose Your Own Adventure*–style game, became so ambitious that Netflix opted for a feature-length runtime as opposed to the standard length of a *Black Mirror* episode. Set in 1984, Bandersnatch is the story of a young video game coder named Stefan, who sets out to build a multiple-choice game based around a science-fiction book. The viewers also follow the multiple-choice formula, where they have multiple options to choose from on how the story plays out.

The worldwide success of Bandersnatch has, according to Netflix, ensured that gamified TV will continue because it looks to be a potential gateway to a higher level of audience engagement, with great potential to be an extremely lucrative medium.

Nissan: CarWings

Electric cars are exploding into the automotive market with exciting and technologically advanced features. The whole premise of electric cars provides an excellent platform for car manufacturers to initiate innovative gamification marketing campaigns — and this is precisely what Nissan has done with CarWings.

Nissan released its Leaf electric car with a video game tracker, which is displayed on its 7-inch LCD screen. The campaign creates a competition with all other drivers and rewards the winner with the Platinum Leaf Cup. Based on their performance, drivers can then earn medals, from bronze to gold, and eventually reach the coveted platinum cup.

Drivers can see how many miles they're getting per kilowatt hour of energy, and how they stack up against others drivers in their country and around the world. The competitive desire of drivers will naturally lead them to better driving habits, which is exactly the message Nissan wants to promote with the electric car.

According to Nissan, the gamification marketing campaign is a success, with half of Leaf drivers opting to participate in CarWings. From Nissan's research, one of the top features of the campaign has been the ability of drivers to view their position in worldwide rankings of driving metrics.

Magnum: Pleasure Hunt

Magnum, an international chocolate company, wanted to create a novel campaign for the launch of its ice cream bar, Magnum Temptation. Its gamification marketing campaign was centered around an adventure game similar to Nintendo's Super Mario. However, the campaign went one step further and integrated the playing field across pages on the Internet.

The players, who can select from several playing themes (such as hand gliding), are encouraged to accumulate "bonbons" in order to build their ranks on a leaderboard.

Cleverly, Magnum raised awareness of this gamification marketing campaign through social media — so much so that the URL managed to become the most tweeted one around the world in one day.

On a final note, Magnum's campaign team not only advertised its product, but also provided a window of exposure to its partner brands, guaranteeing them advertising.

Chapter 16

Ten Common Gamification Marketing Mistakes

G amification marketing campaigns can be extremely rewarding for both your audience and your company. However, that also means there is a lot of room to get things wrong. When they do go wrong, your campaign can completely fail to engage.

Every campaign makes mistakes. Over the years, I've seen and experienced my share of gamification marketing mistakes. As with any mistake, it's important to learn from your errors and prevent them from happening again.

In this chapter, I share some of the top gamification marketing mistakes that I've seen in the hopes that they'll help you correct the things you may be doing wrong.

Offering an Unengaging User Experience

Your gamification marketing campaign should aim to offer a legendary user experience. User experience is defined by your audience's interactions and ability to engage with your campaign's objectives and goals.

TIP

But you need to account for many types of experiences. Here are some tips:

» Make sure that your game's visual experience is consistent across all devices, including mobile phones, tablets, and computers.

» Don't force your user to register before offering your game. Your audience came to your campaign to experience your game, and they'll be turned off if they come up against a request to sign up to a mailing list or some other form.

» Try to offer your audience a user experience that is interesting and worthy enough for them to naturally want to keep engaging with the campaign. In other words, make the value and engagement so pleasant that asking them to register will feel like a natural action and not something that feels forced.

» Don't force your audience to learn new game mechanics unless you have some serious reason for it. Otherwise, you risk your audience exiting your campaign. When you use time-tested designs and gameplays, your audience will engage immediately.

» Whenever possible avoid overcomplicating your campaign. Try to keep your gamification model simple. Your designers may fall into the trap of overdesigning or overengineering the gameplay. If they do, this will make your campaign more complicated and unengaging.

Leaving Your Audience Screaming, "Help!"

TIP

The whole point of launching a gamification model for your marketing is to offer something new and disruptive for your audience. However, there is a danger that the campaign will leave your audience confused and frustrated. So, make sure that you give feedback on every action your audience makes. For example:

» Clearly give the audience some kind of confirmation that they've completed a particular task. Offering more feedback confirmation is better than offering less — feedback confirmation will remove doubt in all actions performed by the audience.

» Give simple visual cues to show your audience their actions are right or wrong, or that something is happening in the background.

>> Add small tooltips throughout the game instead of providing one large help page. Small tooltips show text when the user hovers or clicks the help icons. This ensures your audience gets the help they need right away, without having to navigate away from the game.

>> Offer short videos that play seamlessly on a top layer above your game. Similar to the tooltips, each video should be relevant to the audience's stage of the game.

Having a Flawed Game Structure

Your campaign should be designed and engineered around your business or product, but it still needs to appeal as a gamification model. Every game option has its own standardized controls and structure. All you have to do is apply these standard design patterns, which will make it easier for your audience to understand how your campaign works.

TIP

Don't try to come up with new creative solutions for your game mechanics. Use popular options, layouts, and icons that everyone will recognize and intuitively know how to use. Place all game elements where your audience expects them to be.

REMEMBER

Never underestimate the importance of getting your game designs and mechanics checked by someone who is not on your team. The more you work on your campaign, the less capable you'll be of clearly and objectively reviewing the game. This essentially is getting your game mechanics and designs beta-tested by an external tester at an earlier stage than normal.

Leaving the User Waiting

Years ago, people would wait for a couple of minutes for a service, but today's audience lives in an age of rapid technology. This means your servers need to deliver your campaign immediately, every time. If your audience has to wait for the campaign to load, half of them may just give up.

TIP

One of the most effective ways to ensure that your campaign stays online, even when you're dealing with viral levels of traffic, is to use a content delivery network (CDN). A CDN helps to ensure that everyone who comes to your campaign will quickly receive your landing page. (Turn to Chapter 12 for more on CDNs.)

REMEMBER

The problem may continue without proper website optimization. If you fail to optimize, the campaign could start to lose traffic along with its overall engagement. Your campaign optimization strategy could include the following:

>> Optimizing the size of images on your website

>> Reducing the number of third-party plug-ins and application programming interfaces (APIs)

>> Minimizing the use of JavaScript files, the number of CSS files, and the number of web fonts required

>> Using website caching

>> Optimizing your database

Scoring Pointless Goals

Gamification marketing campaigns can be a powerful way to engage with audiences, but there is a delicate balance between engagement and frustration. Instead of focusing on developing interest in your audience, you can easily get caught up in the novelty of gaming, which means that you lose sight of the true purpose of the campaign. This results in an experience that offers a plethora of goals and game elements like badges but overlooks the core game mechanics. By doing this, your campaign's experience can feel trivial and pointless.

WARNING

Attempting to gamify a campaign without careful thought leads to visual noise that clutters the interface and distracts your audience from the main marketing objectives you were hoping to achieve.

TIP

To avoid this mistake, use gamification to help and engage your audience as they move through your campaign, instead of simply entertaining them for the sake of entertainment.

Not Establishing Clear Big Data Goals

Big data is a technique used to help your team create more efficient and engaging campaigns in the future (see Chapter 11). This is done by following these four steps:

1. **Identify the reason for you and your team to work on this campaign.**

2. **Set the goals you want to achieve in the campaign.**

3. **Collect your campaign data.**

4. **Apply data analysis when the campaign has ended.**

If you don't set all your big data goals during the start (in Step 1 or 2), it'll be too late by Step 3. Having a clear data strategy is absolutely vital when you consider the sheer volume of data that is available for you to collect.

Too many campaigns get caught up trying to collect as much data as possible, without really considering what the end goal will be. It's easy to become overwhelmed by all the options available.

REMEMBER

Instead of starting with the data itself, every campaign should start with the data strategy. Don't be overly concerned with what data is out there; instead, concentrate on what your gamification marketing campaign wants to achieve and how the data collected can help the campaign get there.

TIP

To avoid drowning in data and missing your big data goals, you need to develop a smart strategy that focuses on addressing specific business needs that will help your marketing team reach their strategic goals. This will result in real value for your company.

I still notice a widespread perception among businesses that data and analytics are for their IT teams to focus on. Unfortunately, all this will do is create big data strategies that focus on data storage rather than the company's long-term strategic goals. Your campaign's big data strategy should be planned, led, and executed by the marketing team.

Looking Great on the Desktop, But Not So Much on Mobile

Your gamification marketing campaign likely will be played just as much on mobile devices as it will on desktops or laptops. Actually, in my experience, there is a pretty good chance that the percentage of mobile users will be considerable higher than the percentage of desktop or laptop users.

For your mobile device audience, you want to prevent the frustration and difficulties that result from navigating a poorly designed mobile version of your campaign. Unfortunately, this means that you'll need to support as wide a range of mobile devices as possible, each of which has its own frustrating display resolutions.

Your priority should be to create the best possible experience for your audience, no matter where they view your campaign. This could be on a mobile device, desktop, laptop, tablet, or even a smart TV. Your audience's journey can be on any of these devices, and a poor experience will turn them away from your campaign instantly.

TIP

Search engines such as Google reward mobile-friendly sites and punish ones that are not. This means that your search engine optimization (SEO) rankings will suffer.

Your audience will most likely move between multiple devices, so making a consistent experience is important. Most campaigns are designed for a desktop view, and after that's approved, it's refined to work on mobile views. Here are some issues you need to look out for when preparing your campaign for mobile devices:

>> Make sure your campaign doesn't load slower on mobile devices.

>> Make sure the navigation isn't unfriendly and unusable when viewed on a mobile device.

>> Optimize your calls to action (CTAs) for mobile devices.

>> Look out for any clickable elements within the gameplay that rely on mouse movements and are, thus, not optimized for touch.

>> Make sure that all your images have been optimized for mobile devices. For example, it's important to be aware that a Retina display (used by most Apple devices) will make any low-resolution images you use in your campaign look fuzzy and pixelated.

>> Check that all text, especially text that appears in small modal windows within the gameplay, are still readable on mobile devices.

>> Design for a browser-based view that supports many different screen resolutions and adjusts for landscape and portrait orientations.

>> Keep in mind that web-based code for a desktop browser won't always work for a mobile browser without importing another API or tweaking your code in some way.

>> Check that you aren't using excessively large media files for your gameplay.

Not Checking Up on Absentees

If your campaign allows your audience to register, make sure you have a strategy to check up on absentees. An *absentee* is any member of your audience who hasn't come back to your campaign for a considerable time. How long this time is varies, but generally speaking, a week is enough time for you to classify someone as an absentee.

TIP

You should be able to contact all audience members via email through your admin portal system. However, go one step further and get your developers to build in automated trigger emails. For example, an email can be sent to all audience members who haven't logged into the campaign for at least seven days.

REMEMBER

There can be many reasons for absenteeism, and your emails need to try to capture the reasons. Some of these reasons could be the following:

>> **The audience member didn't understand your campaign.** Send them some helpful tips along with a link to a short video that explains how to engage with your campaign.

>> **The audience member got bored.** This may happen, but it's worth trying to understand why. Did they not manage to progress past the first level? Or did they not manage to obtain any goals? Send them some secret guides or insider tips to nudge their interest back to your campaign.

>> **The audience member got busy and forgot about the campaign.** Remind them of their personal progress and encourage them to get back to the campaign by letting them know how close they are to reaching their next goal.

>> **The audience member didn't have a positive experience.** Give them an outlet to express their frustration and show them you care. Chapter 10 covers multiple ways to gather audience feedback, including dedicated feedback forms and polls.

Using these techniques will result in a far higher success rate when your email reaches the absentees.

Missing Out on Social Interaction

In Chapter 10, I discuss the importance of constantly interacting with your social channels.

Unfortunately, most of the interactions you see from your audience will be to announce their grievances with your campaign. Here are a few tips to help you to deal with these complaints:

>> **Never take it personally.** Your audience is upset with your campaign, not with you as an individual, so don't respond personally or negatively. If you do, you're in danger of making the matter worse and encouraging them to respond far more aggressively.

>> **Try to respond quickly.** Even though you may not have the answers they need, as a starting point, try to reply right away with an acknowledgement. That way, they'll realize that their issue has been seen and is being looked into.

>> **Be consistent with your response times.** Consistently provide this same level of response on social channels, even on weekends. Avoid creating a flurry of responses in the space of 1 hour to complaints made in the last 24 hours.

>> **Take ownership.** Instead of hiding your mistakes, own up to them. Apologize for any errors in your campaign, and do what you can to rectify them.

>> **Try to take the conversation offline.** By talking to the person offline, you remove it from the public eye. Quite often, when dealing with negative comments, other people can be triggered to join in. By taking it offline, you prevent the situation from escalating. Plus, it helps calm the customer, because you're working with them one-on-one to help fix their issue.

>> **After you've responded to their issue, don't assume that you've fully resolved it.** Within a few days, follow up to make sure you've met their needs.

TIP

Propose a hash tag for your audiences to adopt when discussing your campaign (see Chapter 10). Then keep an eye on your hashtag and respond to everyone who has used it. Keep your comments light and, if possible, humorous. At the same time, constantly drum up interest by using the hashtag yourself when providing information and news on your campaign.

Launching without Marketing

A truly effective game launch for your campaign involves a number of different marketing channels and tactics. This means that you need to make sure you have all the right tools in place before you execute your campaign.

In Chapter 9, I look at a number of effective ways to have a successful game launch. This includes the need to build interest for the game via a pre-launch marketing campaign.

Your pre-launch strategy should aim to include the following:

>> **Optimizing your landing page for speed:** Your audience won't be patient enough for the site to load if it takes too long.

>> **Setting up a separate Google Analytics for your landing page:** Monitor these analytics independently from your main website stats.

>> **Setting up tracking pixels on your landing page:** This way, you can start gathering information on your traffic.

>> **Testing your game repeatedly:** Your audience typically won't give the game a second chance so make sure it works.

>> **Preparing a blog post for your launch:** People love to see the personal side of game development, so talk about the people who brought the game to life.

>> **Teasing your followers with posts that give them a preview of the game:** Do this in a fun and entertaining way on social media.

>> **Preparing a video demo of your game:** Keep the demo short and fun.

» into your marketing campaign

» **Developing a more sustainable and appealing marketing campaign**

» **Determining real-life benefits in using gamification**

Chapter **17**

Ten Benefits to Gamifying Your Marketing

For good reason, marketers everywhere are looking for new and innovative ways to reach their target audiences. In fact, this goal has become even more challenging as consumers are turning away more than ever from traditional online advertising. In a recent survey, respondents stated that online ads have little or no influence on their behavior.

Gamification can provide the answer to the problems in traditional marketing. Gamification taps into the basic instinct for humans wanting to "play." It also provides a way for all marketing campaigns to provide real value to the audience, as well as a positive digital experience.

Gamification marketing can help build a successful campaign for your company, one in which you build brand awareness, drive engagement to your brand, and develop a long-lasting loyalty program.

Building Brand Awareness

By using gamification, you can attract new customers in an original way and draw back old customers when they notice your branding, set against an innovative and fun campaign. Your audience, old or new, will experience your marketing campaign in a fun and interactive way — an experience that will leave your audience happy.

Happy audiences instantly spread the word about your brand in the form of social media mentions, as well as word-of-mouth marketing and online reviews. All these scenarios result in a stronger brand awareness than you can achieve in a traditional marketing campaign.

By exploiting rewards, points, ranks, leaderboards, and competition (see Chapter 4), you can encourage your audience to follow, share, and like your brand on social media. This way, with gamification marketing, you can increase your reach and, ultimately, your brand awareness.

Increasing Reach

No matter what kind of campaign you run, one of the main objectives will always be to gain new customers. It doesn't matter what market segments you're targeting or which sector your company works in, increasing your consumer reach will always be a fundamental part of your marketing.

Ideally, every company would have access to a marketing budget that would instantly bring its marketing campaign vision to the required audiences. With an unlimited budget, your market reach could be limitless; however, in the real world, most companies have limitations in terms of how far they can go with their marketing plans.

The brilliance of gamification marketing campaigns, in which everyday situations are turned into games, is in creating a layered and multifunctional campaign that naturally improves both audience engagement and brand reach.

REMEMBER

Here are some of the ways reach can be increased through gamification:

> **» Word of mouth:** Word-of-mouth marketing is more powerful than ever and it has only increased its dominance as a prominent motivator of social influence. Gamification is one of the most efficient ways to influence word of mouth;

as your audience has fun and enjoys your campaign, they'll talk about and share it. If the game options (see Chapter 2) are developed properly, your audience will have an engaging and fun experience. This increases the chances that they'll discuss it with people in their lives.

>> **Social media:** Social media is the avenue by which almost all sharing trends take place. Social media has the unique ability to encourage sharing and even propel marketing campaigns from simply okay to full-on viral.

Gamification campaigns tend to do exceptionally well when it comes to going viral. The reason for this is simple: Games are perfect for encouraging social behavior. From incentives and rewards to collaboration and leaderboards, a well-developed campaign can become viral and return tremendous results.

>> **Incentivization:** As your audience enjoys and engages with your campaign, they'll need to be incentivized to share it, thereby increasing your reach. With gamification, incentives can take many forms (see Chapter 4). From awarding user-generated achievements to rewards, you can create the motivation required for your audience to promote your campaign in their social spheres.

Instantly Appealing to a Younger Audience

Your business can build lifelong audiences if you manage to find ways to make your brand appealing to younger people. As the famous marketing rule goes, "If you brand them while they're young, they'll be your customers forever."

As we've seen in recent years, younger audiences have been quick to adopt the newer digital and social technology revolutions. This makes gamification an even more important method of marketing if you want your campaign to appeal to young people. Gamification forces your marketing to practice creativity, which in turn creates an engaging and motivational platform for younger audiences.

Often obsessive about their phones and any new technology, younger audiences are naturally intrigued by gamification marketing. By promising a fun and engaging experience, your campaign will grab a younger audience's attention instantly, the way Coca-Cola's Shake It campaign did (see Chapter 15).

Driving Engagement

If your marketing campaign is engaging, it will be worth sharing. Gamification can help drive this engagement so your audience can connect with your brand and campaign in a fun and engaging manner. However, there are certain methods you can use to ensure your gamification model drives engagement:

>> **Using rewards cleverly:** To attract new audiences to your campaign, you need to offer them rewards for playing, purchasing, loyalty, and referrals (see Chapter 4).

>> **Educating audiences:** Gamification can help your audience leave the campaign more educated on your business or product. Instead of creating a campaign that simply talks about the message you want to convey, embed the message into the game (see Chapter 7). This will compel your audience to read and understand the message as they have fun playing for their rewards.

>> **Promoting a new product or service:** With a fun, informative game, you can introduce your new product or service to both current and new audiences. By installing discounts into the rewards, your audience will actively play until they gain the discount and make a purchase to redeem the reward.

Injecting Fun into Your Brand

To put it simply, gamification makes fun and competition part of a marketing strategy. This is good news for your brand, because your gamification marketing campaign will actually generate fans — people who want to participate, follow, and share your brand.

Gamification can inspire user engagement in a more meaningful manner, which in turn fosters loyalty. The best example of this strategy can be seen in Starbucks Rewards (see Chapter 15). Loyal Starbucks customers can earn points and receive benefits. This entices customers to choose Starbucks over the competition.

Gamification forces your marketing team to think of more creative, fun elements for your campaign, which ensures all audiences will have an entertaining and engaging experience with your marketing strategy. By using fun elements in your marketing, you build customer loyalty.

Influencing Customer Behavior

Gamification has a major advantage over normal marketing campaigns when it comes to influencing customer behavior. A gamification marketing campaign engages universal experiences such as stimulation and motivation, which allows you to influence customer behavior.

Influencing audiences to make the decisions you want them to make is the holy grail of marketing. In Chapter 15, I discuss how Nissan's use of gamification influenced drivers to practice better driving habits, which is exactly the message Nissan wanted to align itself with.

Gamification's ability to influence behavior can help you build a stronger and broader social network for your brand, too. For instance, interactive gamification options such as quizzes are a great incentive for sharing with your social connections. The desire to earn rewards will encourage users to ask for help on their social networks, which will spread the word about your campaign and your brand.

Accruing Big (Customer) Data

Big data offers insights from all kinds of structured and unstructured data sources to help improve how companies operate and interact with consumers (see Chapter 11). Gamification, which allows you to connect with your audience in a more interactive and intimate way, gathers valuable data that you can turn into new insights to create detailed market segments for future campaigns.

Gamification creates a lot of data that can be analyzed, especially when users are asked to sign in via a social network where a lot of your audience's public data can be captured. More interestingly, this data can be integrated to provide context with all the other gamification data you're storing.

You can also use gamification to better understand how your audience behaves and performs within the campaign. For example, in Chapter 15, I look at how Netflix introduced the era of gamification of TV. By giving viewers an interactive choice of how the story pans out, Netflix was able to gather more information on each audience segment. This information could then be used to improve its future productions.

Personalizing Brand Experiences

Gamification marketing can customize your brand's message for your audience, creating a more personal experience during the campaign. Segmentation and personalization are critical to drive conversion, develop trust, and build customer loyalty (see Chapter 9). The more you tailor your marketing to your target group, the more effective your campaigns will be.

You can create custom game experiences targeted to specific audience segments and then develop these game experiences to your brand values. By doing this, your marketing campaign will connect with your audience on a deeper level.

Gamification allows for two types of personalization:

>> **Audience demographics:** Select game options that appeal to the demographics you're targeting. For example, if you're aiming for people with young families, a game that they can play together with their kids would be ideal.

>> **Audience likes:** If your audience shares something in common (for example, an activity or type of entertainment), you can customize your game to feature this shared preference.

Building Customer Loyalty

Your audience is being bombarded by noise — options, offers, and advertising messages are everywhere. For your marketing to be successful, your campaign desperately needs to engage customers, retain their interest, and more important, develop loyalty. With so many options aggressively competing for your audience's attention, this task is becoming more and more difficult.

Gamification can power effective customer loyalty programs, which creates a more valuable and sustaining customer relationship. When done well, gamification loyalty programs have an impressive impact. Identifying the right gamification strategy with the right rewards will elevate your loyalty program and keep your customers engaged (see Chapter 4).

TIP

Here are two tips to elevate your loyalty program:

>> **Introduce a competitive element.** The idea of gamification is to offer some form of competition to your audience. This could be a leaderboard or badges for audiences to work toward.

>> **Introduce elite clubs.** Being part of an elite club makes your audience feel like they share a special relationship with your brand, which goes a long way toward building loyalty. In gamification, this elite status is developed as an "achievement." When customers achieve a particular goal, they become part of that exclusive set of customers with additional benefits.

Gathering Great Customer Feedback and Research

Your audience is being inundated with brands and websites requesting feedback. Sadly, it has become rare to generate meaningful customer feedback for a traditional marketing campaign. This leaves you with no clear picture of what your audience feels about your company, your brand, and more important (in the short term), your campaign.

Gamification helps make the process simple by offering a more engaging and fun campaign, which increases response rates. Gamification generates an emotional and immediate response from your audience because they respond without thinking about the answer. So, even though your audience is being bombarded with requests for feedback, gamification helps your campaign stand out by making the process simple, seamless, and fun.

TIP

Focus on the following two areas:

>> **Playability:** Concentrate on the overall playability of your game. The key here is to have a game that can be picked up easily and one that your audience will want to keep playing. Stay away from advanced 3D graphics and ultra-complex gameplay. Develop a game that is simple enough to appeal to the majority of your audience while maintaining a competitive edge.

>> **Rewarding feedback:** If you want to encourage feedback, particularly over the long term, enabling your audience to earn points and rewards will be instrumental. Your audience will want to feel that their feedback is earning them privileges or rewards.

Index

About the Author

Zarrar Chishti is a software and games development consultant who has developed and marketed more than 500 games for companies around the world.

Zarrar is sought after to advise on the development of viral games for major marketing campaigns. His work can involve him liaising with marketing directors for new launches and project managing teams of game developers and designers for large-scale development projects. He's also involved in organizing and running game development courses and events.

After graduating from Glasgow University in 1996 with a prestigious joint honors degree in software engineering, Zarrar contracted as a software developer in both London and Los Angeles for five years. In 2001, he opened his own software firm in Glasgow, and within two years he was employing ten staff. By 2005, when he began to offer games development to his clients, his company had grown to a team of 30 people.

Recently Zarrar has been expanding his company, Tentacle Solutions, by opening offices in Southeast Asia and Eastern Europe, as well as partnering with key companies in Africa. Zarrar encourages you to engage with him on Twitter (@zarrarchishti) and LinkedIn (zarrarchishti).

Dedication

To Papa Gee.

Author's Acknowledgments

This will not take long at all. Some very special people in my life need to be mentioned; without them, neither this book nor the success I've found in my professional life would have been possible. I will start with my closest friend, who has been (and continues to be) there for me at the times it matters most: my brother, Ibrar. Thanks also to my one constant and partner in crime, my wife, Sadia; and to my son, Yahyaa, and my "janno-jaan" daughters, Sara, Aisha, and Rushda, all of whom I am so immensely proud of. Thank you to my parents, who gave me the most amazing education and start in life that I could have hoped for. I would be in a tremendous amount of trouble if I did not also acknowledge Bella, our completely useless but irreplaceable cat.

I would like to convey a heartfelt thank-you to my agent, Carole. You continue to understand me despite my thick Scottish accent! Your guidance and patience at the start will always be remembered and appreciated. Also, thank you to Steven Hayes, Elizabeth Kuball, and their awesome team at Wiley.

Finally, I would like to thank all the staff, dotted around the world, for their dedication and hard work. Love and peace to you all.

Publisher's Acknowledgments

Executive Editor: Steven Hayes
Project Editor: Elizabeth Kuball
Copy Editor: Elizabeth Kuball
Technical Editor: Alexandr Khlopenko
Proofreader: Debbye Butler

Production Editor: Tamilmani Varadharaj
Cover Photos: ©metamorworks/Shutterstock

Leverage the power

Dummies is the global leader in the reference category and one of the most trusted and highly regarded brands in the world. No longer just focused on books, customers now have access to the dummies content they need in the format they want. Together we'll craft a solution that engages your customers, stands out from the competition, and helps you meet your goals.

Advertising & Sponsorships

Connect with an engaged audience on a powerful multimedia site, and position your message alongside expert how-to content. Dummies.com is a one-stop shop for free, online information and know-how curated by a team of experts.

- Targeted ads
- Video
- Email Marketing
- Microsites
- Sweepstakes sponsorship

20 MILLION PAGE VIEWS EVERY SINGLE MONTH

15 MILLION UNIQUE VISITORS PER MONTH

43% OF ALL VISITORS ACCESS THE SITE VIA THEIR MOBILE DEVICES

700,000 NEWSLETTER SUBSCRIPTIONS TO THE INBOXES OF

300,000 UNIQUE INDIVIDUALS EVERY WEEK

# of dummies

Custom Publishing

Reach a global audience in any language by creating a solution that will differentiate you from competitors, amplify your message, and encourage customers to make a buying decision.

- Apps
- Books
- eBooks
- Video
- Audio
- Webinars

Brand Licensing & Content

Leverage the strength of the world's most popular reference brand to reach new audiences and channels of distribution.

For more information, visit dummies.com/biz

PERSONAL ENRICHMENT

Staying Sharp dummies

9781119187790
USA $26.00
CAN $31.99
UK £19.99

Facebook dummies
Carolyn Abram

9781119179030
USA $21.99
CAN $25.99
UK £16.99

Guitar dummies
Mark Phillips
Jon Chappell

9781119293354
USA $24.99
CAN $29.99
UK £17.99

Investing dummies
Eric Tyson, MBA

9781119293347
USA $22.99
CAN $27.99
UK £16.99

Beekeeping dummies
Howland Blackiston

9781119310068
USA $22.99
CAN $27.99
UK £16.99

Digital Photography dummies
Julie Adair King

9781119235606
USA $24.99
CAN $29.99
UK £17.99

Meditation dummies
Stephan Bodian

9781119251163
USA $24.99
CAN $29.99
UK £17.99

Pregnancy all-in-one dummies

9781119235491
USA $26.99
CAN $31.99
UK £19.99

Samsung Galaxy S7 dummies
Bill Hughes

9781119279952
USA $24.99
CAN $29.99
UK £17.99

iPhone dummies
Edward C. Baig
Bob "Dr. Mac" LeVitus

9781119283133
USA $24.99
CAN $29.99
UK £17.99

Crocheting dummies
Karen Manthey
Susan Brittain

9781119287117
USA $24.99
CAN $29.99
UK £16.99

Nutrition dummies
Carol Ann Rinzler

9781119130246
USA $22.99
CAN $27.99
UK £16.99

PROFESSIONAL DEVELOPMENT

Windows 10 dummies
Andy Rathbone

9781119311041
USA $24.99
CAN $29.99
UK £17.99

AutoCAD dummies
Bill Fane

9781119255796
USA $39.99
CAN $47.99
UK £27.99

Excel 2016 dummies
Greg Harvey, PhD

9781119293439
USA $26.99
CAN $31.99
UK £19.99

QuickBooks 2017 dummies

9781119281467
USA $26.99
CAN $31.99
UK £19.99

macOS Sierra dummies
Bob "Dr. Mac" LeVitus

9781119280651
USA $29.99
CAN $35.99
UK £21.99

LinkedIn dummies
Joel Elad, MBAs

9781119251132
USA $24.99
CAN $29.99
UK £17.99

Windows 10 all-in-one dummies
Woody Leonhard

9781119310563
USA $34.00
CAN $41.99
UK £24.99

SharePoint 2016 dummies
Rosemarie Withee
Ken Withee

9781119181705
USA $29.99
CAN $35.99
UK £21.99

Fundamental Analysis dummies
Matt Krantz

9781119263593
USA $26.99
CAN $31.99
UK £19.99

Networking dummies
Doug Lowe

9781119257769
USA $29.99
CAN $35.99
UK £21.99

Office 2016 dummies
Wallace Wang

9781119293477
USA $26.99
CAN $31.99
UK £19.99

Office 365 dummies
Rosemarie Withee
Ken Withee
Jennifer Reed

9781119265313
USA $24.99
CAN $29.99
UK £17.99

Salesforce.com dummies
Liz Kao
Jon Paz

9781119239314
USA $29.99
CAN $35.99
UK £21.99

Coding dummies
Nikhil Abraham

9781119293323
USA $29.99
CAN $35.99
UK £21.99

dummies.com

dummies
A Wiley Brand

Learning Made Easy

ACADEMIC

9781119293576
USA $19.99
CAN $23.99
UK £15.99

9781119293637
USA $19.99
CAN $23.99
UK £15.99

9781119293491
USA $19.99
CAN $23.99
UK £15.99

9781119293460
USA $19.99
CAN $23.99
UK £15.99

9781119293590
USA $19.99
CAN $23.99
UK £15.99

9781119215844
USA $26.99
CAN $31.99
UK £19.99

9781119293378
USA $22.99
CAN $27.99
UK £16.99

9781119293521
USA $19.99
CAN $23.99
UK £15.99

9781119239178
USA $18.99
CAN $22.99
UK £14.99

9781119263883
USA $26.99
CAN $31.99
UK £19.99

Available Everywhere Books Are Sold

dummies.com

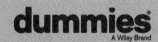

Small books for big imaginations

9781119177173
USA $9.99
CAN $9.99
UK £8.99

9781119177272
USA $9.99
CAN $9.99
UK £8.99

9781119177241
USA $9.99
CAN $9.99
UK £8.99

9781119177210
USA $9.99
CAN $9.99
UK £8.99

9781119262657
USA $9.99
CAN $9.99
UK £6.99

9781119291336
USA $9.99
CAN $9.99
UK £6.99

9781119233527
USA $9.99
CAN $9.99
UK £6.99

9781119291220
USA $9.99
CAN $9.99
UK £6.99

9781119177302
USA $9.99
CAN $9.99
UK £8.99

Unleash Their Creativity